IT'S THE ECONOMY, STUPID

ECONOMICS FOR VOTERS

VICKY PRYCE
ANDY ROSS & PETER URWIN

Biteback Publishing

First published in Great Britain in 2015 by
Biteback Publishing Ltd
Westminster Tower
3 Albert Embankment
London SE1 7SP
Copyright © Vicky Pryce, Andy Ross and Peter Urwin 2015

ISBN 978-1-84954-745-1

10 9 8 7 6 5 4 3 2 1

A CIP catalogue record for this book is available from the British Library.

Set in Adobe Garamond Pro

Printed and bound in Great Britain by
CPI Group (UK) Ltd, Croydon CR0 4YY

IT'S THE ECONOMY, STUPID

IT'S THE ECONOMY, STUPID

ECONOMICS FOR VOTERS

VICKY PRYCE
ANDY ROSS & PETER URWIN

Contents

Introduction

THIS BOOK LOOKS at the economic issues that will decide the general election of May 2015. Written by three economists with differing political perspectives, it belies the old joke that three economists will have six opinions. Sometimes, but certainly not always, the most interesting bits of economics are those where economists do disagree. We could simply give an overview of these various positions and the evidence produced by the variety of economists, but a balanced exposition can be as dull as an academic literature review – that is, very dull indeed! So instead, this book gives rein for each author to go beyond the dry, non-committal formulisations of academic rigour and to express her or his personal judgements – and, on a few occasions, for another author to take issue where they feel they just can't hold their tongue any more!

Each chapter brings together analysis and evidence to inform policy prescriptions. Where there is serious disagreement we do resort on occasion to being the infamous 'two-handed economist',[1] offering the alternative view – or at least not rubbishing it completely! But the authors have not been allowed to use the usual academic's cop-out that 'more research is required'. It's always true that more research is needed and it makes more work for academics, but a professional practitioner is required to make a judgement on incomplete information today to address an uncertain tomorrow. That is, they are asked to answer the policy-maker's question, 'Given what you know now, what do you recommend that I do?' A professional practitioner of policy economics is very used to this, as Vicky Pryce, no stranger to that world herself, points out: 'At the decision point, economists who tell the decision maker that "it is all very difficult and uncertain" are not much help and will soon find themselves not invited back.'[2]

The electorate does vote emotionally, of course, but only up to a point. Pollsters worry about the voters' perceptions of politicians – who looks best when they are eating a bacon sandwich, should they be eating a bacon sandwich at all, do they dress well, do they know how to relax, what do their other halves (usually wives) look like? The newspapers then refer to leaders being 'unelectable' because of those perceptions. Well, in reality and for the most part, voters are not stupid. What matters to them is the economy and jobs. That much is clear. But the information they're given to base their decisions on is often biased, wrong, wilfully distorting the truth or even a downright lie. Getting to the bottom of the issues for the voter is what this book is all about.

PART ONE

The Great Recession: Kicking the Economy When It's Down

CHAPTER I

The Importance
of Being Economists

'IT's THE ECONOMY, stupid.' James Carville, President Bill Clinton's successful election campaign strategist, coined his famous maxim to leave no doubt about what matters most to the electorate. He knew that even those voter concerns that are runners-up to the clear winner, the economy, are mostly also about economics, as opinion polls in the UK consistently confirm. Politicians are acutely aware that democratic outcomes are largely determined by economics. Economics is covered daily, nightly and 24/7 on news channels. Indeed, the media typically place far too much emphasis on fluctuations in economic statistics, often billing the inevitable peaks and troughs as 'breaking news'. Economic statistics are bound to fluctuate, but few doubt the longer-term importance of economics for our prosperity and social cohesion. Among those featured in *Prospect*'s 2014 list of fifty top world thinkers, seventeen were economists – the next highest category being philosophers, with thirteen entries. Economists are sought for business decisions, for policy advice, or simply to explain to non-economists what is going on in the world.

Some media commentators had grown a little complacent on the importance of economics during the fifteen years or so of continuous growth, now known as 'the Great Moderation', that followed the UK's dramatic exit from the European Exchange Rate Mechanism in 1992. During this 'Great Moderation', also known as the 'NICE' period (for 'non-inflationary continuous expansion'), economists who ought to have known better boasted of having 'cracked' how to run an economy. Perhaps it was a euphemism, but whosoever might have been sleeping on the job was rudely awoken by the crisis that began in 2007, which by 2011 had seen the UK lose a bigger percentage of GDP and world trade than any other major economy. What is GDP – and why do we care?

We will use the term 'GDP' a lot in this book, so best to explain it here up front. GDP stands for 'gross domestic product': this is a measure of the value of all goods and services produced within the boundaries of the UK within a year. If we add the income we earn from our overseas assets we get gross national income. It's 'gross' because we haven't deducted the depreciation of our capital, i.e. machines and infrastructure; if we do, we get net national income or just plain national income, but the depreciation adjustment is notoriously arbitrary and inaccurate. GDP tells us most about changes in the level of output, i.e. product, in a country and so is the most widely used measure. You won't be missing much in this book if you simply think of GDP as national income. GDP is useful for tracking the general direction of travel of the output of an economy, and is usually correlated with other important things such as the level of employment and overall tax receipts, but be wary of it as a measure of welfare (see Chapter 10). For example, its measurement has recently been extended to include prostitution and drug trafficking, and these dubious contributions will now be deemed to have boosted GDP by between £7 billion and £11 billion, whereas the wholly praiseworthy contribution of somewhere between 1.7 and 2.1 billion hours of extra help each year provided by informal volunteers in the UK remains excluded!

Good economic news generally boosts the popularity of the incumbent party in government. If bad economic performance becomes associated with a particular political party, it can blight its election chances for a long time. This is true even when the rival parties had near identical economic policies, as did the Conservatives and Labour during the run-up to the financial crisis that caused the recent 'Great Recession' – falling output followed by a flat-lining economy. In fact, economic policy often works with time lags, so measures taken by one government may well not have an effect until after the next one is in power, but the public tends to associate the party in power only with the good or bad news that is in the headlines during their term of office. Politics is a *post hoc ergo propter hoc* business.[1] A grasp of economics helps you sort out who, if anyone, is responsible for what, or at least to make a more informed judgement.

The current Great Recession is an example of an economic event that has its origins decades earlier. After a long post-war regime of close bank regulation, reflecting the bank failures of the Great Depression, the UK financial sector was 'liberated' by Mrs Thatcher in the 1980s by what was called the 'Big Bang'. The Big Bang helped to release banks from their role as strict disciplinarians imposing prudence on themselves and their clients, and increasingly turned them into hard-sell purveyors of credit. This successfully preserved and bolstered London's position as a world-leading financial centre, making the City of London the powerhouse for UK economic growth and providing welcome tax revenues for the Treasury's coffers, but it, and similar deregulation in the US, started the long chain of deregulation that led to near financial meltdown in 2007. The hugely respected *Financial Times* senior journalist Martin Wolf observed:

The economic, financial, intellectual and political elites mostly misunderstood the consequences of headlong financial liberalisation. Lulled by fantasies of self-stabilising financial markets, they not only permitted but encouraged a huge and, for the financial sector, profitable bet on the expansion of debt. The policy-making elite failed to appreciate the incentives at work and, above all, the risks of a systemic breakdown. When it came, the fruits of that breakdown were disastrous on several dimensions: economies collapsed; unemployment jumped; and public debt exploded.[2]

The Labour Party was unlucky enough to have been in power in 2007 when financial hell broke loose as the global financial credit bubble finally exploded, plunging economies across the world into recession. There had been no dire warnings from the Conservatives; there was hardly a fag paper between the parties. David Cameron had agreed to match Labour's spending plans, yet now often blames the crisis on Labour's 'profligate' public spending. Public spending, or at least the government's deficit, was too high, but any good economist can shoot down in seconds the claim that it caused the financial crash in 2007, the crash that would lead to the Great Recession over the six years from 2008 (see Chapter 2). Certainly, Gordon Brown as Chancellor was running a Budget deficit during a time of economic growth even though economists of all persuasions advise that it's wise to run a Budget surplus during growth, so as to replenish the government's war chest for later downturns. And, after first presiding over falling debt, Gordon Brown then perversely allowed the public sector's debt-to-GDP ratio to rise, so that public money could be spent in areas that would guarantee further Labour victories (which indeed was the case, in one of Labour's most successful political periods). Even so, the debt-to-GDP ratio was still one of Europe's lowest and, until the crisis, less than Labour had inherited from the previous Conservative government. But all of this is trivial compared to the scale of the financial crisis that was the real cause of the downturn. Economists may quibble on the details, but the famous McKinsey graph clearly shows that it was the build-up of private debt, not government debt, that caused the economic fragility: government debt actually fell dramatically as a percentage of overall debt.

FIGURE 1: UK BORROWING GREW TO 466 PER CENT OF GDP, DRIVEN BY GROWTH OF THE FINANCIAL SECTOR

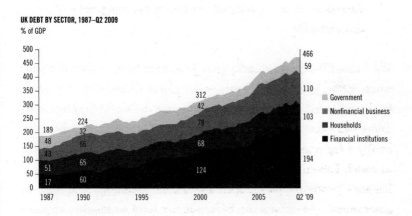

UK DEBT BY SECTOR, 1987–Q2 2009
% of GDP

Source: Haver Analytics; McKinsey Global Institute

Overwhelmingly, it was not reckless public spending that caused the economic crisis: it was reckless banking that took place unchecked by governments and often encouraged by light-touch financial regulations. Some commentators argue that banks were forced to seek higher returns on their lending by the low interest rates that prevailed at the time, but this is hardly an excuse for their reckless and sometimes downright corrupt behaviour.

Another graph, from the Treasury itself, makes it clear that the massive increase in the deficit was driven not by government expenditure (even though government expenditure always tends to rise in a recession as more people become eligible for welfare payments), but by the collapse in tax revenues caused by the crisis:

FIGURE 2: UK GOVERNMENT INCOME AND SPENDING

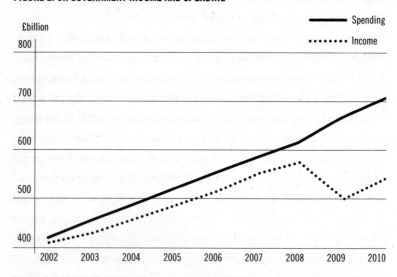

The unbroken line of government spending shows a pretty unremarkable rate of expansion albeit with a detectable upward kink in 2008 as the onset of recession automatically impacts on welfare spending. In stark contrast, the broken line of tax income collapses in 2008 as profits and incomes fall. The gap between the lines is the government deficit and you don't have to do much reading between the lines to see that the deficit was the result and not the cause of the recession. Economics helps you spot when decisions and claims are motivated by politics rather than good economics. Once so armed, you will have a busy time! Of course, a lot of economics leaves a lot of room for reasonable people to disagree, but politicians courting the electorate provide copious examples of out-and-out spin for the economists to debunk. Examples abound: one might be the Conservatives' populist July 2014 'crack-down' on EU migrants claiming jobseeker benefits, even though EU migrants don't tend to claim benefits and so the 'problem' is economically insignificant, the changes probably affecting fewer than 10,000 people. Another example might be a 'Help to Buy' scheme for house buyers that doesn't really help house buyers but could risk creating a housing bubble, causing Mark Carney, the Governor of the Bank of England, to intervene.

Of course, other parties are just as guilty of spin and hypocrisy too. With his election defeat becoming ever more certain, Gordon Brown hastily introduced a 50p top rate of tax as a trap for the incoming Conservative government. For various reasons, not least tax avoidance, the tax would raise a trivial amount in terms of overall public finances and risked damage to incentives, but reducing it to 45 per cent, as George Osborne did halfway through the coalition government, allowed the Labour Party to rail against the 'Conservatives' tax cut for millionaires'. It proved a popular cause among voters, so much so that Ed Miliband has (reluctantly) committed to its reintroduction. In truth, it's a small price for the rich to pay for the privileges, security and support they receive from the nation, and there are much easier and less risky ways of taxing the rich. That respected referee of all things to do with government revenues and taxes, the Institute for Fiscal Studies, has backed HMRC's estimate that the tax has brought in as little as £100 million, a paltry contribution towards a deficit of well over £100 billion, and one that can easily increase tax avoidance and damage incentives and so damage the growth that is actually the most important contributor to getting the deficit down.[3] Yet, following Chancellor Osborne's last pre-election autumn statement on 3 December 2014, Rachel Reeves, speaking on Radio 4's *Any Questions* two days later, was still insisting that Labour's promise to raise the 45p tax on everyone earning over £150,000 back to 50p if they come to power would raise £3 billion extra – and presumably be used to help the NHS, thus necessitating fewer spending cuts from elsewhere! In short, Labour's motivation for the 50p rate of tax is political not economic.

It is perhaps not surprising that politicians often make policy to get elected: in a democracy, political parties are rewarded not so much for telling it like it is as for telling it like the electorate wants to hear it. So, after initial attempts to disabuse the electorate of the myth that profligate public spending by Labour is the main culprit for economic woes, as is so energetically portrayed by much of the press, Ed Miliband turned the

Labour Party instead to attacking a 'cost of living crisis'. This is an old political ploy: 'If you can't win the argument, change the conversation.' Banging on about the public finances was only serving to remind the electorate that they had read that the crisis was all caused by 'Labour's debt'! Move on and attack something else. And say it often enough – you personally may be bored by it by the hundredth time the mantra is repeated, but this is the way politics works.

All this is not just of consequence for the fortunes of political parties. The size of the public debt caused by the financial crisis will affect us all, but how governments approach the problem can affect us even more. Political spin alone cannot change the underlying forces that determine the course of economic fortune, those powerful forces that determine the real world, regardless of whether political parties or the electorate understand them or even know of them! Individual countries, whose national economies operate within a global economy, are much less able to govern their own fortunes than is commonly supposed, but their policies do interact with these underlying forces and can often change what happens in economies. When governments get it wrong it can hurt you whether or not you voted for the party in power. And economics doesn't only rule in democracies. Nikita Khrushchev, once the all-powerful leader of the Soviet Union, boasted he understood how economies work: 'About the capitalist states, it doesn't depend on you whether we [the Soviet Union] exist. If you don't like us, don't accept our invitations, and don't invite us to come to see you. Whether you like it or not, history is on our side. We will bury you.'

He later lamented, 'Economics is a subject that does not greatly respect one's wishes.'

You need economics if you are going to pick through the daily avalanche of misinformation and spot the spin. Without economics you can vote but you are really disenfranchised. You will be an innocent, subject to manipulation by vested interests using economic smoke and mirrors to pull the wool over your eyes. Without a grasp of economics you will be bemused by the contradictory statistics that spin doctors throw at you. Media coverage is often grossly misleading – as you will see in this book – but vote for the wrong economics and we are all in for a lot more pain!

Despite the many misconceptions held by voters, they do mostly appreciate that if the economics is wrong then the other things aren't usually right either. When the economy stalls, millions of lives suffer, even in rich countries. Enterprises – and entrepreneurs – which might otherwise have flourished, fail. Dreams are dashed by unemployment and reduced opportunity. Paying for social services and health becomes harder. Often, social tensions rise: as the great economist John Maynard Keynes predicted of Germany being forced to pay excessive reparations after the First World War, when the economy gets smaller the risk of conflict gets bigger.

Even charities have to know how to control their costs and get the most bangs to their bucks – as shown by the appreciation of those economists who volunteer for pro bono work.[4] In short, economics is ubiquitous, so we need to study economics to help us address our many dilemmas, to reveal the trade-offs at stake in our choices and to provide metrics for good decision making. We need to be able to assess the economics that lies behind so many of our decisions: should we try to stimulate the economy into growth through government spending to generate incomes to pay off debts, or should we cut back on government spending because of the debt? Should we build that airport, bridge or railway, or should we do something completely different? Should health provision and education be more market-based? Does inequality serve a purpose or is it merely corrosive? Do we benefit from being in Europe? Should I buy a new car or renovate the kitchen? Would that country prosper if it was independent?

Economics, much maligned, is important, useful and fascinating. The eloquent economist Tim Harford has done a lot in his *FT* columns, books such as *The Undercover Economist* and radio programmes such as *More or Less* to explain and simplify economics and it is useful to demystify it as much as possible. The economist's approach to evidence allows you to interrogate the world a lot more closely, and often to come up with intriguing and counter-intuitive explanations.[5] Economists have contributed so much to statistical methods that they even have a branch of statistics named after them! It's known as econometrics and it can be applied to an astonishing range of topics. For example, we hear a lot about obesity and see the government react in various ways, such as limiting the availability of chocolate in schools, investing in public service advertising and engaging Jamie Oliver to construct better menus, or that it is the children of mothers who work who are the most obese, immediately making every working mother guilty for going out to earn a living rather than valued for contributing to the economy and relying less on welfare. But all that could simply be nonsense. That two trends appear to be linked may not be in any way proof that one thing causes the other. Econometrics on the other hand helps you to cut through all these half-truths and prejudices and determine causality – i.e. gives you proof that indeed one thing does cause another thing to happen. So, the closing and selling off of school playgrounds under both Conservative and Labour governments is probably as much to blame for our fat teenagers as anything else.

Everyone talks about an obesity epidemic and there are suggestions that the NHS should either stop treating obese patients or should charge them for their treatment. But what do we really know about weight and health – for example, is it good or bad to be slightly overweight? Recent research seems to suggest that a BMI of between 25 and 30, which is classed as 'overweight', is likely to lead to a longer life![6] Economics allows you to question the statistics, in particular the correlations that people present to us all as proving things one way or another. We were told it was good for you to eat fruit, lots of fruit, even more fruit – until everyone then started worrying about the sugar content of fruit. Certainly fruit in reasonable quantities, like most things, must be good for you. But try to prove it unequivocally. Indeed, there may be a close correlation between eating fruit and being healthy but is there actually another reason for that health other than the fruit consumption? You may equally find a correlation between reading the *Times* newspaper every day and being healthy. Or is your neighbour healthier because he reads *The Independent*?

The job of economics is to try to warn you that a lot of what is served to the electorate as facts is, at least, much more nuanced. Causality is seldom proved beyond reasonable doubt. And yet decisions are often made on inadequate or even distorted evidence. And whether one likes it or not, it's all about the quality of the evidence. Question what you read as much as you can, including this book, before casting your vote.

The disadvantages of being an economist pale into insignificance in comparison, but they are still frustrating! First of all, most of us did not see the financial crisis coming. So the Queen famously asked in November 2008 during a visit to the London School of Economics why we had failed to see it. But the sad truth is that no matter how much economics you learn you will always be acutely aware that you could do with knowing so much more. Second, if you admit to being an economist, social events can be ruined by being collared by those graceless bores with all the answers but never a clue. That polite obligation to feign amusement at hackneyed jokes about economists can also become quite tiresome. George Bernard Shaw quipped, 'If you laid all the economists in the world end to end they still wouldn't reach a conclusion.' It's amusing the first few times, but as wearisome to an experienced economist as a dentist finds 'you've been looking down in the mouth lately'. But it's best to resist explaining to inflictors of such endlessly recycled humour why it misses the point, unless you wish to open yourself up to more pontifical drivel.

It's a sad fact for democracy that so many people, from taxi drivers to politicians, believe that they know all about economics despite never having made the effort to learn any at all. Alan Johnson, of course, was a notable exception: when asked in 2010 what his first move would be after his surprise promotion to shadow Chancellor of the Exchequer, he joked, 'Pick up a primer – *Economics for Beginners*.'

Like gravity, you can't escape the effects of economics. It affects your life whether you understand it or not. You might try to ignore economics but there is no escaping economics. John Maynard Keynes famously put it like this:

> The ideas of economists and political philosophers, both when they are right and when they are wrong, are more powerful than is commonly understood. Indeed, the world is ruled by little else. Practical men, who believe themselves to be quite exempt from any intellectual influence, are usually the slaves of some defunct economist. Madmen in authority, who hear voices in the air, are distilling their frenzy from some academic scribbler of a few years back.

Economists actually agree far more than is commonly appreciated, but most of this agreement goes on quietly behind the scenes, as thousands of economists work day-to-day advising businesses, charities, government and the media. By contrast, their disagreements are often very high profile indeed. Economic issues can and do have the greatest importance for politicians and the public, and crucial, complex problems often leave room for experts to disagree, as is just as true at the forefront of physics. In the long run, physics is more important, but decisions on economic policies, and whatever is around the corner for our economies, directly affect our interests now. That is why economics figures so prominently in the news and why public debate can be heated and distorted by vested interest.

And we should stop worrying about diverging views – as long as the right one wins, of course! As the economist and commentator John Kay puts it, 'We should end all this irritating nonsense that we don't want economists who say "on the one hand but then on the other hand". I'm sorry, but much of the world is about on the one hand but then on the other hand.'[7]

How did we get where we are today?

Economics has shaped our world. After millennia of only gradual change, sometimes for the worse, economic progress, allied with scientific advance, traces a 'hockey-stick' graph through time (see Figure 3). There's a long, flat handle of little or no growth, always around subsistence, and then a 'sudden' upward kink in material living standards when industrialisation, overwhelmingly brought about by capitalist revolution, transforms living standards.

FIGURE 3: WORLD PER CAPITA GDP
10000 BCE – 2003 CE (1990 INTERNATIONAL DOLLARS)

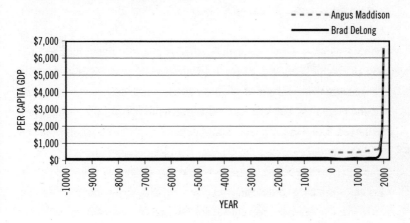

Source: Kruse Kronicle, http://www.krusekronicle.com/kruse_kronicle/2008/03/charting-histor.html#.VBQtzpRdVqV, accessed 24 January 2014

Nations that had only ever known comparatively minor fluctuations in GDP per head, caused by weather, wars and disease, saw a 'sudden' uplift to sustained growth in living standards that transformed their societies. It also brought unprecedented inequality between nations, as industrialised nations achieved unprecedented wealth. Today, Luxembourg has the highest GDP per head at $78,000 a year while the lowest is in the Democratic Republic of Congo at $365 per head. Economic growth allowed population growth and gave another hockey-stick graph for the world's population: less than one billion until the nineteenth century, it took off to rapidly climb to over seven billion today. Most of us could not and would not exist if not for economic progress! In this century, economic growth may well solve the 'problem' of world population growth as the citizens of enriched countries demand better conditions for their children and better economic opportunities for women: world population growth has almost halved since the 1960s and the latest United Nations projections indicate that world population will nearly stabilise at just above ten billion after 2062[8] – still a large size to deal with, presenting challenges for food, transport and the environment.

Economic and population growth have impacted negatively, of course, on the natural world. Scientists are near unanimous that the accumulation of the by-products of human economic activity is dramatically changing the planet's atmosphere. Today, atmospheric carbon dioxide is at 400 parts per million for the first time in millions of years (see Chapter 11). Some scientists even believe this may have prevented a new ice age, but unchecked global warming may lead to huge costs and destruction from shifting areas of habitable and arable land and increasingly regular extreme weather events.

Despite recessions and quite a few crises along the way, the world's pace of economic change is accelerating. For example, and a very big example, in the last thirty years, economic reforms in China have lifted well over 600 million people out of poverty, about ten times the current population of the UK, an unprecedented and truly astonishing rate of poverty relief. In 1990, the British economy was 2.5 times larger than China's; by 2013, China's was 3.5 times larger than Britain's! In 2013, for the first time, less than 50 per cent of world GDP came from the advanced economies. In 1988, 44 per cent of the world's population lived on less than $1.25 a day, but by 2008 this had almost halved to 23 per cent in real terms. The emerging economies, the ones Jim O'Neill called the BRICS – Brazil, Russia, India, China and South Africa – and perhaps next the MINTs – Mexico, Indonesia, Nigeria and Turkey – are reshaping world politics just as older patterns of wealth and power have long continued to shape the world and society. Without knowing about economics it is impossible to understand what drives our world.

With capitalism came increased competition and the transformation of traditional life. New means of transport, canals then railways carrying the inputs and outputs of industrialisation, meant that local producers now had to compete with the best from elsewhere. Mostly they could not, and so industry and population gravitated towards the industrial, commercial and finance centres that grew into the vast cities that still dominate the world's economy. Today, competition is really between these cities rather than between nations. London has become the richest global economic city, with a life of its own, often standing alone and seemingly unattached to the rest of the UK.

In the twentieth century some of the most brutal aspects of capitalism were counter-balanced to a considerable extent by increased competition over available labour and by the social reforms that were made possible by the ending of subsistence living standards. Capitalist economic growth gave birth to socialism and other social reformers. Against opposition, the welfare state we often take for granted now came into being after the Second World War. Its size, effects and role are still being contested at the centre of the political debate (see Chapter 2). If the Conservatives win the next election, will they be able to achieve their pledge to return the government's consumption of goods and services, much of which goes on welfare spending, to its smallest share of national income since 1948? Could even a Labour government sustain the welfare state at anything like the level of provision we have grown accustomed to? Economics continues to be the very substance of politics and is still what drives the world and our futures.

Using economics to make choices

Economists analyse and advise on the best use of available resources; they appraise projects, identify economic and market trends to spot opportunities; they recommend and trouble-shoot policies, warning of potential threats. The economist will often seem to be a party-pooper; economics is not known as the dismal science for nothing. Economists often have to provide the reality checks that others would rather ignore. Efficiency means getting the most from resources, so even while the party is swinging, the economist's job is still to ask if it's the best party for the money. Project A may be a good idea, but is it better than project B, which will no longer be possible once resources are sunk into A? Economics has developed powerful cost–benefit analysis tools for revealing what a decision actually entails and what would be forgone by pursuing it. Good economists have this 'opportunity cost' in their gut: that's why they're handy people to have around to temper misplaced enthusiasm and cut through the spin.

Cost–benefit analysis (CBA) can be applied to a very wide range of decision making. In demonstrating the benefit-to-opportunity cost ratios of project A against project B economists are really asking the annoying but intensely practical question 'Are you really sure you want to commit your resources to this and not that?' Should a new high-speed railway be built? Should we spend less on defence? Should I rent or buy a home? Should I go to university? Should I get married? Should I have children? Should I be an economist? CBA forces you to quantify and so challenge values and priorities. We often hear that 'Health is the most important thing' (see Chapter 7), but the entirety of our GDP could easily be sunk into health care. So how much improvement do we really want to tax more for, and cut back elsewhere to provide? 'You can't put a price on justice!', but justice does have a cost, so do you really want to cut back on health spending to catch every litter-bug out there? Are prisons an effective use of resources anyway?[9]

The ubiquity of economics and the advances in its techniques mean that economists now have something interesting to say about a hugely diverse range of phenomena. The 'Big Data' revolution encouraged by the digital economy (much more is now known about consumer preferences and behaviour, for example), better survey techniques and the ability at last to interrogate at the same time data held by different government departments to check linkages have all hugely increased the ability to test the impact of various courses of action – whether private or public. Economists are loath to say that anything is endless, but it is now an astonishingly long list of topics that have been explored using the techniques of economics. It includes: should we put an airport here or there or anywhere? Did bankers cause the recession and how do we stop them doing it again? Are charities effective? Can we instil lifelong habits of charity in kids? Are cities really quite green and why are they so astonishingly productive? When is competition good and when is it bad? How can we best address crime? At what level does debt matter? How much discrimination exists and what are its costs? Should drugs be decriminalised? Should we spend more on education? What are the returns to education? Did educational maintenance allowances work? Should we charge for a university education and if so, how much? What determines election outcomes? How much should we invest in new energy sources? Should we put folic acid in bread? How can governments raise more funds from auctions? Is gambling harmful or rational? Is immigration good or bad for the incumbents? What drives the dynamics of inner cities? How can market mechanisms be applied to matching kidneys? How much value do we put on a human life; when is it too little or too much? Which partner gets the most in marriage? Why are so many commercial TV and radio channels the same? What should and shouldn't you get on the NHS? Should nursery care be heavily subsidised? What's the best way to prevent an obese society? Do we spend too little or too much on passenger safety? Does performance-related pay actually make people work harder? Can we afford our pension commitments? Is privatisation always best? How much does regulation cost the economy and is it effective? If not, how might it be made effective? Is trade protectionism ever justified? Should the BBC keep its licence fee system going? Should we stay in Europe? How much do psychological quirks affect economic decisions and when is it important to know about this? Do economic considerations affect sexual behaviour? Do we spend enough on science? Would an independent Scotland be better or worse off? Can we measure social capital? Is social mobility increasing or decreasing? What are the costs of social immobility? Are we taxed too little or too much? How can we incentivise tax compliance? What makes a good team? What is the value of time? Do we spend enough and wisely on transport links? What causes unemployment and how damaging is it? What is well-being and how much does it cost? What causes wars?

In addition, of course, we have the wide-ranging and huge economic questions which are often mired in controversy: how should we use economics to cost in and avoid the environmental damage that could lead to catastrophe? (See Chapter 11.) Are austerity measures the best way to tackle recessions or do they make them worse? (See Chapter 2.) How can we foster economic progress for poorer countries? (See Chapter 12.) How will the newly rich countries change the world economy, and with it the balance of powers?

At another level there's all the Freakonomics of Steven Levitt: do teachers and sumo wrestlers cheat? Did the availability of abortion reduce teenage crime? Do doctors pump up their earnings by performing unnecessary operations? Freakonomics, Happinomics, Socionomics, Wikinomics, Greekonomics, Prisonomics... Of course no one wants 'Bollonomics'; good economists are always concerned with peer review and the quality of their data. Not everything goes and that's why it's so important to look for good economics.

If nothing in the above interested you then economics is definitely not for you. Carry on reading the newspapers.

If you have chosen to read this book, you are no doubt the sort of person who is eager to know more about lots of the things mentioned. Economics matters hugely in the conduct of our everyday life. If poorly understood, it may lead to the wrong decisions being made, with negative long-term consequences, not only for us but for many others around us. But knowledge is power. So read on. Unfortunately, we cannot cover everything in a book still light enough to be carried around, so we have concentrated on the issues that will be central to the 2015 election and beyond.

What the book is also arguing is that, in the end, most political decisions are anchored in economics. On 14 August 2014, reporting on the latest jobless figures, *City AM*, a daily finance paper given out free to central London commuters, had 'IT'S THE ECONOMY, STUPID' plastered in huge letters on its front page as a headline to an article that was arguing that jobs and growth were going to be the main issue deciding the 2015 election in the UK. Slightly irritating given our title, which we had opted for quite some time before! But of course economics is crucial and for a meaningful democracy, expertise should be harnessed through the democratic process: unless the public is informed by basic economic theory and facts, they will vote for bad decisions. As the controversial economist Ha-Joon Chang writes:

> People have strong opinions on all sorts of things – gay marriage, Iraq, abortion, global warming – without having any qualifications to make informed judgements. I don't have a degree in international relations but I have a view on Afghanistan. How come everyone thinks that economics is too difficult, too technical? People make strong judgements on the basis of having some basic knowledge about international politics or some climate science, they are not making this judgement based on sophisticated expert knowledge, and that's all I'm asking when it comes to economic matters as well.[10]

This book attempts to make important issues intelligible for voters. Without this, what we have is a false democracy. Economists should not always make their writing so technical and obscure; they must take the time to provide accessible versions for those who are expected to vote on economic matters. We seek to go some way towards achieving that in this book. We would be lying if we said that economics can always be made easy, but a lot of it can be made accessible – and it is the duty of economists to make it so.

CHAPTER 2

Balancing the Books
or Reckless Austerity?

The crisis: whose fault was it?

YOU'VE PROBABLY HEARD the one about how the UK economy was going really well until Gordon Brown started squandering tax-payers' hard-earned money and borrowed so much that he almost bankrupted us all. It goes as follows: just a few months after Brown became our unelected Prime Minister, in June 2007, the economy began to fall apart. A year later it was deep into the worst crisis seen since the Great Depression. Luckily, having waited impatiently for ten years to be PM, Brown chickened out of an election, even though he probably would have won it; he preferred the certainty of staying on uninvited to the risk involved in becoming our properly elected Prime Minister. That left him with 'only' three more years to drive the country into unprecedented debt before George Osborne, supported by Lib Dem Danny Alexander's brain, came to the rescue. As soon as the letter handed down from the previous Chief Secretary to the Treasury was read out, informing the coalition that there was simply no money left, the new Conservative-led government took the tough decisions needed to start paying down the deficit to restore the world's confidence in the UK.

The coalition did something complicated about those greedy banks that nobody likes, too, whereas Labour's Alistair Darling had given those same banks even more squillions in bail-out money paid by us, their poorer victims!

Despite the dire predictions of many so-called expert economists, and the protestations of those who had helped get us into the mess in the first place, the coalition stuck to their guns and so now we can all see for ourselves how well their tough love has worked. At the time of writing, the UK is the fastest-growing economy of all the major developed nations. Hooray! Despite all the pain that was necessary to clear up Labour's mess, and even despite the widespread distaste for a Cabinet with so many 'Tory toffs' in it, a grateful public rewarded the Conservatives in May 2014 with their first opinion poll lead for over two years. Ed Miliband's Labour saw its poll advantage fall from a 16 per cent lead to low single figures as the economy continued to recover. As always, it's the economy, stupid!

So it's a convincing story: Labour's profligacy got us into a right mess and the coalition's painful but effective medicine got us out of it. Speaking on BBC's Radio 4 in June 2014, Lord Lawson, the veteran Tory ex-Chancellor, summed it all up:

> Clearly, the economy's doing extremely well, and that is great news, that the recovery is going, across a broad front, very well indeed. George Osborne has, to his great credit – the Chancellor – been proved right, and his critics, whether among Keynesian economists or the Labour Party or the IMF, have been proved totally wrong, and this is good news for the British people.[1]

Or was it those greedy bankers?

There is another, less well-known, version of the story. It goes like this: in the 1980s, the Tories' revered PM Mrs Thatcher reversed the even more revered Churchill's maxim that finance should be 'less proud and industry more content'. She and her friends in finance began to unravel the restraints that had long reflected Lord Keynes's advice from the 1930s that casino banking should always be kept 'expensive and inaccessible'. It was unwise to ignore such a formidable economist as Keynes. The bankers rose and industry fell. The creation of shed-loads of 'funny money' by casino banks let rip was, not surprisingly, extremely profitable and extremely dangerous for the economy.

Although this unbalanced the economy towards higher unemployment and greater inequality, both Conservative and Labour governments were seduced by their dependency on the taxes from banks flowing into the Treasury's coffers, not to mention the substantial direct bank contributions to the political parties themselves. It is little publicised, for example, that more than half of the Tory Party's donations since the 2010 general election have come from individuals and businesses working in finance.[2] New Labour had also sought to reduce its reliance on union funding by courting donations from financial institutions, which allowed the Lib Dems' Vince Cable to say to great applause in the BBC's 2010 pre-election debate between three would-be Chancellors, 'Now they want to have another turn to get their noses in the trough and reward their rich backers.'

Financial bubbles can build up over decades. Reagan and Thatcher, as kindred neo-liberal spirits, set the direction for the deregulation of finance that continued through to the present century, with an increasing arrogance and belief in the efficiency of markets. A belief strengthened by sophisticated-sounding embellishments of new and apparently impressive academic proofs about 'efficient markets' from neo-liberal mathematical economists. Indeed, many of these economists became quite hostile to anyone who disagreed with them, especially other economists. So, through the final repeal of the USA's 1930s Glass-Steagall legislation in 1999 – an important part of the regulation that had long prevented the traditional prudence of the retail banks becoming too contaminated by the speculative ventures of investment banks – restraints on speculative greed were swept away to serve the interests of big finance.

To add to the momentum of the bubble's long build-up, all sorts of exotic 'parallel banks' were deliberately set up just outside the reach of any remaining regulation, and in the new 'financial markets are always efficient' regime they were allowed to flourish. Banks, and other rejuvenated finance institutions, were raking in unearned fortunes by flogging off trillions in iffy debts to anyone unwise enough to take them on. Sometimes the activity of banks was what in any other walks of life would be called organised crime. For example, vital interest rates were fixed in close-knit inter-bank stitch-ups, and some even advised their own clients to buy junk assets and then made money from this by betting on the side that these investments of their own customers' hard-earned money would go belly-up! If all this sounds far-fetched then go check it out by watching Charles Ferguson's jaw-dropping documentary *Inside Job* about the origins of the financial crash. If it was a made-up slur, be assured that the banks, with all their financial clout, would sue; instead, it won the documentary film Oscar.

With the ending of regulation and the removal of the protective barrier between casino banks and traditional high street banks, finance in the US and the UK became increasingly complex, with the creation of new and exotic financial instruments and the growth of myriad interconnections between finance institutions which, when mapped, resembled networks of brain neurons. Few, if any, really understood the complexities of this monstrous tumour. For those involved, both personal and corporate, their interests seem best served by just carrying on partying while profits could be made. Only a few wise observers such as Warren Buffet, who has amassed his fortune using the same long-term investment methods Keynes had used to such good effect, warned long before the collapse that highly complex financial instruments are time bombs and 'financial weapons of mass destruction' that could harm not only their buyers and sellers, but the whole economic system. Buffet was proved right.

From mid-2007, serious debt default problems began in the US sub-prime mortgages sector, where huge volumes of mortgages had been sold to persons who previously would not have been deemed sufficiently credit-worthy. Sub-prime mortgages and many other dodgy and often fiendishly complicated financial instruments such as 'derivatives', often in effect bets placed on the fortunes of third parties, were then all mixed up together with more solid assets in 'securitised' packages of different types of assets and then sold on widely across the financial sector. This was all greatly helped by private sector 'rating agencies', employed by the banks themselves, granting 'Triple A' status to these pig-in-a-poke bundles, known as collaterised debt obligations, or CDOs. CDOs in effect hid the real risks and facilitated a massive growth of newly created asset/debt bundles with over-inflated values. These were then used as collateral to create even more funny money – using other people's money for your own bets is called leverage – and so the debt bubble grew. It looked like growth, it felt like growth as it produced income for bankers and tax for government, but it was as fragile as a house of cards.

But was Brown blameless?

No. He and Ed Balls did nothing to reverse the liberalisation of banks. As we saw in Chapter 1, it was also true that for a short while before the crisis Gordon Brown was running what economists call a structural deficit. This is when the government is a net borrower even though the economy is growing at or above its normal trend level. This is generally frowned upon by all economists, as government debt should be repaid in the good times so as to save up 'fiscal ammunition' for the bad times, and as government borrowing can help fuel credit bubbles as the government both spends the money it borrows and leaves a gilt-edged IOU in the economy that can be used as collateral to create more loans. Although much of the borrowing went to sound investments, most economists regarded this structural deficit as poor form, and so it gave Brown's critics a good excuse for blaming the crisis on Labour's debt. But the public debt amounts were trivial compared to the size of the build-up in private debt, created by finance run amok. The elimination of the UK's structural deficit would not have been even a sticking plaster in the face of the haemorrhaging of the finance sector's jugular.

The crucial thing to notice in the McKinsey graph in Chapter 1 is that government debt – that's the little stripe at the top – doesn't explode, or even swell, after Labour came to power in 1997. In fact, up until shortly before the crisis it falls as a percentage of GDP, so that by 2007 it was actually below the level inherited from the Conservatives, and more of the borrowing was being used to finance investment rather than the day-to-day running costs of the public sector. At this time the UK's debt levels were the second lowest level in the top group of rich countries, the G7, higher only than Canada's. It's clear that it was not the public debt that was bloated, it was private debt, and in particular the debt created by the unbridled greed of the financial institutions.

Labour's critics made much of some countries having lower structural deficits than the UK, but in the face of the debt tsunami to come, these differences are simply swamped. No saving for a rainy day would have helped very much, given that, as a direct result of the recession, public borrowing had to be increased about fivefold. The Treasury's own chart in Chapter 1 shows that the deficit was overwhelmingly the result of collapsing tax revenues, not high spending, following the financial crisis that caused the recession.

The financial collapse that caused the Great Recession

Eventually, as always happens, the bubble burst. Only a few defaults were needed to expose the risks, but these caused the values of other assets based on similar debts to fall, and this led to a chain reaction as the values of a host of financial institutions' holdings of dodgy asset bundles collapsed in an electronically networked implosion of banks' capital. Banks in turn became more likely to default and so all the assets that depended on them also fell in turn, further spreading the risk of default like a contagion. The whole Ponzi scheme of iffy debt tumbled like a pyramid of cards. Worse, because the bad assets had been so thoroughly and deliberately mixed in with the good, it was now difficult or impossible to isolate these 'toxic assets'. It was as if a million pies had been made from fresh meat but with some rotten meat thrown in, so no one now trusted any pies. So paper asset values tumbled across the board, adding even more fuel to the fire, decimating the asset values of even famous and long-standing banks. As trillions were written off, many finance institutions moved towards insolvency from positions that only months earlier had seemed completely secure. Even banks that had practised 'micro-prudence' were caught out by the now exposed lack of 'macro-prudence' as the debt of bad banks took out capital from even the best banks.

The first banks to face complete bankruptcy were those that had been particularly reckless during the good times. Banks in general have to make a living from borrowing short-term (e.g. taking deposits) to lend longer-term (e.g. loans), but some had taken advantage of deregulation and the 'liberalisation' of the finance sector to fuel rapid but ultimately very fragile growth. They took on liabilities in the good times that they would be unable to pay for if bad times came. This lack of prudence was in part because the bank employees involved did not bear the risk themselves; they pocketed their bonuses from selling toxic debts and assets and then moved on before fan and excrement met. With no regulations or sanctions to punish them, and with a new breed of smart City executives taking the place of traditional finger-wagging bank managers and aggressively urging them on, there was seemingly no personal downside for finance traders. Engaged in a veritable frenzy to sell, they created more and more dodgy debts. As corporations, the banks were also aware that they had become 'too big to fail' – that is, too big for the government to let them fail. Knowing that the government would be forced to bail them out, banks could indulge in what economists call 'moral hazard': making decisions about how much risk to take, safe in the knowledge that someone else will pay the price if things go wrong.

Northern Rock was one bank that had built up massive short-term debt by borrowing in short-term money markets to finance long-term debts which they then sold on to other financial institutions through 'securitisation'. So long as Northern Rock could keep selling securitised long-term debt it could service its short-term loans, but by August 2007, as the global demand from investors for securitised mortgages had sharply decreased, Northern Rock became unable to repay its loans. In September 2007 it sought and received 'liquidity support' from the Bank of England through the Bank of England's 'lender of last resort' facility, to replace the funds it was no longer able to raise from the money market. This led to panic among Northern Rock depositors, not helped by the psychological effect of the widely published phrase 'lender of last resort', a technical term that was not to inspire confidence in Northern Rock's customers!

Depositors feared that their savings might not be available should Northern Rock go into receivership. The result was a bank run, the UK's first in 150 years. Long queues formed outside Northern Rock branches as depositors sought to withdraw all of their savings, and to do so as quickly as possible before others doing the same exhausted the reserves of the bank. Even Bank of England support for the bank proved inadequate and by February 2008 Northern Rock had been nationalised. Private excesses had been converted into socialised debt. By then, the crisis was overtaking even those financial institutions that had exercised prudence.

In September 2008, Lehman Brothers, a large and respected US-based investment bank, collapsed under the strain of falling asset values. To guard against further moral hazard, governments on both sides of the Atlantic resisted bailing out Lehman Brothers; with hindsight, this was a big mistake. Lehman's went bankrupt with $613 billion of debts. This sent panic right across the whole finance sector and the banks, fearful of their own positions and the credit-worthiness of others, ceased to lend to each other. The money markets had frozen up. This left even some of the most major banks completely exposed as their asset prices continued to collapse along with their credit-worthiness. Further bail-outs and nationalisation followed. At one point the UK government's commitment to supporting banks exceeded £1 trillion, though much of that was 'bluff' money offered as reassurance rather than actual aid; banking is all about confidence. No one knows quite how much was actually paid out to bail out the banks – it depends how you count it – but the usually fierce watchdog of public spending, the National Audit Office, was unequivocal: 'If the support measures had not been put in place, the scale of the economic and social costs if one or more major UK banks had collapsed would be so large as to be difficult to envision. The support provided to the banks was therefore justified.' In short, poor Alistair Darling had no choice but to bail out those misbehaving banks.

So, were the bankers grateful and ready to make amends by lending to businesses to get the economy moving again? No, they raised their interest rates to protect themselves against further risk, even as the Bank of England cut the rates at which it would lend to commercial banks and provided billions in bail-outs. To reduce their debts the commercial banks actually cut back their lending to consumers and industry and so the financial crisis spread to the rest of the economy, locking the US, UK and the rest of Europe into the deepest recession since the Great Depression of the 1930s. In some ways it was deeper, and certainly much longer, as was shown by the National Institute of Economic and Social Research's chart showing the course of recessions since 1920. The black dotted line shows the recent Great Recession. We took quite some time for GDP to get back to where we were before the recession. By the end of 2014 real GDP was some 3 to 4 per cent above but we've yet even to get back to where we were in terms of GDP per head:

FIGURE 4

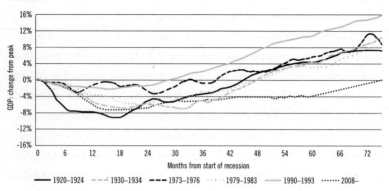

Months from start of recession

—— 1920–1924   – – – 1930–1934   ━ ━ 1973–1976   ····· 1979–1983   ～～ 1990–1993   ······ 2008–

Source: National Institute of Economic and Social Research[3]

The deregulation of the banking sector that had accompanied the re-birth of free market macro policies, as encouraged by Mrs Thatcher's government, had allowed banks to take on risks, and a bubble of credit and debt was created out of thin air through exotic and highly complex financial instruments. It was noticed, most famously by the Queen, and in stark contrast to the previous hubris of many economists, that the vast majority of academic economists had failed to anticipate the worst financial crisis since the Great Depression. Some, mostly more Keynesian economists, had warned of impending meltdown, and so suddenly Keynes was back in fashion – for a while at least, until the neo-liberals could regroup. As the crisis began, Alistair Darling, Gordon Brown's successor as Chancellor, provoked PM Brown's fury by declaring that the economic climate was the worst for sixty years and that the effects of the financial crisis would be longer-lasting and more profound than people thought. In the event, even this was an understatement.

A short-lived recovery killed off by austerity

Darling looked to both monetary stimulus (cheap money) and fiscal stimulus (raising government expenditure and – particularly in this case – cutting tax) to fight off the deep recession, and this Keynesian prescription did indeed seem to lift the economy and begin the recovery. At the same time, Gordon Brown successfully campaigned for similar stimulus packages across the EU. Nick Crafts, the eminent economic historian, wrote: 'Monetary and fiscal policies were pursued on a scale that would have been unacceptable during the 1930s but, crucially, these bold initiatives prevented financial meltdown … the "experiment" of the 1930s shows only too clearly the likely outcome in the absence of an aggressive policy response.'[4]

Although history will judge Labour's response to the crisis more kindly, none of it failed to revive the popularity of the Labour government. By the time Brown's period of office had run out, in the general election of 2010, the Labour government was still being blamed by the electorate for the crisis. The recession had inevitably led to a greatly increased fiscal deficit, as tax revenues always fall and welfare spending rises during a recession, but it suited the Conservative's emphasis on Labour's 'reckless borrowing' to repeatedly and loudly announce that it was making 'fiscal consolidation', i.e. austerity, its number one priority (despite an immigration policy that, in making fiscal consolidation harder, showed that getting elected was the real number one policy!).

Fiscal 'austerity' also suited those Conservatives, and others, who had perennially longed for any excuse to cut back on government spending – they wouldn't let a good crisis go to waste! So Osborne rejected Darling's target to halve the deficit over four years as 'not enough'; instead, he committed the new coalition in June 2010 to eliminating the structural Budget deficit completely by March 2016. This forced many Lib Dems into a painful U-turn when they signed up to the coalition agreement, particularly the more Keynesian Vince Cable, he who had correctly predicted the financial crisis. In the event, it turned out that Osborne was not only to fall short of his own targets: he also failed to meet Alistair Darling's more modest deficit reduction targets. Embarrassingly, Osborne was forced to repeal even the legally backed milestones Darling had put in place for himself!

Back in the 1930s, Keynes had explained how one person's spending was another person's income. Hence, cutting spending reduces the incomes of others. As their incomes fall, total spending falls some more, thereby decreasing all incomes even further and hence multiplying the original cuts and producing a downward spiral. Demand for products falls, so output falls, and so businesses stop investing and consumers save for the uncertain days ahead – or are made unemployed and can't spend anyway. So again, spending falls and then gets stuck at low levels as pessimism towards future prospects gets locked in, and a Chancellor banging on about the need for 'austerity for years ahead' is unlikely to raise optimism either! Not only does this create unemployment, it also reduces the taxes needed to pay for a deficit and, worst of all, increases the debt-to-income (GDP) ratio, which is what really matters. This will tend to rise as its denominator, GDP, falls. Play all this back in reverse and you can see what Keynes meant when he said 'look after the unemployment, and the Budget will look after itself'.

The coalition's austerity killed off Alistair Darling's nascent recovery. A long period of 'flat-lining' GDP followed, mimicked by Ed Balls's childish flat-lining hand motions whenever the Tory Chancellor spoke in the Commons, a gesture that even the usually implacably aloof Osborne found intensely irritating. Austerity was not only preventing the economy from recovering, it was also keeping down the tax revenues needed to pay off the government's deficit. Worse, it destroyed business optimism and decreased business investment. Public infrastructure, vital for the UK's long-term growth and now available at rock-bottom unbeatable low interest rates, might have been used to kick-start the economy, but instead it was cut. It's a common feature of periods of austerity that public investment gets cut; maybe it's because the future generations that it would have benefited are unable to complain or, more importantly, to vote now. An example of such false economy is the failure of successive government to build homes that has resulted in 95 per cent of the government's housing budget now being spent on rent subsidies rather than construction!

Instead of government borrowing being used to boost the economy and provide the vital infrastructure for future growth, it was instead used to pay for the effects of not doing this – that is, to pay for the Great Recession.

For example, in the calendar year 2007, the Labour government borrowed £37.7 billion, of which £28.3 billion was invested in big projects; in 2013, the Conservative-led coalition borrowed £91.5 billion with just £23.7 billion invested. So tax revenues stayed low and welfare spending stayed high, and flat-lining growth meant that the deficit was flat-lining too. Even the minority of economists who had originally backed his austerity package now felt George Osborne and his ally in 'austerity', the German Chancellor Angela Merkel, were ignoring the vital lessons of Keynes.

The respected senior *Financial Times* economist Martin Wolf in his excellent book *The Shifts and the Shocks: What We've Learned – And Have Still to Learn – From the Financial Crisis* blames the premature and severe tightening in policy in 2010, which followed the massive fiscal and monetary relaxation in 2008 and 2009 that was stabilising the situation. The collective opting for austerity resulted in a downward spiral from which some of the European countries are only now beginning to recover, and at the time of writing even this is looking increasingly precarious because of the continuing lack of demand across European economies.

Osborne followed and promoted the austerity line too. He argued that he was successfully maintaining the confidence of the markets and that it was only this that was allowing the UK government to continue to borrow at such low interest rates. He claimed that if he was not seen to be strict on reducing the fiscal deficit this would spook the markets and cause interest rates to rise, hence reducing borrowing and making things much worse. Most economists found this a risible argument as the UK, the sixth and sometimes the fifth, largest economy in the world, with its own central bank and therefore bottomless money supply, was never even close to default. This was especially true as there was a severe lack of other safe havens across the world for finance to be stored anyway. If Osborne's claim that it would spook the markets unless he tackled the deficit in his way had been true then we would have found out by now, for in the event he did fail to meet his deadlines for deficit reduction and was then forced by the dire performance of the economy to ease back on austerity. And as we shall see, the

UK has successfully survived far worse debts than these in the past. The story that the markets would punish Britain was exaggerated as a bogeyman to scare the electorate into accepting the need for austerity. In the event, a couple of the rating agencies, who were by now discredited anyway because of their awful record of having given their highest credit ratings to toxic debt packages, did show their disillusionment by downgrading the UK a notch, but it wasn't because Osborne wasn't austere enough: it was because of the poor growth outlook and therefore weaker fiscal outlook that austerity was causing.

Today, the debate is still largely framed in terms of austerity measures versus Keynesian stimulus, often called the 'Austerians versus the Stimulards' debate. It's pretty much the same debate that was had in the 1930s. What the analysis has gained in technical sophistication since then it has perhaps lost in terms of economic wisdom from such giants of economics as Keynes and Hayek. As we will never know for sure what would have happened if Labour had not been in power and Osborne hadn't taken over, we can never say for certain which side is correct. That's what economists are for, to try to make sense of economic phenomena. But which economists do we trust to be impartial? A good place to start must be the economists in the body that George Osborne himself set up to be the impartial watchdog on economic prospects; the Office for Budget Responsibility (OBR). Amid the many voices commenting on economic policy, the OBR is intended to be the referee that governments must heed.

The PM, David Cameron, claimed the authority of the OBR in March 2013 as proof that the long economic flat-lining wasn't caused by austerity: 'They are absolutely clear, and they are absolutely independent. They are absolutely clear that the deficit reduction plan is not responsible; in fact, quite the opposite.'[5]

Unfortunately for Cameron, it turned out that the OBR is more independent than he may have bargained for. Economics flatly refuted his claim that austerity had nothing to do with lack of growth, and hence the OBR had said no such thing. So Robert Chote, the well-respected economist at the head of the OBR, felt compelled to rebuke the PM in a public letter: 'For the avoidance of doubt, I think it is important to point out that every forecast published by the OBR since the June 2010 Budget has incorporated the widely held assumption that tax increases and spending cuts reduce economic growth in the short term.'[6] In short, austerity had hit growth.

But the Conservatives wouldn't have got us into this mess in the first place!

Wrong. As we have seen, by far the most important cause of the Great Recession was a failure to control the credit/debt bubble. Ed Balls, the Labour shadow Chancellor of the Exchequer, has since confessed that Labour didn't do enough to regulate the banks, but it is largely forgotten that George Osborne, when shadow Chancellor, had severely criticised Gordon Brown as Chancellor, and urged him to go much further in deregulating the banks: 'In an age of greater choice, he offers more overbearing control; in an age of greater freedom, he gives us more interference ... In short, in an age that demands a light touch, he [Gordon Brown] offers that clunking fist.'[7]

David Cameron, so critical now of Labour's record of letting finance rip, had told big finance in 2006: 'The lessons from the City are clear. Low tax. Low regulation. Meritocracy. Openness. Innovation. These are the keys to success.' In his last big speech on this before becoming Prime Minister, at the Mansion House in June 2007, just as the financial crisis was about to break, Cameron praised the bankers for their remarkable achievements and predicted 'the beginning of a new golden age for the City of London'. It wasn't a great forecast.

Whatever mistakes Labour made in lessening bank regulation, the Conservatives would have gone even further in the wrong direction.

But would they have ended Gordon Brown's excessive spending? No, not at all. There hadn't been a peep from Osborne about Labour's spending pre-crisis and this is how the *Telegraph* – or the Torygraph, as it is often called – reported George Osborne's own pre-election spending plans: 'In an echo of New Labour's own 1997 manifesto promise to match the Tory government's projected spending levels, George Osborne vowed last night to stick to Gordon Brown's plan of increasing public spending by 2 per cent in real terms over the next three years.'[8]

In short, pre-crisis there was never a gnat's whisker between the two parties on public spending.

But the economy is now recovering, so doesn't that prove Osborne's austerity was right?

No. Nigel Lawson is a better economist than he is climatologist (see Chapter 11), but he forgets to mention that of course economies eventually recover! Recessions always come to an end eventually – that's why they are called 'recessions' and not 'business as usual'. To illustrate, suppose that for some perverse reason the Chancellor had the inclination and power to close down the UK pharmaceutical industry. Employment would fall directly by the 70,000 or so employees in the industry, and then by much more indirectly because of the multiplier effects we have already described. Output would fall dramatically, but this would also 'free up' a lot of previously employed labour and other resources. Eventually, the displaced labour would find jobs (though probably not as good ones) elsewhere, and resources would move into their second-best uses. Output would begin to rise again from the trough caused by the policy of throwing away such a valuable industry. Employment would start to rise, even though productivity, i.e. output per head, had been lowered by this madcap policy. Indeed, the more resources that had been 'freed' by the policy, the more that would be available for the recovery. That is, the deeper the trough that had been created, the faster the economy would tend to rise once it started to recover.

This fictional story may sound familiar because it is close to what actually happened, forgetting about the pharmaceuticals metaphor, of course. Because of its large financial sector and early austerity policies, the UK shrank more than other countries – in fact, in terms of constant purchasing power, much more than any other major economy.[9] So it is hardly surprising then that it is now recovering more quickly than most other countries, especially as those countries had got back to pre-recession GDP long before the UK did in mid-2014. The most salient points are that it took some six years for the UK to recover, that it will take considerably longer to get back to the same GDP per head, and that productivity is still well down compared to other countries. Despite some improvement in 2013 and in 2014, output per hour worked in late 2014 was still some 16 per cent below where it would have been if pre-recession trend growth in productivity had been maintained.

Many of the new jobs are in reality simply people scraping about: for many it is a case of an 'any income is better than none' recovery as they form a new 'precariate' of low-income workers with jobs prospects that are often uncertain week to week, even day to day, with 'zero-hour' workers and the reluctantly self-employed. In November 2014, the TUC estimated that the number of part-time employees who say they want to work full-time is still almost double the number before the recession, at 1.3 million.[10] At the end of October 2014, the Resolution Foundation announced that the numbers earning less than two-thirds of median hourly pay, equivalent to £7.69 an hour, had reached a record of 5.2 million workers. Wages have seen their biggest squeeze since 1860. Despite the increase in GDP from its depths, at the time of writing earnings are so low that tax revenues are insufficient to prevent the government's borrowing actually rising by 10 per cent per annum! This is hardly a success story and exactly what an economist would expect from a deep recession in which a lot of good jobs were lost. Repeatedly stomping on the economy for ideology-driven reasons and then claiming a victory when the economy belatedly lifts itself off the floor again may be good politics but it is very bad economics.

Perhaps the above is a biased condemnation of Osborne's austerity, since, as already admitted, we can never know for certain what might have happened had things been different. So let's turn again to George Osborne's own independent referee, the OBR. In October 2013 the OBR produced a chart[11] that tracked the effects of fiscal consolidation, using an average of a range of estimated multipliers, not even the higher multipliers many authorities claimed. We have seen that the fiscal deficit automatically increases in recession, but the OBR chart picks out the element of fiscal policy that is at the Chancellor's discretion. The rectangles show the impact of each year's fiscal policy in the year it was enacted and then follows its 'echo' effect through subsequent years. We can see that before 2010 Alistair Darling was using fiscal policy to inject demand into the economy, and the effect was indeed to lift GDP: this was why there were the beginnings of recovery. Osborne's fiscal impacts, after the 2010 election, are all below the line, showing the effects of austerity in choking off Darling's recovery. We can also see that Osborne lost his nerve after 2012, as the new fiscal consolidation rectangles are smaller after 2012, so his claim to have kept up the pace of his fiscal consolidation was not supported by the evidence from even his own authoritative watchdog that he had set up to adjudicate on such matters, the OBR.

FIGURE 5: IMPLIED IMPACTS OF DISCRETIONARY FISCAL POLICY ON THE LEVEL OF GDP

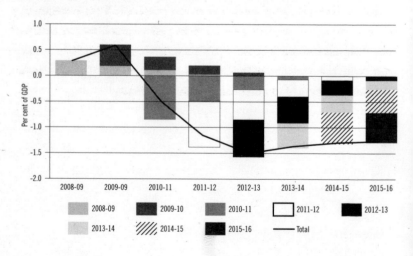

Source: Office for Budget Responsibility

Our banning-the-pharmaceutical-industry metaphor explains why the effects of fiscal consolidation eventually wear off, as the workers and resources displaced by recession are gradually reabsorbed by the economy. Had Osborne continued with rapid fiscal consolidation he may well have driven the economy down still further, allowing for even faster later recovery, but by slackening the pace of fiscal consolidation, and missing his original targets, the fiscal rectangles pushing the economy downwards after 2012 get smaller. As the effects of the bigger fiscal consolidations wearing off are not replaced by equal-sized rectangles the overall depressing effect of the Chancellor's chosen fiscal policy reduces after 2012.

In short, although they would never put it so starkly, the OBR is saying that a major reason why the economy is now recovering is not because of Osborne's austerity policy but because he backed off austerity and so its depressing effects and the effects of his earlier fiercer austerity are now wearing off. In Osborne's March 2014 Budget he claimed, 'We set out our plan. And together with the British people, we held our nerve.' The truth is plain to see, much to the annoyance of neo-liberal commentators: Osborne did not hold his nerve and from 2012 thankfully backed off on austerity. Unfortunately, we do not have a graph of all the unnecessary misery, and even deaths, that the austerity policy caused, but we do have one that puts Osborne's boasts of his 'successful' economic policy in context. With the exception of Italy, and despite a faster rate of growth lately, Britain still lags behind other comparable countries.

FIGURE 6: G7 REAL GDP

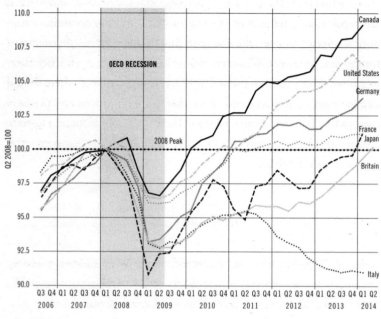

Source: Macrobond

Another generation lost

In the 1980s, Mrs Thatcher's 'monetarist experiment' saw unemployment rise to over three million. The effects were long-lasting; it took twenty years to come back down to where it had been before Mrs T. This chronic legacy of high unemployment is known as 'hysteresis' in our trade. It's a technical term that does nothing to describe the social and personal decay caused by recessions. Unemployment, and also hidden unemployment, of which there has been much, leaves deep scars. Young people aged 16–24 have suffered disproportionately from the 2008 Great Recession. There is a wealth of research that demonstrates the damage unemployment does to skills, self-esteem and work ethic; for unemployed youth, this imposes costs for individuals and society that last a long time into the future.[12] The economic, personal and social costs of hysteresis are massive, and are part of the reason why spending on welfare support is forecast to overtake the spending of government departments for the first time ever. Whatever risk of losing market confidence there might have been, and we think that was very slight indeed, there should also have been a greater concern for the economic, social and personal costs caused by such a long recession. These costs will damage long-term growth, and history shows that long-term growth is the most effective way to reduce a deficit.

Shades of Orwell?

Although he would never say it himself, Simon Wren-Lewis is probably the UK's best macroeconomist. He clearly despairs at the quality of public debate and media coverage about Osborne's austerity policy:

> We have this Orwellian world where the Chancellor says we have a recovery because he stuck to his plans, when it appears exactly the opposite is true … if he keeps on repeating that rapid growth shows critics of austerity are wrong, he will get away with it. Just as he has with the myth that much of our current problems are down to the fiscal profligacy of the previous government. Most of the press will parrot his arguments (even those that really should know better). Any hope that the BBC might provide some objectivity has disappeared as a result of threats and intimidation … This will all mean that the public will never find out that many of the minority of UK academics that originally supported austerity have changed their minds, that it is difficult to find prominent academic macroeconomists currently supporting austerity, and that more widely the academic argument for austerity has been decisively lost. Unfortunately, as Paul Krugman, the Nobel Prize-winning

economist, suggests, there is evidence that this strategy of initially closing down parts of the economy so you can claim credit when it starts
up again can help win elections.[13]

But didn't something have to be done about the deficit?

Yes, but that should not have included an ideologically driven policy of
austerity that prevented recovery in a depressed economy and thereby
lengthened, rather than shortened, the time it will take to eliminate the
government's deficit. The time to mend the government finances is when
the economy starts to grow again, not when the economy was so on its
knees that cutting spending merely reduced tax revenues, and so self-defeat-
ingly prolonged the deficit we were supposed to be tackling. Osborne's
claim that without austerity world markets would be spooked about the
UK defaulting on its debt, and so charge us higher interest rates on loans,
was always nonsense. It was never going to happen as, again: a) there were
no other comparatively safe havens for speculators' money, and b) most
importantly, the Bank of England can 'print' limitless amounts of money
if needs be (although because markets know it can do this it doesn't actually have to do it), and, related to this, c) the British government has never
failed to repay its creditors.

We also need a bit of proportionality on the size of the current UK
deficit. For example, the size of the current public debt can be made to
look absolutely terrifying when shown like this:

FIGURE 7: UK PROJECTED PUBLIC DEBT 1900–2015

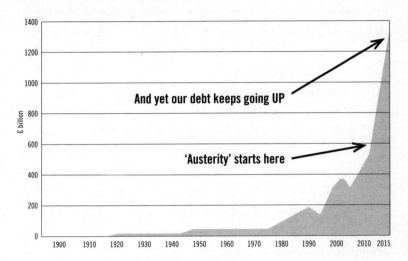

Source: Money Week 'The End of Britain'[14]

That is, unadjusted for inflation and in absolute terms, rather than, what matters more, as a percentage of GDP. But it looks much tamer when shown like this:

FIGURE 8: PUBLIC NET DEBT, UNITED KINGDOM FROM FY 1692 TO FY 2011

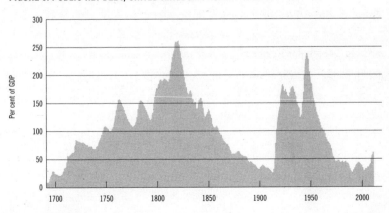

Source: ukpublicspending.co.uk

43

'Public debt is at about the average for the last 300 years' sounds a lot less frightening than the much more publicised 'disaster of unparalleled public debt'. In fact, Britain, an international leader in the management of government finances, has maintained a national debt without default for more than three centuries; mostly, the ratio of debt to GDP has been higher than it is today. For example, in the early 1950s, UK national debt was over 200 per cent of GDP, compared to about 75 per cent of GDP today. It was the legacy of the Second World War, supplemented by spending on the welfare state and nationalising industries. Some say that the UK could only have raised these funds because the US backed her, but then capital markets are more globalised today and the world is much richer, and anyway the Treasury has had no problem at all in selling UK government debt. The bigger point is that this level of debt didn't prevent three decades of growing economic prosperity. And there are plenty of people with mortgages whose debt-to-income ratio is very much higher, yet most people don't feel this is irresponsible. Mrs Thatcher was famously a grocer's daughter; she may have wanted to balance the books, but many businesses borrow to expand. Religion may condemn usury, but borrowing is not evil. Whether it is a good idea or not simply depends on why you need to borrow and whether you can pay it back.

In the twenty-five years from 1945 to 1970, we followed Keynes's dictum that the government's deficit is the tail not the dog, that is, that debt is caused by low growth and not the other way around. Keynes's approach saw the ratio of debt to GDP fall from 225 per cent to 67 per cent. OK, the national debt increased by just over 50 per cent, with, for example, huge post-war investments in public housing, but GDP went up by more than five times and so the debt-to-income ratio, which is what matters, fell consistently from 1947 to 1974, helped along by the debt-destroying properties of inflation of course! Compared with the miseries of the interwar years, this was an age of great prosperity. It was an age that had seen the setting up of the NHS, the nationalisation of one-fifth of the economy and a massive expansion of the welfare state under Attlee's Labour government

– innovations that were not much reversed by the next Conservative government. There was then a consensus about the mixed economy and the
welfare state that was to last more or less right up to Mrs Thatcher's government. Harold Macmillan, the Conservative Prime Minister from 1957
to 1963, faced with higher levels of relative debt than today, boasted to the
electorate, 'You've never had it so good.' The Conservative Party campaign
slogan of the time was 'Invest in Success'. That is still the right approach
to recession, invest for growth and pay back the deficit when the economy
recovers. Austerity, particularly when encouraged internationally, starves
the economy of oxygen and simply makes debt harder to carry.

Oops! We made a mistake!

Given that the weight of academic advice and the lessons from history
were against him, how did Osborne mount a convincing argument for his
austerity policies? A very important part of the academic evidence used
to support austerity programmes was provided by seizing on an article
by two eminent Harvard economists, Carmen Reinhart and Ken Rogoff.
Their article 'Growth in a Time of Debt' was published in the journal of
the American Economic Association in 2010. As the paper was published
in an annual 'Papers and Proceedings' edition of *The American Economic
Review*, it was not subject to the usual peer-review standards that other edi-
tions use before publication. It used international data to compare about
twenty countries and its conclusion was stark: 'When gross external debt
reaches 60 per cent of GDP, [a country's] annual growth declines by about
2 per cent ... in excess of 90 per cent, GDP growth is roughly cut in half.'[15]
   Such an adverse impact of debt on growth would of course have made
it difficult to reduce the debt-to-GDP ratio other than by cutting back on
government spending, i.e. austerity. The paper was widely cited at the highest level of government to provide credible support for the implementation
of austerity policies, but then in 2013 it was revealed that an economics

student doing his homework had cast doubt on the methods used in the paper. The University of Massachusetts Amherst gave a graduate class an assignment to choose an economics paper and see if they could replicate the results. Thomas Herndon chose 'Growth in a Time of Debt'. No matter how he tried, Thomas just couldn't replicate Reinhart and Rogoff's results. He tells how 'my heart sank ... I thought I had likely made a gross error. Because I'm a student, the odds were I'd made the mistake, not the well-known Harvard professors.' When Thomas still hadn't cracked the puzzle at the end of the semester, his supervisors became intrigued. 'We had this puzzle that we were unable to replicate the results that Reinhart–Rogoff published,' Professor Ash said. 'That was really a mystery for us.'

So Ash and his colleague Professor Robert Pollin encouraged Thomas to write to the eminent Harvard professors. After some correspondence, Reinhart and Rogoff provided Thomas with the spreadsheet that they'd actually used to obtain their results. Thomas was astonished: 'Everyone says seeing is believing, but I almost didn't believe my eyes.' Thomas called his girlfriend over to check his eyes weren't deceiving him, but there was no doubt: there were obvious and fundamental errors. Data that would greatly affect the result had been omitted and there were some strange uses of averages. Ash concluded that the 'combination of the collapse of the empirical result that high public debt is inevitably associated with greatly reduced GDP growth and the weakness of the theoretical mechanism under current conditions ... render the Reinhart and Rogoff point close to irrelevant for current public policy debate'.[16]

Other economists then looked more closely at the Reinhart and Rogoff results. They found no convincing evidence for thresholds of debt past which growth becomes negative, that the differences across countries made averaging largely meaningless in any case, and to the extent that any negative association between debt and growth existed it was likely to be the result of Keynes's observation that if you look after unemployment, debt will look after itself: that is, that debt is caused by low growth and not the other way around. This ambiguity was belatedly conceded by the two, by now highly embarrassed, Harvard economists attempting to distance themselves from those politicians who had seized on their findings to justify austerity. 'Our view has always been that causality runs in both directions,' they said in their *New York Times* op-ed, 'and that there is no rule that applies across all times and places … Nowhere did we assert that 90 per cent was a magic threshold that transforms outcomes, as conservative politicians have suggested.'[17]

Paul Krugman summed it up in 2013:

> What the Reinhart-Rogoff affair shows is the extent to which austerity has been sold on false pretences. For three years, the turn to austerity has been presented not as a choice but as a necessity. Economic research, austerity advocates insisted, showed that terrible things happen once debt exceeds 90 per cent of GDP. But 'economic research' showed no such thing; a couple of economists made that assertion, while many others disagreed. Policy-makers abandoned the unemployed and turned to austerity because they wanted to, not because they had to.[18]

But what about the debt?
No matter whose fault it was it still has to be dealt with!

Yes, it does need to be addressed. Other things being equal, low levels of debt are better than high levels of debt, but economic theory tells us that deficit reduction should be fairly slow if it is not to be self-defeating and the cause of much social misery. At the moment, interest rates are so low that in relative terms it actually costs less to service the national debt than it did under Mrs Thatcher. If interest rates were to rise without sufficient economic growth to offset this, and hence keep the debt-to-GDP ratio down, it could cause big problems. But, as we have seen, cutting the growth of the economy through sustained austerity when the economy is weak is not the answer: this only exacerbates the problem. That is why the Bank of England has refrained for so long from raising interest rates. At the time of writing, interest rates have been unchanged since March 2009, and they won't have moved much by the time you read this either.

There are good reasons to be optimistic that interest rates will not be raised. Firstly, we know that interest rates can be kept low for a very long time by the Bank of England: during the long post-war consensus, a central policy plank was precisely to keep interest rates low, not only to encourage business investment but also to reduce the interest burden of the national debt. But it is harder to maintain this if UK interest rates become much lower than elsewhere. So the period of capped interest rates between 1945 and 1979 also saw capital controls to limit the mobility of finance, that is, to prevent low interest rates leading to a flight of capital to countries where it can earn high interest. Given the tight curbs on capital that existed, it is probably no coincidence that this period of 'financial repression' saw far fewer financial crises than earlier or subsequently. Capital controls remain a rather unwelcome but nevertheless available option, but then we are unlikely to see a massive rise in rates in the foreseeable future.

Sir Charlie Bean, outgoing deputy director for the Bank of England, in June 2014 estimated, 'It might be reasonable to think that in that very long term you would go back to 5 per cent but it's probably quite a long way down the road.' Mark Carney, the Bank's Governor, predicted that 2.5 per cent would be reached in slow stages and then be the norm for at least the medium term. It is also important to note that rising interest rates will not affect existing government debt: the interest rates on existing 'gilts', as government debt is known, have already been set. Also, interest rates will only rise if the strength of the economy improves greatly, which means that reduced welfare payments, and particularly increased tax revenues, will be available to cope with the increased cost of servicing new debt. But what seems to be happening is that despite the pick-up in demand and the creation of 2 million new jobs since the coalition came to power, wage pressures have remained low. It is therefore possible that until productivity starts to improve, inflation will remain below target despite employment levels that are considerably higher than used to be the case in the past. It is entirely possible that changes in the structure of jobs in the economy and increasing globalisation have resulted in the UK having to wait longer for an improvement in the economy to translate itself to higher wages in a consistent manner. Paul Gregg and Stephen Machin[19] argue that serious pay pressures may not occur until we see the unemployment rate falling to at least 5 per cent. Three decades ago, pay pressures would have been begun to be seriously felt when unemployment was at 10 per cent.

So what is the best course of action – and is there room for manoeuvre by whoever comes to power in May 2015? One constraint will clearly remain the level of debt. But it is easy to exaggerate the debt problem faced; indeed, 'Austerians' do deliberately exaggerate it. For example, another myth put about is that the debt is somehow a terrible burden on future generations as it is owed to someone other than us UK citizens and will therefore have to be repaid. But in fact less than a third of the debt is owed to foreigners. The rest is owed to ourselves. Much of it is held by our own pension and insurance funds: UK citizens will be the beneficiaries of these funds and the proceeds can be redistributed among us by future governments if needs be. About a quarter of the debt is owed to the Bank of England, and there is an easy solution for this debt: don't pay it back! It was never actually there in the first place: the advantage of having our own central bank is that it can create money out of thin air. It's a pity we didn't make much more use of that facility. For, instead of real borrowing, we could, EU rules aside, have simply printed money to get out of the recession. Non-economists, and even some economists, find this will-of-the-wisp nature of money difficult to believe. But money is like a myth: it requires only imagination for its creation but faith for its effectiveness. And as there is such enormous confidence in the Bank of England, both here and abroad, it simply has to say it has the money and, hey presto, it does have the money!

This ability to create money at will is not to be abused. It is rather like adrenalin: very useful in exceptional circumstances but it damages health if used too much. In particular, excessive 'printing' can create inflation, but in such a deep recession inflation has been the least of our problems. Indeed, a greater danger has been deflation, and at the time of writing this still is a very real European risk. This is to be avoided at all costs, for it can trap the economy into a downward spiral as deflation sends real interest rates soaring, increasing the real value of debt and stopping people spending.

'Reneging' on paying back the Bank of England will not bankrupt it, or us, and is unlikely to produce inflation. This is because economists now know that money is not pumped into the economy but rather sucked into the economy. For all the special measures the Bank of England has engaged in – mostly, creating money through 'quantitative easing' – they did not, unfortunately, create much more rapid spending. The money provided by commercial banks simply follows the economy rather than pushes it along. When the economy picks up speed, businesses and consumers will start to borrow again; if this threatens to overheat the economy, that is the time to act. Now is not the time to act, for monetary policy, like a string, can pull even where it cannot push, so allowing interest rates to rise would further weaken demand and act as a drag on the economy, endangering a fragile recovery. In any case, a little inflation can be a very effective way of reducing debt!

In short, yes, we should be looking to reduce debt, but trying to do this too quickly presents much more danger than doing it more gradually. This is implicit in the OBR's announcements that accompanied Osborne's December 2014 'autumn' statement: 'The government's fiscal plans imply three successive years of cash reductions in government consumption of goods and services from 2016 onwards, the first since 1948. The corresponding real cuts directly reduce GDP.' The Chancellor had massively failed to meet his target of eliminating the deficit by 2015, but now the OBR estimates that for the government to meet its new goal of eliminating the budget deficit by 2019 public spending as a percentage of GDP would have to fall by much more over the next five years than it has over the last five. Indeed, they note that government consumption of goods and services would fall to its lowest share of GDP since 1938.

Osborne/Merkel austerity did enormous damage last time; an unyielding commitment to even sharper austerity poses a new and enormous threat. As David Blanchflower, respected economist and former member of the Bank of Engand's Monetary Policy Committee notes,

> Many of us tried to explain that to George before he embarked on his reckless austerity path that produced the third worst recovery in 650 years, behind only the Black Death and the South Sea Bubble. The economy was growing at escape velocity when he inherited it in May 2010 but then the economy flat-lined for three whole years until picking up in 2013. GDP per head remains well below its peak level at the start of 2008. Most of the growth we have seen has come from a rise in the 16+ population, which is up 2.5 million (5 per cent) since January 2008 and 1.5 million since May 2010 (3 per cent), mostly through immigration.[20]

Any mitigation in Osborne's poor economic record has mainly been through the failure of Conservative policy on the deficit and immigration, but a common definition of insanity (or should that be stupidity?) is doing the same thing again and expecting a different result.

Conclusions

There are three major flaws in the commonly repeated narrative, a story neatly summarised by Mrs Thatcher's famous phrase, 'The problem with socialism is that you eventually run out of other people's money.' Firstly, whatever Labour had supposedly done to cause a crisis the Conservatives were committed to do too, or to go even further in the same direction.

Secondly, government spending had nothing to do with the causes of the crisis. Thirdly, the UK could not have fully protected itself from the global financial crash in any case. The truth is that poverty and misery have been inflicted on people of modest incomes and less, by the sins of very rich bankers. It is a great irony that, led by a Tory-dominated press, the electorate's response to this has been to (almost) elect a Conservative Party funded by the banks and led by a man whose family wealth comes from banking.

As we saw, panicked by the poor performance of the economy and in the light of the impending election, Osborne has eased up on austerity. In any case, the so-called automatic stabilisers had limited the extent to which people felt the impact on austerity in their own lives. Automatic stabilisers limit fluctuations in the economy through counter-cyclical changes in the fiscal balance between government expenditure and taxation. As the economy declines government expenditures automatically rise in relation to taxes thereby boosting demand and this prevents GDP falling by as much as it would otherwise. For example, there is more unemployment benefit that needs to be paid and higher welfare payments that need to be made and more tax credits for those still at work but in lower-paid jobs or faced with higher bills as VAT and other taxes rise. As fewer people are employed or more work part-time or become self-employed, often earning much less than before, less income tax is collected. Indeed, partly through the progressive raising of the income tax threshold to £10,600 and the fact that many of the new jobs created have been either at or near minimum wage, part-time or on zero-hour contracts and that many of the new jobs are made of the self-employed who have seen their real wages go down by some 20 per cent over five years, tax collection has suffered much more than the OBR had predicted. This also correspondingly boosted welfare benefits being paid, including working tax credits. It is calculated that during the five-year coalition government the Chancellor collected £65 billion less in taxes and paid some £25 billion more in benefits than had been forecast.

In addition as profits suffer, companies pay less corporation tax. VAT receipts are affected if people don't spend. There is less stamp duty paid if shares do not exchange hands as frequently, or their value drops, and similarly if fewer houses are sold and at a lower price. This tends to leave more money in the system and that is basically tantamount to a real relaxation in fiscal policy – in other words, the government stance is more expansionary – and indeed was more expansionary throughout the early austerity years in general – than had been envisaged. After so severely damaging the economy from 2010 to 2012 with his austerity measures, Osborne then chickened out some on seeing its effects, much to the chagrin of many of his soulmates on the right.

At the same time, government investment spending started to recover. Most economists had argued at the time of the emergency Budget in June 2010, a month after the coalition came to power, that the savage cuts to government investment would have serious consequences for the economy as whole, particularly as private sector investment often depends on government spending as a trigger (such as in infrastructure, for example). As Nick Clegg, the Deputy Prime Minister, admitted in January 2013, the coalition made a mistake in cutting back capital spending when it came into office.[21]

But the real loosening of policy that has helped hold up demand in the economy has come in terms of monetary policy, helped along by a much lesser but not insignificant boost of £12 billion of bank repayments for their mis-sold payment protection policies. Interest rates are at a record low – lower than has ever been the case since the Bank of England was created in 1694. At the beginning of the recession, the government intervened heavily to assist the banks as their loan books deteriorated rapidly and to inject new money in the economy. In effect, two banks were partly nationalised – RBS and Lloyds – and others were either closed down or merged with the bigger banks. Crucially, there was also quantitative easing, amounting to £375 billion, which consisted of the Bank of England buying assets, mostly government bonds, from banks to improve their liquidity and capital position. This was followed in 2012 by extra injections of money through 'Finance for Lending' – cheap loans worth some £80 billion to banks to use for lending to companies and individuals – and through the Help to Buy scheme, both of which have resulted in a considerable amount of money being made available to consumers who have kept up their levels of spending by cutting their savings. As George Osborne had hoped, this has managed to get the economy moving again in time for the elections, but a longer-term solution to the economic hangover may need more than the hair of the private sector debt dog that bit us.

So this government has done what many other Conservative governments have done through the generations: austerity when they come in followed by a couple of years of 'boom' conditions as the electoral cycle throws up the prospect of another polling day. And this time has been no different except for the language used, which, confusingly, is still a language of austerity – at a time when the UK was the fastest-growing economy in the Western world in 2014, growing by 3.5 per cent according to some forecasts. By the time of the next election, GDP will likely be considerably higher than it was at the beginning of the recession (complicated by some re-estimates of the raw data which we must ignore for the moment) and unemployment will be well below 6 per cent – that is, back to about the level it was before the Great Recession in 2008. The question is, of course, whether real living standards will have improved. Real disposable incomes, i.e. the money left in your pocket that you can actually spend on yourself, despite a rise in the threshold from which one starts to pay tax, are still in fact below where they were at the start of the recession. Wages are some 2 per cent below their pre-recession levels, and those of the self-employed some 20 per cent below. In short, there is still real hardship around. Wage growth has been below inflation for a very long time and that is an issue that will feature greatly in the election debates, even if wages pick up a bit before then.

But looking ahead, if elected, the Conservatives have promised to bring the government's current account into surplus by 2018/19, in part by reducing public spending as a proportion of national income from 46 per cent in 2010/11 to about 37 per cent in 2018/19. Osborne has called for an additional £25 billion of cuts for 2016/17 and 2017/18, on top of the £20 billion cut already announced for 2015/16. Most economists thought Ed Balls was correct when he used to chant 'too far, too fast' at George Osborne, but so effectively has the public debt caused by bankers been attributed to Labour that even he now refrains from this refrain, promising instead that 'the next Labour government will balance the books and deliver a surplus on the current Budget and falling national debt in the next parliament'. This is all unnecessarily fast and risks a renewed suppression of growth. So, as Martin Wolf of the *Financial Times* says, 'It is the hair shirt for the indefinite future. Welcome to Austerity Britain.'

By contrast, Osborne's erstwhile EU partners in austerity may be having second thoughts. At the end of November 2014, the European Commission announced:

> The European Commission has today presented a comprehensive plan to drive Europe's recovery from the current economic crisis. The Recovery Plan is based on two mutually reinforcing main elements. Firstly, short-term measures to boost demand, save jobs and help restore confidence. Secondly, 'smart investment' to yield higher growth and sustainable prosperity in the longer-term. The Plan calls for a timely, targeted and temporary fiscal stimulus of around €200 billion.

Too little, too late – but at least it's in the right direction!

Back in the UK, fiscal consolidation will need to be pursued in the next parliament, debt does need to be addressed somehow and the markets will need to retain trust in any incoming government's commitment to fiscal prudence. But only up to a point. As we have seen, we have moved to a realisation that the structural deficit is much more difficult to shift and eliminate, as the OBR is now suggesting. To achieve the proposed balanced budgets requires savage spending cuts and sizeable tax increases, or indeed both – all rather scary for the voters. And the truth is that austerity can indeed be overdone. Any new government will have to talk the talk of retrenchment and have to make difficult decisions. But the bottom line remains that there is nothing sacrosanct about achieving balance and then moving to a sustained surplus – and nothing sacred about the date when that needs to be achieved. A consideration implicitly conceded by Ed Balls in December 2014 when he admitted, 'How fast we can go will depend on the state of the economy', as he astutely allowed himself space for £50 billion less in spending cuts or tax rises than the Conservatives' commitments over the next parliament. So, voter, when looking at the various manifestos bear in mind that in reality there is no critical doomsday date for a surplus. And also be aware that all political parties know this. So expect lots of tough talk but no real details and much less action in the end unless they want to commit economic and with it political suicide. Osborne realised it and moved to Plan B two years into the 2010–15 parliament. Evidence everywhere does show that too much austerity stops recovery in its tracks while also having the perverse effect of worsening government finances.

The markets want growth – and growth above balanced budgets. In truth, it is more than likely that the date of reaching balanced budgets will gradually shift to later years, as fundamentally changing the structure of the UK economy to a more sustainably productive one with a strong investment and export sector is likely to prove a much harder challenge than the authorities had anticipated. But watch out nevertheless, as 'rebalancing' and 'much needed cuts' and 'much needed restructuring' and 'continuing to do more with less' and 'administrative efficiencies' and 'outsourcing to achieve these' and 'the role of the public sector' and 'continued crisis' feature strongly in pre-election oratory. In particular, the continued fiscal problems present just too good an opportunity for some of the parties to miss and thus will use the chance they have under the guise of needing to respond to the crisis in order to attack their pet hates. More taxes for the rich for some, even if they don't raise much money; for others, a long awaited excuse to slash away at the welfare state or reduce the influence of an independent civil service which, despite its weaknesses, by and large believes in evidence-based policy.

As part of their measures, the Tories have introduced an arbitrary cap on welfare spending. Voters should ask if an unnecessary, ideology-driven reversal of the gains in welfare provision since the Second World War really is an appropriate policy for an ageing population, a population hit by unnecessarily prolonged austerity, and a population that has seen large increases in inequality since Mrs Thatcher's government. They should also ask themselves whether a mansion tax isn't just there for show, given that property taxes in the UK, equivalent to some 4.3 per cent of GDP, are among the highest in the developed world – and will remain so after the stamp duty reform announced in the autumn statement of December 2014. Even the Conservatives' coalition partners, the Liberal Democrats, who from the word go were often even more fanatical in their avowed zeal to achieve fiscal consolidation, suggesting that without immediate action the UK would end up like Greece, have changed their tune. They no longer believe – or so they say pre-election – that austerity should be a long-term goal and now warn that the Conservatives want to use it as an excuse to reduce the size and role of the state...

CHAPTER 3

There's No Business Like Grow Business

(… And create a safer banking system in the process)

What to do with the bankers? Chaining the golden goose

B ANKS AND OTHER financial institutions are an integral part of the economy. Without them, the system would not allow transactions to happen efficiently. A poor financial system hampers economic growth. Financial intermediation that allows savers to lend to investors who then build capacity for future output is clearly productive, and even some credit money creation may be a good stimulus at times. However, there is general agreement that speculative bubbles that create mountains of illusory paper wealth that will later collapse like a house of cards is counter-productive. It is a cause of human suffering and grossly inequitable. And yet this is precisely what happened and it brought about a recession in the developed world that was the worst since the Great Depression of the later 1920s. Regulation had failed to stop this from happening. And, more recently, the unearthing of long-standing illegal practices such as the manipulation by market practitioners of crucial financial indices like interest rate benchmarks and foreign exchange rates, on which most international transactions are priced, e.g. the London Interbank Offer Rate (LIBOR), have shocked the markets. Fines have been imposed and banks have also been paying compensation to customers for mis-selling products. Personal protection insurance mis-selling, for example, has already cost the banks in the UK some £12 billion in the past two years alone – and there is still more to come. But now governments across the world have turned to tighter regulation to stop reckless and corrupt banking practices.

The UK is at the forefront of new regulation. But when considering what is appropriate, the question has to be whether the remedies we are imposing on the financial sector are still trying to deal with a situation which has now moved on, rather than with the here and now which may necessitate different thinking. And certainly a balance needs to be struck between increasing regulation while still allowing the UK's vital finance sector to thrive.

As outlined in Chapter 2, the hard-selling of easy credit as financial markets increasingly deregulated in the years before the financial crisis fuelled many of the excessive behaviours that are now the subject of modern political debate. In the search for high returns at a time of low interest rates, financial institutions offered huge bonuses many times over basic pay as compensation for high short-term profits created by their employees. In this environment, ethical behaviour often went out of the window. Short-termism became rampant, market practitioners looked for high yields in areas where such yields should never have existed, and often, though not always, underestimated the risks they were taking. Indeed, credit rating agencies failed to perceive the real underlying risks in many of the instruments created and traded in vast quantities around the world or held as supposedly secure assets by banks and other financial institutions and effectively gave their blessing to what was going on. In the UK as in most places elsewhere, no attempt was made to prick various asset bubbles.

Easy credit conditions were helped by the fact that lax monetary policies were accompanied by expansionary government fiscal policies and helped create a credit boom, while the regulatory authorities were in awe of the organisations they were meant to supervise. Banks expanded their balance sheets exponentially. And the credit boom gathered pace more or less unrestricted.

All this was reinforced by lax monetary policy more or less everywhere in the world, which, in the Eurozone, had occurred since the introduction of the euro. Globalisation had led to low prices around the globe and inflation seemed to have moved to a perpetually low rate so interest rates everywhere could be kept low too. At the same time, high savings rates in the emerging economies as export receipts mounted gave rise to huge sums of money needing to be invested somewhere around the world, and bodies holding these savings were also chasing returns internationally.

Are capital markets and financial institutions inherently short-termist?

Economists are always accused of believing in efficient markets – in other words, that somehow or other capital will flow to the most productive and valuable assets and the markets will clear in an orderly way. But in an environment where interest rates stay low for a long period and markets become so globalised that large flows of capital between borders makes finance too freely available, capital markets are no longer able to identify and allocate resources to the most efficient possible uses. The pursuit of more profitable returns either results in or is accompanied by the acceptance of questionable practices and a lack of incentives to consider the long term.

For instance, for the past fifteen to twenty years or so, financial institutions have been using mathematical and econometric models for the pricing of risk that did not use a long enough time horizon and that did not therefore incorporate 'exceptional' circumstances; and yet, as is now clearly obvious, these exceptional events do happen more frequently than people assume, and should be built into expectations when pricing risk.[1]

The emphasis therefore has been on short-termism rather than long-termism. But were financial actors really to blame for their behaviour? Some would argue that even knowing the extent of the miscalculations made in the run-up to the crisis, with hindsight, it was not irrational for financial actors to adopt this approach in a booming market. The collective experiences of the finance sector and the capital markets they operate in suggest that, ultimately, their 'bets' have been underwritten by the taxpayer. During the long boom of the 1990s and up to 2007 it was therefore rational to assume that there would be a bail-out if such extreme events were to take place. This is called 'moral hazard' by economists: there was no incentive to write in extreme events to models, as such extreme events trigger government intervention that covers their risk. Therefore, the implicit underwriting of the bulk of risks in large financial institutions provides little incentive to create models that predict events that will be the subject of large government bail-outs.

Further, in finance a trader will look only at their private returns from creating credit, but they will ignore the cumulative effects of all trades on asset prices. So if credit is created to buy assets, the prices of these assets rise and they are then used as collateral to secure even more loans. This amplification, or spill-over, effect, whereby rising asset prices create more credit and yet more asset price rises, is known by economists as a 'credit externality'.[2] Credit externalities fuel booms and make busts more likely. Together with the moral hazard implicit in the taxpayer in effect underwriting risk in modern finance, there are clearly potential market failures that increase the likelihood that credit creation and asset prices will bubble up like a Champagne bottle out of control. It is not widely recognised – or it is ignored – that these factors were at the root of short-termism. And it is not at all clear that effective solutions to these intrinsic instabilities have been found yet, other than restricting finance so much that there is nothing left to bubble. Great in one respect. But as we have already seen as lending both within countries and also across countries has dried up, the danger is that overdoing it could be at the expense of permanently depressing the whole economy. Capitalism needs capital!

Equity markets and corporate leverage

How do these incentives translate into equity markets and the corporate environment of firms? There is short-termism here, too. With the world awash with cash chasing returns, the criteria for lending and the judgement of the financial viability of borrowers became more lax, sometimes reckless and too often immoral. This shift in attitude frequently seems to accompany financial bubbles when there is a frenzy to lend.

For example, for consumers, the opportunity to secure large amounts of credit/debt (for instance, in housing finance) with little or no evidence of ability to pay became increasingly common. The UK followed the US, which actively encouraged mortgage lending institutions – the state-supported Fannie Mae and Freddie Mac – to extend credit to poorer individuals who did not have to prove their income but were allowed to self-assess their ability to repay the mortgage they were being granted. As we saw in Chapter 2, lenders were able to package up this risky debt and pass it on mixed up with other debts, removing the incentive for initial lenders to carry out due diligence on borrowers' ability to repay.

Similarly, ratings agencies, non-executive directors and private equity investors became enthralled by the possibilities of leverage. 'Leverage' is when you use a little bit of your money to access a lot of someone else's money and then invest the lot. All of these supposedly well-informed agents systematically undervalued the risks of this excessive borrowing and leverage.

However, during a time when interest rates were at record low levels and credit was widely available, expansion and acquisition through leverage appeared to be a profitable corporate strategy. The excessive amounts of finance flowing into equity markets meant that companies were more likely to have the finance (on paper) to justify their expansionary plans. So there is a corporate short-termism here, but it is one that is analogous to the short-termism implicit in the risk-pricing models employed by financial institutions and, again, it was behaviour that was completely predictable in the environment that preceded the bust. The experts (financial institutions) were willing to bankroll extensive corporate spending and acquisition sprees and nobody stopped to ask what would happen if interest rates increased or if they were not able to roll over short-term loans. Why would they have? The problems that emerged later leading up to the financial crisis and beyond were outside the lifetime experience of most financiers and corporate operators.

Appointing the CEO and remuneration

In the environment described, just try to imagine the incentives facing prospective CEOs who wish to secure a new post. They have no incentive (and would not secure appointment) if they were to suggest in interviews that they are 'a safe pair of hands'; that the company should retain cash reserves and reduce leverage. In such a booming environment, corporations appoint those who are going to outdo their competitors and achieve an even faster rise in their share price. This risk-taking is not perceived as risk, of course, if everyone else is doing the same. There is, in people's minds, security in numbers. And outdoing competition is the surest way to achieve big bonuses for all. And remember, the risks are usually borne by the shareholders and creditors, not the management, or at least not directly (see below).

But this does not explain why their remuneration should continue to rise: we would expect a focus on appointment of 'risk-taking' CEOs to have both an upside and a downside, with some cancelling-out in the aggregate. More risks should mean more CEOs winning (and their remuneration growing) but also an offsetting fall in remuneration for those who lose their corporate bets. However, in an environment where consumers, governments and corporations were taking on excessive debt with little apparent fall in their credit rating, the balance of wins started to outweigh the balance of losses. As we have just described, up until 2007 there was clearly a massive misallocation of capital in investments that were not sustainable (i.e. they would eventually result in losses), but they were not uncovered until the bust. Corporations (and the CEOs who ran them) were making bad bets, but these were seen as good bets in an environment where risk was under-priced.

Are we that surprised that in an environment where the owners of capital (shareholders) continue to make a return on very poor investments, the managers of those investments see their remuneration packages rise substantially? A little reality check is needed here. Anybody who purchased a house at certain points over the last twenty years will have made tens, maybe hundreds of thousands of pounds in capital gains by doing nothing at all. Is this justified by their incisive investment acumen? No – they were simply operating in an environment where the possibility of losing a bet was substantially reduced and the possibility of winning was almost assured – even bad purchasing decisions made a profit for most of that period.

Again, as was the case in the financial markets, such a situation would eventually lead to re-adjustments and reversals. However, during the period of boom, the pressure to secure ever more phenomenal returns and the need to secure the services of the (apparently) charmed CEO who has won all of their corporate 'bets' for the last fifteen years results in corporate laxity and recklessness. The appointment of non-executive directors becomes window dressing, rather than a serious position of oversight; ratings agencies fail to take a long-term view of risk; accountancy firms start to secure large 'consultancy' contracts with firms they are supposed to be 'independently' auditing; and regulatory bodies become increasingly toothless.

So why has this not now changed? Clearly, many of these corporate bets have been uncovered as losses and we are now expecting to see remuneration packages tumble as a result. However, as with the wages of lesser mortals, the wages of corporate high flyers are 'sticky' downwards: in other words, it is difficult to see them taking a pay cut. This happens across most sectors and not just in banks or large corporates. Even in the public sector and in quangos, the most that has happened is a pay freeze. Again, yes, some people have lost their jobs. But many companies have been able to argue that particularly at a time of crisis what is needed is the best person (usually a man, apparently) for the job, whatever the cost. And as soon as things stabilise the remuneration committees seem to want to compensate and motivate the leaders even more, and the merry-go-round continues.

But bonuses are set to decline. The public revulsion with their size – particularly at times of hardship and in organisations which have been saved by public funds – has led both here and in Europe to attempts to limit the scale of these bonuses. The EU directive fought and lost – or rather, abandoned – by the Chancellor in the autumn of 2014 will now restrict bonuses in the financial sector to only 100 per cent of basic salary – or 200 per cent if shareholders agree. And there are also already schemes that tie bonuses and also share options to long-term achievements rather than short-term gains which may prove illusory. The bonus cap may indeed be bypassed by higher executive pay, which may be more difficult to cut when things slow down again, but at least the new regime should start shifting the incentive to one where longer-term sustainable performance becomes comparatively more important than short-term but temporary gain. Hopefully the remuneration committees will also apply this increasingly to the man (or woman) at the helm and help change corporate culture throughout whole organisations.

Short-termism versus long-termism

In an environment running on what was essentially a Ponzi finance scheme, no board had an incentive to adopt a long-term approach. In the present environment, do we expect boards to be able to adopt a long-term focus now?

The long boom, removal of regulation and availability of credit resulted in an unprecedented misallocation of resources. For a number of actors, both financial and corporate, the incentives were further skewed because of the implicit assurances provided by the public sector. In such environments, short-termism, inflated corporate remuneration and asset price bubbles are predictable. These fundamentals have not changed. All the mechanisms for the next bubble remain in place in this respect.

Managing the economy better at a macro-level will better assure a long-term approach to finance, but it is questionable whether an interventionist approach is appropriate, and it may now be too late. We have entered a stage of one regulation or initiative being heaped on another. Following a review for the Department for Business, Innovation and Skills (BIS) and the Treasury by Sir John Vickers, we are about to ring-fence retail banking from investment banking within financial organisations in the UK, well ahead of anyone else. We have tightened mortgage approval processes, raised the toughness of capital requirements well ahead of the rules that will come with the implementation of the new European Basle III regulations, implemented tighter solvency rules for insurance companies and pension funds, imposed a payday lenders interest rate cap and have embarked on a new competition market authority (MCA) review of the regime for SMEs lending. What a reversal of trends! The City complains about rules and regulations being imposed by Europe and elsewhere, and yet the regime here in the UK is now one of the toughest across the globe. But rules can be bent and circumvented. Indeed, imposing complicated rules geared to and reacting to the previous downturn risks creating an armoury of measures that are needed for battles which only arise rarely and could indeed leave the underlying situation unchanged. Remember, of course, that the crisis in the UK started with Northern Rock, a small retail bank, not with a large investment bank engaged in activities of the type we now gaily refer to as 'casino banking'. So have we actually learned from the past mistakes or are we just reacting? And are we focusing on the right thing? As Sir Richard Lambert outlined in his 2014 review[3] and as the recent scandals regarding PPI, LIBOR, foreign exchange manipulation etc. have demonstrated, the real problem is the culture in the banking system. The banks have realised this and the UK's seven largest lenders have followed up Richard Lambert's recommendation and set up a Banking Standards Review Council, chaired by Dame Colette Bowe, to promote high standards in the sector. Self-regulation in this area should help, but only up to a point. The key is having structures in place which provide a group of policy-makers with an incentive to call a halt to the party. The problem is that across government, corporate boards and financial institutions, there is simply no incentive to turn off the stereo and stop the party when there are no complaints from the neighbours; at an individual level it is simply a no-win situation. Nobody can say that by turning the music down they have avoided the police coming round, so the incentive is to party until the police arrive and then hope you will be able to make your escape. The problem for many of them was that when everybody tried to escape at once, the exits couldn't cope.

It's clear that the remuneration of directors was not appropriate and nor were many of the company acquisitions and takeovers that took place in the boom years. However, this is symptomatic of a wider misallocation of resources (and a long period of securing returns to such misallocations) that pervaded most economies that experienced a boom in credit, rather than just a failure of corporate institutions: they were often complicit, sometimes bankers were immoral, even criminal, but they did not alone create the dysfunctional frenzied environment they operated in.

Is better corporate governance the answer?

Booms and busts are a characteristic of economies and acceptance of this may be a first step in creating a realistic environment for policy-making. What we have learned with reasonable certainty as outlined above is that we cannot blame companies' short-termism alone for the spectacular crash and the slow growth experienced since. Nevertheless there is no doubt that if the way companies are motivated and run is improved, this should lead to more sustainable growth.

Short-termism as we discussed in this chapter is an integral part of the problem. But company structures often encourage it. In listed companies, owned by general shareholders, there is the issue of what is called the 'principal/agent' problem, which arises from the separation of ownership and management and which at times leads to management putting their own interests ahead of that of shareholders and the managers, who generally only stay with a firm for a relatively short period and are motivated by their remuneration arrangements to achieve short-term gain, often against the long-term interests of the shareholders.

As a result we have seen a clamour for different ownership structures that would, it is thought, inevitably lead to more long-termism. John Lewis workers' shared ownership has certain attractions, as do partnerships where the owners are also the managers, or other structures such as mutuals. But that didn't stop Arthur Andersen, the accountancy firm run as a partnership, from collapsing after being embroiled in the Enron scandal in 2001, while the problems recently faced by the Co-op bank, whose major attraction was meant to be the ability to better combine business with ethics, have all cast doubt on whether alternative ownership models are sustainable in the long term. What's more, the ability to raise capital under these ownership models is generally more limited and that tends to constrain growth prospects.

The financial crisis also exposed the fact that even the best governance structures were often lacking in quality or in the ability to exercise sufficient control over management to avoid excesses. The worrying thing was that in many cases bank boards did not have sufficient understanding of the deals done by people further down but seemed happy to accept them as they seemingly boosted profits – at least until the crisis hit. The competence of non-executive directors has been challenged in what have been some spectacular failures, such as at RBS and HBOS, both of which overextended themselves and had to be rescued by heavy government intervention to prevent the whole UK banking system collapsing. There have been attempts, including through legislation, to ensure that shareholders exercise more control over issues such as strategy and remuneration, but there are too many passive shareholders around, so that often the dissenting votes remain in a minority. So regulation alone is not the answer.[4] It should go hand in hand with a change of culture throughout an organisation that can only happen if it is clear that society expects them as part of their licence to operate to be accountable to all their stakeholders. And that, of course, automatically means caring for the long-term condition of customers, suppliers, employees, the environment and the community in which they operate – as well as the organisation's own shareholders/owners.

It is too important an issue to ignore come the next election, as we need companies to start up, grow, employ more people, invest and contribute to the well-being of society. Without them, there will not be the wealth created to support the services we all want. But as John Kay[5] has argued, 'Markets and corporations serve citizens when and only when they are embedded in the societies of which they are part.'

Conclusion

But how optimistic can we be? It is true that there is overall revulsion with the huge bonuses which had been handed out during the boom years but which in many cases resumed as soon as the recovery started – in some cases, even before. Labour minister Michael Dugher observed:

> We know that bank bonuses are actually higher this year [2014] than last
> year: bonuses at Barclays are up 10 per cent at £2.4 billion, they are up
> 8 per cent at Lloyds at £395 million, HSBC bonuses are up 6 per cent at
> £2.3 billion, and the RBS bonus pool this year is £588 million.[6]

Barclays chief executive Antony Jenkins can expect be paid up to £7.2 million this year, while Lloyds expects to pay boss Antonio Horta-Osorio a maximum package of £7.8 million.[7]

True, the European Commission has now come up with suggestions to cap bonuses to no more than 100 per cent of the salary of the lowest-paid employee. The UK has bucked the trend and seems to be allowing 200 per cent. But, as we know, every target or restriction imposed on a market tends to encourage the finding of ways to avoid it or circumvent it, as the extremely wise 'Goodhart's law', named after a previous Bank of England chief economist, Charles Goodhart, reminds us. The focus on the target obscures what happens all around it, which might negate the intended outcome of the legislation to begin with. So we are seeing salary increases to make up for lost bonuses; bonuses being delayed or finessed in a way that still meets targets but has a lesser impact; and payments in kind, including higher housing allowances and travel perks, children's school fees or being paid partly in shares. In the end, these can very well bring bankers' take-home pay up to the same level it would reach if the bonus cap did not exist. It is not surprising that all the political parties are turning their attention to this.

The Conservatives have spent over £20,000 of public money in fees for its legal challenge to an EU cap that limits bankers' bonuses to the same level as their base salary, and EU officials are said to be increasingly 'disturbed' by reports that UK banks are bringing in novel forms of pay, such as cash and share-based adjustable allowances, in order to get around the bonus cap. The Treasury, until it abandoned the pursuit in November 2014, had defended its legal challenge, saying, 'These latest EU rules on bonuses, rushed through without any assessment of their impact, will undermine all of this by pushing bankers' fixed pay up rather than down, which will make banks themselves riskier rather than safer.'

Labour had said that if it came to power in 2015 it would make bankers pay back bonuses if it turned out that the bank had made a loss or taken an inappropriate decision for its customers, so any remuneration which might have increased profits temporarily would have to be returned. Shadow Chancellor Ed Balls said, in July 2014, that the Bank of England is 'fundamentally doing the right thing' with its plans to claw back rule-breaking bankers' bonuses up to seven years after they are awarded. He spoke as the Bank of England was set to unveil plans to make badly behaved or incompetent bankers pay back bonuses even if they were given out in shares and had been cashed in. This is designed to punish bankers who misbehave or make a significant error, causing a serious financial loss for their bank, as well as those who have failed in risk management. Antony Jenkins, boss of Barclays, described the claw-back as 'extremely useful', saying that 'recklessness should be punished' and that the plans were a good idea in principle.

While writing this in 2014, the latest pay figures were indicating that average earnings in the economy as a whole were growing at just 0.4 per cent, well below the 1.9 per cent inflation rate of July 2014, and real incomes were therefore continuing to be squeezed. A few days later, on 16 August, the papers reported that the head of the nationalised Royal Bank of Scotland's US retail banking division was in line for a package of up to $9.4 million this year and up to $11.2 million in future years as the American unit starts to loosen its ties to the UK state-owned bank.[8]

It does not therefore look as if the issue is being tackled in any meaningful way despite so much debate, and voters will have to take a view on the rival alternative proposals come May 2015. We say more about it all in Chapters 5 and 6.

CHAPTER 4

Getting Out of the Hole: Why Productivity Matters

Is our education system fit for purpose?
Are we doing enough to foster innovation?
Are we helping our budding entrepreneurs?

THE PAST EIGHTEEN months have seen the beginnings of an unexpectedly strong UK recovery, with GDP growth in 2013 estimated to have reached 1.9 per cent.[1] The December 2014 autumn statement, in line with other forecasts, suggested that 2014 growth, likely to have been some 3.4 per cent, was the fastest in the developed world. Growth in 2015 is predicted to be slower at 2.4 per cent, but still higher than most large Eurozone countries. And yet public debate still rages over whether the programme of public spending cuts introduced by the coalition government was too harsh and too early (a view forcefully put in Chapter 2); or whether the present recovery provides evidence that austerity has worked. Both sides can claim some support in the figures. On one side, those who argue that we cut 'too much, too young' (for instance, Jonathan Portes at the National Institute of Economic and Social Research (NIESR) and Simon Wren-Lewis of Oxford University) see the recent rebound in growth as an inevitable consequence of the fact that we lost more growth than we needed to at the start of the recession, while the present government would obviously argue that their policy of austerity has worked.

Figure 9 shows how the size of government has varied in the UK since 1979, when the first Thatcher administration embarked on a period of austerity to reduce its size. We can see that during the 1980s the size of government dropped from just under half the total value of economic activity (total managed expenditure) to around 39 per cent at the end of the decade. The recession of the early 1990s raised government spending back to 43 per cent of all economic spending in the mid-1990s (as unemployment benefits and other expenditures increase during recession), and then we see a fall to 35 per cent at the end of that decade. A rise back to around 40 per cent just before the start of the present recession reflects the more redistributive policies of Labour governments in the early noughties, and the present recession returned the size of government back to a level in 2010 similar to that at the beginning of the 1980s.

FIGURE 9: HOW BIG IS TOO BIG, HOW SMALL IS TOO SMALL?

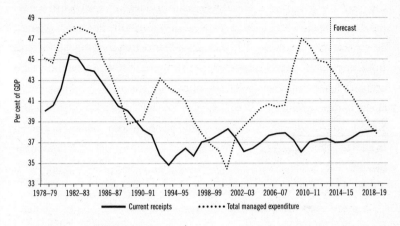

Source: ONS, OBR; excludes Royal Mail and APF transfers

The unbroken line represents the value of receipts (VAT, income tax, stamp duty etc.) that are used to cover the levels of government expenditure just described. In most years this is not enough to cover spending and necessitates some borrowing by government.[2] From the start of the noughties onwards, the gap between what government spends and what it receives has grown, and dramatically so, as the Great Recession pushed the government sector further into debt. The Office for Budget Responsibility expects the total level of government debt that has accumulated as a result of this gap between spending and receipts to peak at around 80 per cent of GDP in 2015/16. The projected continuing fall in government spending from 2014 onwards in Figure 9 would slowly lower this level of debt.

The aim here is not to get into philosophical arguments over how big or small government should be. These arguments are important, and a particular perspective is put forward in Chapter 2, but readers can make their own minds up over what Figure 9 means for them. More importantly, any debate over how big government should be must take place within a broader consideration of how strong the underlying economy is. For instance, a recession increases the money needed by government to support those affected. The peaks in the '80s and after 2007 were partly due to the increase in spending required to cushion those impacted by recession. However, as we can see, prior to these downturns government spending was already historically high and this meant piling debt upon more debt, as recession took hold – many argue for fiscal prudence in more favourable economic times to avoid just such an eventuality. If the economy can grow at a steady pace (above 2 per cent GDP growth per annum), we would expect the receipts in Figure 9 to pick up (as more people pay income tax, VAT etc.), and we need that level of economic growth if we are to create the extra jobs that are needed in a country in which the population is expanding.

An economy firing on all cylinders also allows more room for us to rectify some of the inequalities that flow from our reliance on a competitive market economy. As we saw in Chapter 2, there is an argument that overly large government stifles the very engine it depends on to fill its tax coffers and engage in redistribution. In the extreme, we can see that this would happen, but whether this situation occurs when government constitutes above 40 per cent of GDP (as the Thatcher government suggested) or 50 per cent of GDP, or 60 per cent, is debatable and tends to be an issue of faith.

However, there are a variety of social trends that are expected to push up the proportion of spending undertaken by government in coming decades. Health and social care spending will continue to rise as we live longer, and expensive technologies help us achieve this increased longevity. The suggestion is that by 2060, age-related cost pressures could increase spending by 5 per cent of GDP. We can also expect to see increasing costs from global warming, which are much harder to predict (see Chapter 11). No matter what the wider debates over the ideal size of government at present, we need to ensure that the UK economy embarks on a path of sustainable long-term growth: only by securing such growth can we ensure that future debates on how to cope with these rising costs are able to consider the option of increased government expenditure. If we do not secure such growth, these costs will rise at a faster rate than our ability to pay for them and we will face some unpalatable choices.

At present we are nowhere near this ideal of an economy embarking on a sustainable long-term growth path. There are signs that business confidence is picking up, but any boosts to growth at the end of 2014 have been from parts of the service sector such as bars, restaurants and hairdressers. Even those with little economic understanding can discern the problems of an economic recovery based on 'eating, drinking and a new hairdo'. Business confidence and investment are vital to longer-term recovery, but the present recovery in growth is being driven by a housing boom, stoked by continued low interest rates and the printing of money (quantitative easing). New growth is mainly due to increased consumer spending, which is largely credit card-fuelled, because real earnings have stagnated. People are spending extra money that they do not have and running down savings, leaving levels of household debt uncomfortably high. Nevertheless, confidence remains high as employment prospects in the economy as a whole are improving and booming house prices in some parts of the country are making people feel wealthier and therefore more inclined to run down their savings (a trend we term 'the wealth effect' in economics). Most forecasters seem wedded to the wholly unrealistic suggestion that UK growth will be 3 per cent in 2015.

With the level of government debt standing at just below 80 per cent of a year's total output, and interest rates remaining at bargain basement levels, we have an economy wearing some pretty robust water wings – cries of 'look, Dad, I can swim' seem a little premature. We may be about to have at least one of our buoyancy aids removed, as interest rates are predicted to rise towards the middle of 2015. More importantly, our main trading partner looks like its water wings have a 'slow puncture' and as economies across Europe begin to sink a little, they are likely to create a nasty back current dragging us down. As the next section underlines, even if 2015 does not turn out to be quite as dire as this section suggests, the fundamental problems at the heart of the single currency make it highly likely that we will bounce along with low growth for many more years to come. The root of all these problems is the question of 'productivity'.

What determines productivity?

Labour productivity is a measure of how much we can produce (in both goods and services) with a particular level of labour input. For instance, if we consider the example of a factory that is able to produce 1,000 cars using ten employees, with each employee working for 100 hours, then one measure of labour productivity would be 'one car per labour hour'.[3] This may seem like a poorly chosen example, as one hour to produce a car seems very low (and probably is too low), but it does highlight the importance of business investment in this equation. Most car factories are dominated by robotic production lines: the more business investment (in robots), the higher the levels of labour productivity. However, we can also see that the higher the level of business investment, the fewer jobs we can expect for, in this example, production-line workers.

This trade-off is something we will return to, but for now, how has the UK been doing in terms of labour productivity, both before and after the start of the present recession? The UK has historically had levels of productivity that compare poorly with those of other countries, but from the beginning of the 1990s up to 2007 we closed the gap on some key competitors. There are various challenges when comparing productivity between countries, but generally, 'labour productivity growth in the UK has outpaced France and Germany ... and has compared favourably with the US at a time of rapid acceleration in US productivity growth'.[4] Unfortunately, even at the end of this period, this still left the UK with productivity rates in 2007 that were 'some 13 to 14 per cent' lower than these three countries combined.

Figure 10 gives a more detailed indication of the UK's position at the end of this period of improving relative productivity, and combines this with consideration of employment levels. The reason we would like to consider these two aspects together is that, as we have seen, there is some potential for a trade-off between robots and people – in countries that have very high levels of business investment we might see lower levels of employment because robots have replaced workers. In this case labour productivity would be very high, as there are fewer people in employment but each person is working with more robots. The ideal outcome is to be in the top right-hand quadrant of the diagram, where labour productivity and employment are high. The UK is in this quadrant, but it does relatively better on employment than it does on productivity.

FIGURE 10: PRODUCTIVITY AND EMPLOYMENT IN THE OECD COUNTRIES

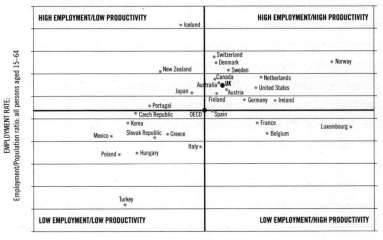

Source: Spilsbury and Campbell (2009)[5]

Since 2007 we would ideally have improved on our productivity performance and at least retained a relatively high employment rate. In fact, we have further improved our employment record, but labour productivity has not budged. As of May 2014, 73.1 per cent of those aged 16–64 were in employment, a high that has not been seen since 1974 and 2004/05. By contrast, labour productivity (output per hour) fell by 0.3 per cent between the second quarter of 2013 and the second quarter of 2014.[6] Perhaps because real wages have fallen in the recession, employers have seemed more willing to retain workers (keeping unemployment low), but these workers have less to do because of the slump in demand for goods and services (putting downward pressure on productivity). The story of employment, low wages and productivity represents two sides of the same coin, with your individual perspective determining which you see as the 'upside': an issue to which we return.

All indications are that the UK's excellent employment performance will continue into 2015, with the 2014 autumn statement predicting a fall in unemployment to 5.4 per cent. In contrast, Figure 10 suggests that when we compare ourselves to countries at a similar stage of development, there is room for significant improvement in productivity. Furthermore, digging a little further into the relative improvement of UK productivity up to the start of recession, there may be even more cause for concern. While labour productivity improved across manufacturing, services, utilities and extraction in the run-up to 2007, much of the improvement in services was due to business services and banking.[7] The present downturn makes it clear that much of this apparent improvement in productivity was illusory, as gains were due to iffy practices or over-confidence (falsely inflating asset prices).

Continuing concerns over UK productivity underpin the less favourable projections for future economic growth at the start of this chapter, and concerns over European productivity further strengthen this downside risk. As we can see from Figure 10, there are higher levels of productivity in the more northerly countries of Europe such as Germany, Belgium, the Netherlands and France; and much lower levels in the more southerly countries such as Greece, Portugal and Italy. Unfortunately these lower productivity countries have tended to have more generous levels of government spending, and this mismatch was a key driver of the Eurozone crisis which began in early 2009. Chapter 9 describes why it is so hard to adjust to such imbalances in productivity within a single currency area and the pressure at the moment is for the more productive north to bail out the less productive south. This fundamental Eurozone productivity imbalance has not been tackled in recent years; there is little prospect of it being tackled; and this leads us to a much less rosy prediction for both UK and Euro-area growth in coming years.

Why productivity matters

'Productivity isn't everything, but in the long run it is almost everything.'
– Nobel laureate Paul Krugman (1994)

Continuous productivity gains in the economy are essential to start us on a path of sustainable growth. So, what economic fundamentals do we need in place and which policies do we need to implement to achieve this? How are governments to re-tune the engines of growth?

First and foremost, the amount of *business investment and innovation* in the economy is a central determinant of future economic growth. There is a continual trade-off between how much we spend now and how much we save and invest, which then allows us to consume more in the future – if I spend all my money now on booze, expensive meals, clothes, parties and haircuts, I will not have anything left to invest in the factories that produce the clothes of tomorrow and give me income to go to all tomorrow's parties. There has certainly been some welcome recent improvement in private sector investment. The OBR estimates that business investment increased by approximately 8.5 per cent in 2013, and revised data by the ONS in late November 2014 indicated that business investment is now some £2.6 billion higher than its pre-downturn peak in Q2 2008. But this is from a very low base, as it had fallen by 20 per cent between 2008 and 2009[8] and still needs to increase dramatically to ensure sustained growth.

In addition, we need a skilled and well-educated workforce to ensure that all the business investment in computers and factories is put to the most productive use – we need to invest not just in the physical capital of business, but also in our *human capital*: education, training and skills.

Of course, if we want to increase the amount of GDP for each person (per capita) and we assume that there is a fixed level of natural resources, then alongside this investment in computers and people we need *entrepreneurs* to drive the levels of *enterprise* in the economy – terms that are widely used and seldom understood. Entrepreneurs are the glue that binds these various inputs, bringing to market new goods and services that shift us to higher pathways for growth. To ensure that the economy benefits from this entrepreneurial input, we need a range of basic rules and regulations in place that ensure we have a competitive economic system. A competitive environment reduces monopoly profits, allows a level playing field and facilitates entry and exit. Proper regulation that ensures this competitive environment is allowed to operate – with ease of entry, ease of firing and hiring and light-touch bureaucracy – is a basic requirement for entrepreneurship to thrive. The question is: what is the 'proper' level of regulation that ensures competition? And how do we balance some of the gains to competition with the apparent loss to some groups in society, who suffer when we introduce policies that increase competition? We look at all these issues in more detail, but first consider the importance of innovation and business investment.

Business investment and innovation

Why do we worry about innovation?

An innovative economy is a more productive one. Attention therefore needs to be paid to the extent to which the systems in a country encourage that innovation rather than detract from it. And that requires many players to interact and work in conjunction with each other to develop the right 'eco-systems' to allow this to happen.[9]

If these 'eco-systems' are not there, innovation will be nipped in the bud. Why is that? Well, people invent things all the time: the question is how we take the idea, develop it further and then commercialise it. The innovation could relate to the products one sells or to the services one delivers. A good measure of the innovative capability of a country is the amount it spends on research and development (R&D) as a percentage of GDP. The UK likes to think of itself as an innovative country with a large creative and design sector. Nevertheless, on current data it seems to spend collectively – if you add the private sector and public sector together – less as a percentage of GDP than most of its direct competitors. This is important. Increased R&D activity accounts for a large part of the difference in productivity between countries. In some ways, that can be explained by the relatively minor role manufacturing plays in our economy, since this is where a large part of the R&D budget is spent. Manufacturing has now fallen to about 10 per cent of GDP, while employment in the sector has fallen by some 3 million since 1982, to 2.6 million. In the '70s, by way of contrast, manufacturing accounted for some 25 per cent of GDP.

But before we start pulling our hair out and feeling nostalgic for our industrial past, it is worth remembering that despite it all, the UK has remained a major manufacturing country – the sixth largest in the world. Despite ups and downs, despite a decreasing share as other parts of the economy have risen faster, actual manufacturing output in the UK has been on a more or less steady upward trend. It is not surprising, therefore, that as employment in the sector has shrunk – manufacturing currently employs only 8 per cent of the labour force, much less than in Germany, where it accounts for over a quarter of employment, or France or even Spain at about 18 per cent – UK manufacturing productivity has risen fast, and considerably faster than in the service sector.

And manufacturing in the UK still accounts for over three-quarters of total business investment in R&D. It needs this investment to stay ahead to compete and keep abreast of technological changes, and requires much more capital investment than the services sector to remain competitive and produce the quantities required. It has had to modernise and become far more efficient in the face of low-cost competition from emerging markets. It has therefore had to increasingly substitute capital for labour. And this has happened to a greater or lesser extent in most other wealthy countries. We have a comparative advantage in services and the sector has flourished though it is not as productive on average as manufacturing. But we are not outliers, whatever politicians calling for a 'rebalancing' of the economy may say. The share of our GDP accounted for by manufacturing is pretty similar to that in the US, an economy that has many similarities with ours, where services also form an important part of the economy and have become increasingly tradable with the rest of the world.

But R&D on its own may give the wrong measure of innovation in the economy. Much of the innovative activity that businesses engage in is not immediately visible or measurable or even easily identifiable. Instead, it is what we term 'hidden innovation', which is not seen immediately and is not spent on technology. A report for the think tank Nesta in March 2014[10] estimated that the UK market sector invested £137.5 billion in knowledge assets whereas it invested only £80.8 billion in tangible assets. Within the intangibles, the largest categories were investment in workforce training, the importance of which has been outlined earlier in this chapter, in organisational change and in software.

However, investment overall, including R&D spending, is only just recovering and it is still lagging behind where it should have been in the current cycle. As investment and innovation tend to go hand in hand, that is something which the policy-makers will need to be looking at quite carefully. R&D spending fell by 3 per cent in real terms for 2012, the latest year for which full data exists. The result was that in that year it amounted to only 1.72 per cent of gross domestic product. This compares with a target set by the previous Labour government of a rise to 2.5 per cent of GDP by 2014, which, at the time of writing, is unlikely to be met. The target for Europe is 3 per cent. Innovation is estimated to have accounted for some 40 per cent of productivity growth in the UK in the ten years to the onset of the recession. A pattern of low business investment and innovation and hence poor productivity growth – as seems to be the current norm – matters hugely for growth.

The current coalition government has made innovation a priority. It has reinforced the operations of the Technology Strategy Board (now known as Innovate UK), originally set up under Labour to disburse funds to companies in various sectors to pursue innovative proposals that could lead to breakthroughs in commercialising ideas. It has also created innovation clusters – the so-called catapult centres – which are there to bring UK businesses, scientists, academics and engineers together to collaborate, under funding they are able to attract as a group, to turn new ideas into new products and services.

All this should help. But in reality what attracts investment in innovation is, as the famous economist Schumpeter outlined, a wave of optimism that creates those clusters of innovation that then move up under their own steam. Of course, a wave of pessimism can bring it all down, as we have witnessed here during the financial crisis. So investment and innovation cycles tend to be very unstable. A period of exuberance as a result of the introduction of new technologies which leads to higher growth can equally accentuate the downswing in the cycle.

But an economy cannot stay still and has to continually innovate to stay in front. Innovation is essential for both large and small firms, and the competition exercised by new innovative start-ups is hugely important for productivity growth. This is why the government has a role to ensure the investment climate remains positive. Whether it can meet the new challenges emerging across the world in new sectors of the economy remains to be seen. The areas the government is now choosing to encourage greater innovation through those 'catapult centres' are: high-value manufacturing, cell therapy, offshore renewable energy, satellite applications, the digital economy and transport systems. There are also many more. The benefits could be significant if the UK plays it right. In one area alone, the Centre for Economics and Business Research (CEBR) has forecast that the big data marketplace could benefit the UK economy by £216 billion and create 58,000 jobs by 2017.[11] What this requires is consistency in policy and an effort to keep the optimism referred to above going for as long as possible now that business investment has started to recover.

And yet in July 2014, in a reshuffle just before the summer recess, the Prime Minister reshuffled his well-liked and extremely able Science Minister David Willetts out of the Department for Business, Innovation and Skills and out of the Cabinet, which he had been allowed to attend. Not a particularly reassuring message to business, which values continuity, often above all else.

Investing in people: education, education, education!

One of the key ways we can improve labour productivity is through investment in education and training. Research suggests that for developed economies such as the UK, increasing the proportion of individuals with degree-level and higher skills has the largest impact on growth.[12] The UK has undergone a substantial expansion in the numbers going to university and other forms of higher education, especially since 1992. This has resulted in 27 per cent of the working-age population, or approximately twelve million people, possessing a degree or equivalent higher qualification.[13] However, during this time nearly all of our competitors have also expanded the proportion qualified to this level, leaving our relative position unchanged.

Is our education system fit for purpose?

When we look across the EU, the UK has the lowest proportion of employees who report that their skills match the requirements of their job.[14] This seems to be largely explained by the fact that the UK has more high-skilled jobs than it has high-skilled people to fill them.[15] For instance, one perennial problem that has plagued the UK economy is the lack of skills among

managers, with only 43 per cent of UK managers having a degree compared to 58 per cent across fourteen countries of the OECD in 2007.[16]

Some argue that the UK does not create enough high-skilled jobs, cit-
ing evidence that many UK graduates move on to work in non-graduate
jobs.[17] However, this 'over-education', as it is called, seems due in part to
a lack of more practical 'non-academic' skills among the 'over-educated'.[18]
The continued wage premium for a UK degree implies that over-supply
of graduates is not the problem. Rather, it seems that variability in the
skills of graduates causes some to be in non-graduate jobs, as well as the
fact that many are studying in areas where there is less demand, e.g. arts
and humanities;[19] while many employers find it hard to find staff in areas
such as science, technology, law and, thankfully, economics.

The UK economy finds it hard to fill skilled jobs in many areas as there
are not enough suitably qualified graduates; while many of our graduates
perhaps shouldn't have studied for a degree, as even after graduation they
secure relatively poor returns to employment. The question of what we do
about the supply and demand of higher-level skills is considered in more
detail at the end of this chapter, as it is key to our future growth prospects.

Any focus on higher-level skills needs to be accompanied by policies
to improve the skill levels of those with intermediate qualifications, often
through vocational learning undertaken in further education (FE) colleges. This is an important issue, as research in the UK has typically found
that those who gain vocational qualifications such as National Vocational
Qualifications (NVQs) at Level 1 or Level 2 (equivalent to GCSEs) have
zero or negative earnings.[20] The suggestion from this research is that these
qualifications provide no return, as employers do not value them. If this
were the case, any investment in these qualifications would be wasted,
as it would have no impact on productivity. However, since 2011 a programme of new research commissioned by the Department for Business,
Innovation and Skills,[21] using large administrative datasets, suggests that
this finding of poor returns is more to do with the limitations of existing methods and datasets. FE colleges are key in ensuring that those with

intermediate qualifications gain the vocational skills that the UK needs, and also allows a second chance to those who have not done as well as they could at secondary school.

However, even with extensive FE and HE education supporting a universal secondary education system, research undertaken in 2008 found that about 14 per cent of the UK working-age population (or about six million people) lacked the basic literacy skills needed to function in the economy and around 8.5 million were missing a similarly basic level of numeracy skills.[22] In England there is now a requirement that everybody participates in some form of education or training until the age of eighteen. This can be fulfilled through apprenticeship schemes or other forms of vocational training. We may expect an improvement in numeracy and literacy levels among the next generation of workers thanks to this and similar policies. The millions with low, or no, skills already in the labour market can access schemes of training and education in local further education colleges.

However, many of the approximately six million people who are functionally illiterate will have been faced with similar opportunities in the past and have still failed to improve their situation. At the end of this chapter we consider the policies that need to be put in place to further enhance the UK's productivity. Secondary, FE and HE education are at the centre of these strategies. Evidence suggests significant returns even for many individuals who take up learning in later life.[23] However, we also have to recognise that many of the millions of semi-literate workers already in the labour force will continue to have low skills. For whatever reason, a significant proportion will not take up these opportunities. It remains an intractable challenge.

Will future economic recovery lift all boats?

A key issue for the UK is the need to ensure that sustained growth is shared by all groups in society, rather than just the highly educated and those at the top end of the income distribution. Social cohesion and a compassionate inclusive society depend on it. We've already hinted at some of the trade-offs we face when considering issues of wages, employment and productivity; we now look in more detail at the – often uncomfortable – policy trade-offs that we are presented with when considering those in the population with few or no skills.

Unemployment in the UK

Unemployment is a key issue for the low-skilled. In 2008, 64 per cent of the unemployed had achieved their highest qualification below A level; and this group of lower-qualified individuals made up only 44 per cent of those in employment. The less-skilled have a much higher probability of being unemployed whether we are in recession or boom, and they are often located on the margins of the labour market, flowing in and out of low-paid employment and unemployment (more recently referred to as the 'precariate', a combination of precarious and proletariat).

Chapter 5, on inequality and the labour market, explains how many of the free market policies introduced in the 1980s by the Thatcher administrations were designed to alleviate the persistently high levels of unemployment experienced by the UK from the late 1970s onwards. We can see from Figure 11 that any 'success' from these policies was delayed by many years, and it was only in 1987 that we see unemployment beginning to fall below 10 per cent.[24] While the recession of the early 1990s pushed unemployment back above 10 per cent, from the late 1990s to 2008 the UK experienced unemployment rates much closer to those of pre-1970.

FIGURE 11: THE UK HEADLINE RATE OF UNEMPLOYMENT, 1971 TO 2013

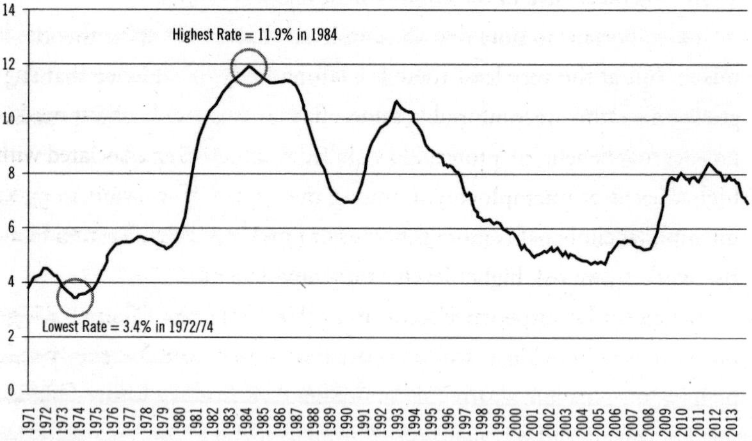

This improved performance on unemployment has not been shared by many of our European competitors. For much of the 1990s the average Eurozone unemployment rate remained above 10 per cent, and only fell below 8 per cent for two years before the recession of 2008, after which point it went straight back above 10 per cent. In contrast, UK unemployment has been much more subdued in the present recession – not rising much above 8 per cent, and falling below 7 per cent in 2014.

> *Why has the UK economy experienced much lower unemployment rates than we might have expected?*

Theoretical models used by labour economists often suggest that stronger unions and higher benefit replacement ratios (more generous unemployment benefits, relative to average earnings) can lead to persistently higher levels of unemployment, especially among the low-skilled. In addition, a number of theories suggest a similar rise in average unemployment rates if we increase the protection afforded to workers (for instance, making it harder to fire workers in a downturn, and more generally increasing the 'power' workers have in the employment relationship).

It is important to note that the empirical support for these theories is mixed, but at the very least there is a strong body of evidence that suggests some rather uncomfortable trade-offs may exist, with labour market policies that benefit, or 'protect', low-skilled workers being associated with higher levels of unemployment among this group. If we want to make unemployment benefits more generous or provide more protection to at-risk workers, we risk higher levels of unemployment.

The recent UK experience seems to fit this description. There is a high proportion of individuals working part-time who report that they would prefer a full-time job; clearly this 'under-employment' is a form of hidden unemployment, and we can expect these individuals to experience hardship. However, this proportion is now falling and it is not at all clear how one would avoid this phenomenon without large increases in government spending and job-subsidy programmes. Some may argue that this is viable in the short run, but there are questions over this policy as a long-term solution.

Perhaps because unions and professional bodies have not been able to push for wage growth that would keep up with prices, employers have retained workers. The earnings of workers have suffered, but unemployment has been kept much lower than we might have expected. This is not much of a comfort if you are on low earnings, and these low earnings are in themselves problematic if you are low-skilled and unemployed: low wages at the bottom of the earnings distribution are not much of an incentive to work. This has been one of the motivations behind policies that attempt to 'make work pay'. Labour governments and the present coalition have both gone a long way to cut the amount of tax paid by those on the lowest wages, thus raising take-home pay. Similarly, both have brought in sticks alongside these carrots. Unemployed individuals can claim benefits only for a limited time before having to attend mandatory interventions to improve their job chances (including skills training), and policies have resulted in relatively less generous levels of UK unemployment benefits.

With all these trade-offs we face the same question as in other parts of this book: where are we on this continuum of trade-offs? Are we at a point where policies to return some power back to unions would produce only very small, almost negligible impacts on unemployment and earnings inflation? Similarly, we have gone some way to mitigate the concerns of business over the perceived costs of employment tribunals[25] – do we really need to cut back further on employment protection legislation (EPL)?

Small businesses and entrepreneurship

In our discussion of the impacts of regulation and legislation, there is an implicit assumption that impacts are the same for all employers and employees. This is not the case. There is an unavoidable rationale that small firms bear a disproportionate burden of regulation, legislation and tax compliance compared to their larger counterparts. The essential argument is that the costs of compliance (with respect to firm size) are regressive, as there are economies of scale in tax compliance[26] as well as fixed costs of complying with regulation and legislation. The cost to a large firm of additional regulation (with its legal and human resources departments) is much less than to the small firm working with perhaps one or two people dealing with these issues and managing the entire firm. Indeed, the costs of complying with the tax system are estimated at 'sixteen times more … [for] the smallest firms than on the largest'.[27]

This argument has often been used to call for specific exemptions from regulation and legislation for small businesses. However, large firms also benefit from economies of scale across many other areas (in addition to regulatory compliance), for example, being able to afford specialists and large indivisible items of capital. As a result large firms tend to be more productive at any given point in time than small firms. If this is the case, should we give serious consideration to small firm exemptions? Surely it is a distraction from the main issues of growth and productivity, if large firms tend to be more productive when we take a snapshot of the economy?

Destroying, but also creating, the most jobs

In 2011, around 41 per cent of employment was accounted for by firms with 250 or more employees. The majority of employment is thus accounted for by businesses that are considered to be *small to medium-sized*, in the following proportions:

- 16 per cent of all those in employment work in a firm[28] with no employees (i.e. they are self-employed without employees);

- 16 per cent work in enterprises employing between one and nine employees;

- 15 per cent work in businesses employing between 10 and 49 employees;

- 13 per cent work in firms employing between 50 and 249 employees.[29]

So the first answer to our question of why small businesses are important is that many people rely on them for employment. However, these figures represent the 'stock' of jobs in firms, and to understand the importance of smaller firms, we also need to consider the 'flows' that drive change in this 'stock'. If you are filling a bath but have also pulled the plug out, water will be flowing into the bath and, at the same time, out of the bath. The level of water in the bath at a point in time is the 'stock', and this is driven by the flow in from the tap (the amount of job creation in our case) and the outflow from the plughole (the amount of job destruction). If we turn the tap on further, then the stock of water will rise (as long as it continues to flow out of the plughole at the same rate as before). The same can be said of the number of jobs in the economy at any one point in time – the key measure is not just the rate of job creation, but also the rate of job destruction, as the difference between the two gives us an idea of additions to the stock of jobs (or 'net job creation', as it is also called).

Within the literature investigating these underlying processes, the suggestion that small firms contribute the most to job creation has its roots in the work of David Birch.[30] Since Birch's early studies, debate has tended to focus on evidence that smaller firms create more jobs but also destroy more in any given time interval when compared to larger firms, and thus the net job creation picture hides a more volatile underlying story.

There have been many studies providing confirmation and others challenging the suggestion that smaller firms predominate in the process of net job creation.[31] Recent studies[32] suggest that the highest rates of net creation are among the youngest business start-ups (which also tend to be small). On average, we can expect somewhere in the region of 266,000 firms to be starting up in the UK in any one year (with some rise during recessions) and at the end of five years, just under half (44.4 per cent) of these remain.[33] It would seem that in any one year it is business start-ups that contribute the most to net job creation and, perhaps more important, recent research by Moscarini and Postel-Vinay (2012)[34] shows that 'large employers on net destroy proportionally more jobs relative to small employers when unemployment is above trend, late in and right after a typical recession; and create more when unemployment is below trend, late in a typical expansion'.[35] If we want to get out of this hole, we need a bit more focus on the small business start-ups that will bring the bulk of growth early in the recovery.

Unfortunately when considering much of the evidence on how legislation and regulation impact small businesses and start-ups (in the context of the job creation and destruction dynamics previously described), one of the most striking features is the flawed methodology used.[36] Similarly, when we consider various academic, practitioner and policy documents, there is an overuse of 'entrepreneurship' and little mention of the 'self-employed'. This is because entrepreneurs are universally recognised as a central driver of economic growth. Entrepreneurs are little understood but 'cool'; by contrast, commentators are increasingly suspicious of the high levels of self-employment. We now shed a little light on this issue.

The importance of the entrepreneur

Many of today's best-known economists consider the entrepreneur and the skills they bring to the economy as central to the process of economic advancement. Jean-Baptiste Say, whose *Treatise on Political Economy* appeared in 1803, was one of the first academics to consider the group of economic agents who, as 'entrepreneurs', 'shift economic resources out of an area of lower and into an area of higher productivity and greater yield', but it is the 'Austrian school' of economics that has the entrepreneur as the central component of a working economy. In the world of the Austrians (who no longer have much association with Austria), we have an entrepreneur spotting opportunities for profit, and moving us towards a more efficient use of land, labour and capital as they pursue these opportunities. This brief discussion is rather abstract, so let's consider an example.[37]

In 1992, there were just under 11,000 self-employed computer analysts and programmers and this had grown to just over 18,000 by 1998. In 2002, the figure had ballooned[38] to 51,000.[39] It would be hard to argue that all of these 51,000 self-employed individuals working in the UK were dotcom 'entrepreneurs'. Some may have been, but the majority will have spotted opportunities for profit in a range of market signals (such as wages) and supplied their labour accordingly. There was a long period of time when demand for IT consultants outstripped supply: a number of people spotted this disequilibrium (through the existence of inflated wages), became self-employed and moved the market to a new equilibrium. This describes a process of 'arbitrage', and in this sense the self-employed are helping the market to move towards equilibrium, but this does not describe 'entrepreneurial insight'.

Consider the small number among these 51,000 who decided to become self-employed because they could see that the traditional role of many intermediaries (record companies, travel agents, insurance brokers, information providers etc.) in the physical world was under threat but that there would be a key role for intermediaries in the online world.[40] Some may argue that there was some hint of this in the price mechanisms (through, for instance, share prices of the time), but essentially this was entrepreneurial insight as it was achieved by *standing back from the signals of the market*. It was an entrepreneurial insight that at once revealed an enormous misallocation of resources and, in each individual manifestation (Google, eBay, lastminute.com, Facebook etc.), revealed the new equilibrium (efficient allocation), which many self-employed IT consultants then followed as the market picked up the information contained in the disruptive enterprises started by these self-employed entrepreneurs.

Entrepreneurs are essential to the discovery of 'unknown unknowns' or the overcoming of 'sheer ignorance'.[41] There have been signs that the ICT revolution has had an impact on the quality of goods and services produced, but we still do not seem to have used this new form of technology in a way that has moved us to a new model for growth. We are walking round with super-computers in our pockets but are still waiting for some key entrepreneurial insights that build on those of Google, Amazon, Microsoft and Apple. While the US upped its productivity growth in recent decades, in 1987 the eminent economist Robert Solow noted wryly that 'you can see the computer age everywhere but in the productivity statistics'.

We can therefore see how important the entrepreneur is to the economy, but also how few of the self-employed are true entrepreneurs. This reflects an ongoing debate. The argument that small firms and start-ups are essential in bringing entrepreneurship to the economy has a long history. It is at the centre of the creative destruction of Schumpeter, where new entrepreneurial firms spring up to 'disturb the economic status quo through innovations'[42] and is often taken as a given. In contrast, with the rise of firms such as Google and Apple that seem more 'entrepreneurial', many argue that large firms now create an environment where entrepreneurship flourishes. This original challenge came from Schumpeter himself, as his approach to entrepreneurship changed from one that emphasised small firms and individuals in the process of entrepreneurship to one that 'include[d] large established corporations and government agencies as agglomerations capable of fulfilling the entrepreneurial function'.[43]

However, when considering the processes of administration within most large firms, there is an emphasis on cooperation, acceptance and adherence to a system. The implication is that the firm requires those who have an acceptance of authority and are willing to work within clear parameters: this seems to be almost diametrically opposed to the definition of an entrepreneur. Some employees in large firms will be tasked with providing the strategic insights that influence the nature of the company and keep it running, but they are not there to unearth the 'unknown unknowns' of entrepreneurship.

The entrepreneur relies on the ability of abstraction to identify opportunities for profit that are not apparent to the majority of the population. The entrepreneur 'upsets and disorganises' and is a 'bold and imaginative deviator from established business patterns and practices'.[44] The skills and dynamics that lead to disruptive entrepreneurial insights are quite different from the administrative and cooperative skills required for management of an ongoing firm. This is not to suggest that there is no room for innovation, insight and originality in larger firms (this is where most scientific innovation occurs), but small firm start-ups and the self-employed are essential in supplying entrepreneurial insight to the economy. Talented individuals are essential wherever they are found but, as Baumol[45] suggests, entrepreneurs are always with us. Unfortunately, when they face economic systems that do not present an outlet or return to their entrepreneurial skills they turn to much less productive activities.

Embracing risk and return

In our discussion of the small firm there is a focus on the upside of job creation and the outcomes of entrepreneurship, but once again we face important policy trade-offs. When we consider the discussions above, there are clear questions for voters:

ENTREPRENEURS: CREATIVE DESTRUCTION OR UNNECESSARY RISK?

In various chapters of this book we consider arguments that the Thatcher administrations of the 1980s initiated policies that, on one side, are argued to have been essential in reversing the fortunes of a broken UK economy, and, on the other, are thought to have been flagrant in their disregard for the lives of the people they had an impact on. Perhaps the only thing that these two camps would agree on is the need to take into account the lives of individuals when there is a need for structural change. If the UK's long-term future no longer required 200,000 miners, the government had a responsibility at the start of the 1980s to put in place retraining and other policies to support families during this transition.[46] There are arguments that suggest the changes of the 1980s had to happen but that such change could have been much more compassionately managed.

Providing an environment in which entrepreneurs, small firms and the self-employed can flourish seems central to our future growth prospects. However, we have also seen that during the process of job creation initiated by small firms and start-ups, there is a lot of job destruction. Similarly, the process of entrepreneurship, bringing economic insights that nobody else spots, requires a process of experimentation that leads to many failed experiments. Not everybody's entrepreneurial insight will work – in fact, the majority will not work. It wouldn't be so bad if the majority of these failures were in big firms, as size and scale act to cushion the blows from failed experiments, but the suggestion is that the really valuable ones are often not.

There is a value in experimentation, selection and learning. A 'failed experiment' has value, as it adds to knowledge and understanding, and ultimately successful experiments are built on the back of what we discover from failed experiments. However, there is an inevitable risk in entrepreneurial ventures, as the market process selects successful ventures and it is not possible to determine in advance those ventures that will succeed. Some consider business failures to be a 'waste of scarce resources' and suggest that one can obtain success with less 'waste' by picking the right sort of firms to support. However, it is very difficult to predict which firms will succeed in advance (the problems of lending to small firms attest to this) and, by definition, the success or otherwise of entrepreneurial insights (uncovering unknown unknowns) is almost impossible to predict.

On this basis, policy needs to ensure that entrepreneurial experiments are not discouraged in general and that the right underlying conditions for entrepreneurs to succeed – such as access to finance, minimal regulatory burden and access to dedicated, skilled employees – are in place from the outset. But we also need safety nets in place so that those who suffer job loss and hardship from failed experiments are 'caught' and protected.

PROTECTED AS EMPLOYEES, TAXED AS EMPLOYEES ... PUSHED INTO SELF-EMPLOYMENT

The increasing ease with which individuals have been able to create companies and therefore become incorporated has further widened the potential gap between the tax treatment of the self-employed and employees.[47] Creating companies provides an opportunity to characterise labour income as income from capital. It has become easier and more attractive (from a taxation perspective) to set up as a self-employed person running an incorporated firm, and this has falsely inflated the numbers of self-employed without employees over recent decades.

In addition, during the years before 2007, increased personal equity resulting from a booming housing market and financial liberalisation[48] increased the numbers who were pulled into self-employment, because they spotted business opportunities in new technology. Besides this, it has arguably become relatively more costly for firms to go down the route of taking on employees in the last twenty years, compared to the option of engaging somebody who remains self-employed.[49]

The increasing cost of national insurance contributions (NICs) and the extensions to employment protection legislation (EPL) have increased the costs associated with a company taking on an additional employee and therefore increased the levels of self-employment. Just as the favourable tax treatment of the self-employed can be thought of as an artificial 'pull' factor into self-employment, EPL can be thought of as an artificial 'push' factor out of an employee job. This will work through reducing employment opportunities to individuals, who may then become self-employed; it will also prompt employers of all sizes to consider outsourcing and engaging in contract for services, rather than engaging an employee.[50]

Between 2008 and 2012 the UK saw the numbers of self-employed increase by 367,000[51] and the recession has obviously been an additional push factor, raising self-employment and keeping the UK's employment figures at an all-time high. There are many possible reasons for this, not least the possibility that, in the face of stagnating wages, employees take the option of starting out on their own. However, the main thrust is likely to be a push into self-employment, reflecting a lack of employee job opportunities elsewhere.

In all of these situations we would prefer that individuals are choosing to go into self-employment because of a 'pull' they feel to be their own boss, to put into place an entrepreneurial idea they have or other decisions that do not reflect the distortions created by the tax system or employment protection legislation. However, even if this were the case, the self-employed without employees face higher barriers to taking on their first few employees, because the costs and risks associated with these first stages of employment expansion are disproportionately high when compared to the burdens they impose on large firms, where they can be spread across a much larger scale of operation. This acts to stop the self-employed without employees from expanding. Evidence suggests that the route from self-employed without employees to self-employed with employees is a particularly important part of the entrepreneurial pipeline.[52] Rather than attempting to reduce obstacles to self-employment without employees through tax breaks, public policy should focus instead on the costs and risks associated with taking on employees in small firms, especially the first one or two.

Is the UK competitive enough?

We worry and fret about competition. A number of the issues coming up in the election have to do with the high price and perceived poor services in a number of core sectors such as energy and retail banking. The newly formed Competition Market Authority, formed by the merger of the Office of Fair Trading and the Competition Commission, working with the various industry regulators, has its work cut out. There are probes now in many areas – high-cost, short-term lending; retail banking in general; the energy supply industry. But it is worth emphasising that surveys trying to discern the strength of the competition regime in the UK consistently rate us in the top three with the US and Germany. We are consistently voted one of the most open countries in the world and in terms of product regulation we are one of the least bureaucratic countries in the OECD,[53] which suggests that despite concerns, the conditions for starting and continuing a business are among the best in the world.

Specific policy prescriptions

We have begun to hint at policy prescriptions, but what are the specific policies that voters should be looking for across the parties? Unfortunately, they are unlikely to find one party proposing a full range of 'sensible' policies, as the suggestion is that we need to a) spend more on certain parts of education, b) reduce the burden on small firms and start-ups, and c) increase the safety net for those who need it (i.e. the unemployed). Voters should remember that policy prescriptions supporting free markets can be pursued hand in hand with those for generous social systems; it is the specifics that count.

RAISING SKILL LEVELS

First, let us consider the problem of skills supply at the high-value-added end of the labour market. Within higher education the response to this has already begun. The raising of a cap on tuition fees has been very unpopular among (mainly middle-class) students, but charging a cost that better reflects the returns to students focuses the brain. Individuals will increasingly consider the returns to their degree (moving them to where employer demand and productivity are highest) before embarking on a costly three-year degree. This will help to sort out much of the mismatch between the subjects demanded by employers and those studied by students. However, a 'market' in HE qualifications creates the wrong kind of incentives; there is a clear risk of grade inflation when universities teach and grade their own students. Market incentives are for institutions to expand student numbers and award these students (no matter how smart or dumb) very good degrees, and the existing external examiner system does very little to stop this. We are likely to see many more 'graduates' working in non-graduate jobs, but this does not mean we go back to the old system of support that acted as a subsidy to the middle classes.[54]

University participation rates are already very high among the middle classes and any future growth in those qualified to degree-level needs to draw in those from lower socio-economic backgrounds. All the evidence points to the fact that the recent rise in tuition fees, paid following graduation via income-contingent loans, has had no detrimental impact on participation among less-advantaged groups. This was to be expected, as work (for instance, from the Institute of Education)[55] has long suggested that the majority of any differences in higher education participation rates between different social classes are determined early in school careers, rather than being the result of barriers, such as fees, at the point of entering higher education. Any savings from the reduction of support to higher education needs to be pumped in to early years education and FE learning.

The present threat to expenditure on further education (within the Department for Business, Innovation and Skills) needs to be reversed immediately. There is now strong evidence that suggests the value added of vocational training has been underestimated, even at intermediate level (GCSE equivalent), where there were questions over apparent negative returns. In contrast, as already suggested,[56] there are close to zero returns to some arts and humanities degrees. It is clearly better to have many more individuals pursuing vocational qualifications rather than degrees that will not provide them with any return and represent a waste of resources to the economy.[57]

Furthermore, FE is central to a focus on helping the low- and no-skilled who are already in the labour market. FE colleges are embedded within communities in a way that the majority of HE institutions simply are not (with some exceptions, such as the University of East London). From a policy perspective, FE learning is not 'sexy' in the way that university education is, partly because the vast majority of MPs from all parties will have had no experience of FE, but most will have experience of elite universities. FE is essential in helping those who have been let down by the secondary education system – for example, people who realise that it is not learning that they do not like, just bad teachers.

The quality of teachers has improved enormously in recent decades, not least because improved salaries have attracted a much higher quality of graduate. However, by all international standards the UK secondary education system is still very poor. The rise in teacher salaries has been accompanied by a variety of policies that have lessened the power of teachers; but perhaps more important have been the consequences head teachers face if their school has a run of poor exam results. The threat of dismissal has focused the minds of head teachers and as a result they are more willing to remove bad teachers. The time is now right to give teachers in this new environment more flexibility in how they teach and what they teach, and to stop dictating this from the centre. Keep the money flowing in, as long as performance improves!

RAISING DEMAND FOR SKILLS

This is all useless unless we have jobs for these people – demand for high-skilled, intermediate-skilled and low-skilled individuals. Here the first argument is that we need to free the entrepreneurial spirit (as opposed to innovation), which largely still comes from start-ups and the small businesses spawned by these start-ups. We have presented a raft of evidence that start-ups make a larger contribution to net job creation at any time, and during the period when we are coming out of recession, small firms have a major role to play.

By contrast, many commentators see the small-firm sector as providing insecure, low-quality jobs at low pay and this was one of the initial responses[58] to Birch's work that started the whole 'large-firm, small-firm debate'. However, as we have seen in our discussions, the self-employed and small businesses are an enormous part of the economy: to lump small firms into one category is ridiculous. The argument here is that they are an essential component in creating the demand for high-value-added jobs *and* the low-value-added jobs.

First, consider the high-value-added strategy. In the present environment for those aged 18–24 with A-level qualifications, incentives are skewed towards enrolment in higher education institutions (HEIs). There are many individuals who will gain a good return from studying at this level, but there are also many going to university whose skills would be better put to use as entrepreneurs. These individuals have very few incentives to create a start-up. While students are now being charged for study at English HEIs, they are still faced with an investment opportunity (in their own human capital) for which they can secure tuition fee and maintenance loans in excess of £40,000 on very favourable terms.

To rebalance incentives, a scheme could be created alongside the one that presently supports students to go to university. This would enable people who have reached a given level of qualification to access public funds to start up a business. The same rules would apply as apply to a student loan, with repayment conditional on the borrower achieving an acceptable level of annual income. Only one such loan could be accessed in a person's lifetime. This scheme would help to overcome the liquidity constraints that are particularly acute at present in the markets that fund entrepreneurial start-ups.[59] Furthermore, the provision of loans would lead to less deadweight, and other, losses, as the loan would be paid back by those who succeed, as opposed to the present situation, where special tax breaks or subsidies can be taken up by those who are often not entrepreneurial but who become self-employed simply to avoid higher taxation. This would also provide more of an incentive to learn for students who have talents that make them good entrepreneurs but who are not interested in further academic study.

This leads us to the second important point. The fact is that many pupils will continue to find that they do not thrive in the academic environment of secondary schools, but many will also not have the skills of an entrepreneur – it is ostrich-like to ignore this issue, but very unfashionable to face it head on. We have underlined the importance of vocational skills in this situation, but even with additional funding to FE to tackle this issue, there will be many who enter the labour market with few or no skills. What are we to do about this group?

Research underlines the importance of small firms in employing groups that are considered to face some form of disadvantage in the labour market. Women, individuals from certain ethnic groups, those with young dependants, those with few or no qualifications, those for whom English is not a first language and those who have recently experienced unemployment make up a much greater proportion of the workforce of small firms than of larger ones. For example, in the UK, whereas 11 per cent of employees of small firms have no qualifications, only 4 per cent of employees of large firms have no qualifications.[60]

The reasons small firms provide a route to employment for disadvantaged groups are debatable and a question for ongoing research. However, even from such a brief discussion we can see that there is enormous variety among the groups of firms that are lumped together as 'small'. Some are essential to the supply of entrepreneurial insight that will create the high-value-added jobs of the future; some are essential to the employment prospects of those who are towards the bottom end of the skills distribution.

What does it mean for policy?

This is where we come to a policy prescription that spans the political divide. The details will be important, but the suggestion is that we will continue to have a group of individuals on the margins of society who continue to cycle in and out of employment. To accommodate this group we need to retain benefits that are time-limited but more generous. The suggestion in recent years that the unemployed need to bear their 'fair share' of the burden of fiscal retrenchment is simply wrong and we need to reverse this. Because wages have been stagnating in the last few years, unemployment benefits (index-linked to inflation) have risen relative to real wages – this has been portrayed as 'unfair' on those in work. However, as Jonathan Portes at NIESR points out, between 1979 and 2011, unemployment benefits dropped from about 22 per cent of average weekly earnings to only 15 per cent. This is a relative decline of about one-third and any concentration on the latest reversal in this trend seems rather cynical. However, alongside this, we need to make sure that small firms and start-ups are able to expand employment easily and with less risk attached: we need to make serious attempts to remove barriers to expansion for small firms and start-ups. Those who put the small-business sector in the low-skill category miss a trick, as do those who focus solely on their role as providers of the entrepreneurial input.

Some will argue that we risk paying a price for improved growth prospects by reducing the protection afforded to employees in small firms. But we must remember that in small firms the only real guarantee of job protection is the survival of the firm. Furthermore, the contribution of each employee is substantial enough to make a difference to the bottom line. As we might therefore expect, the evidence is that employees in smaller firms feel that managers are better attuned to their needs, even though they also report that policies and practices are much less clearly defined. Employment relations in small firms are very different from those in large firms and may warrant a different approach.

In the present environment, government does not have enough financial heft to make a difference to the demand side. Any new initiatives in this area simply re-arrange deckchairs on the *Titanic*. Rather, it is the start-up firms and the entrepreneurs that run them who represent an important opportunity for sustainable economic growth. They create genuinely new value, through their insights into how we re-combine technology, people and places in ways that drag society forward to new eras of expansion. Government cannot predict who these people and enterprises will be, but they can remove many of the impediments placed in their path. In addition, they can also make sure that those who do not do well out of this process of creative destruction are caught when they fall.

What about large firms? Should we care?

Well, as always in economics, nothing is clear cut. And this is an area where there is little consensus. Indeed, some researchers think that 'size does not matter', as once other factors are controlled for, there is no longer a significant correlation between size and entrepreneurship and job creation.[61] Growth, not size, is the thing we need to promote, and we must remember that all large firms were once small. Firms differ hugely and, as we have stated earlier in this chapter, it is ridiculous to lump all small firms in the same category. So a policy-maker who aims at blanket support for *all* small firms may be disappointed with the results. Even if small firms did create most jobs, that is not necessarily a desirable state of affairs. For example, making things easier for small firms compared to big firms may increase employment in small firms at the expense of big firms, which is not necessarily a good thing – although the evidence suggests this may benefit more disadvantaged groups and we need to remember our desire for a 'level playing field'.

A champion of entrepreneurship, *The Economist* sums up the conundrum well, by conceding that 'big firms are generally more productive, offer higher wages and pay more taxes than small ones. Economies dominated by small firms are often sluggish', but also large firms 'can be slow to respond to customers' needs, changing tastes or disruptive technology' and 'to idolise big firms would be as unwise as to idolise small ones'.[62]

In reality, for government policy, it is the benefit 'at the margin' that is important (see Chapter 7 on Health) – that is, the expected benefit from a bit more of one thing and a bit less of another thing. A policy of spending, or allowing exemptions, for all small firms does not mean there will be additional benefits even if small firms as a group are currently important. And we should be looking at data, as we say throughout this book, a lot more forensically, with a lot of scepticism. The growth of many small firms in the Great Recession has been driven by a depressed economy. That's not a trend that we necessarily wish to see continue, but in the absence of other employment opportunities, we have to be pragmatic.

Ideally, a more targeted policy would pick out the aspect that is important: that is, start-ups and fast-growing firms. And indeed the government is trying to do just that through an emphasis on identifying and assisting the few thousand companies with high growth potential which the think tank Nesta has termed 'gazelles'. Nesta suggests that they have identified key firms that move faster than the rest of the pack and if they receive proper assistance can move even faster.[63] With cooperation from a number of universities and also Goldman Sachs, a programme of providing support to 10,000 selected small companies has started, holding their hand in areas of skills, training, marketing and accessing finance, among others.

However, whether we believe in young firms, small firms or large firms, job creation and growth arises from a relatively small group. In the UK there is only about a one-in-a-thousand chance that a new firm will become a large firm. It is almost impossible to predict which firms will become successful, before they are successful. We must remember that Nesta's work looks at data and tells us which firms *have become successful*; there has yet to be any work across academia, in finance or other areas that accurately predicts which start-ups *will become successful*, before the fact. Picking winners is something that government has failed to do throughout history and the new packages of support that are at arm's length (Business Finance Partnership, the Business Angel Co-Investment Fund and Enterprise Capital Funds) seem much more sensible approaches.

Regulation costs disproportionately more for small firms, but so does pretty much everything else, from IT systems to maintenance, from parking to HR. These have traditionally acted as constraints to entry, innovation and growth. Policy has focused on providing extra assistance mainly by reducing bureaucracy and legal demands on small firms. But some would question why we should focus on this, as we may argue that it encourages some small firms to stay small. When big firms can achieve economies of scale and are able to provide workers with more capital to make them more productive, this seems a vital factor for the UK's international competitiveness.

As we have already underlined, while evidence for small firms in general could appear inconclusive, start-ups matter. Large firms that provide productive capital for workers are essential to the UK's competitive advantage, but at a point during the 1990s most large record companies, travel agents, insurance brokers and other information providers were wholly unable to adapt to a new environment. They went bust and were replaced by, at that time, small start-ups – the older larger firms were wholly unable to re-orient themselves towards the new environment. Start-ups matter for productivity and they matter for job growth.

We do need to foster entrepreneurship, start-ups and growth, so venture capital is vital. We must provide start-ups with finance and, as the previous chapter has argued, our highly profitable banks have tended to favour the creation of yet more financial instruments rather than more industry. Clearly in the past there have been bubbles and mistakes made, such as during the first dotcom boom of the early part of the new millennium, when the younger you were, the more money was invested in your idea and many ended up nowhere, or with a venture that remained unprofitable for very many years thereafter. We should encourage entrepreneurship and rebalance the support towards early career individuals with entrepreneurial flair, but we also need to be cautious of encouraging those who are over-enthusiastic but naïve, into failed ventures. As always, there is a trade-off – many of the entrepreneurial may be languishing in jobs that are not a good fit to their abilities, but many would fall foul of the risks inherent in new ventures.

One way forward is to do much more to provide second-chance education, not less, as is suggested by recent funding cuts to FE. We have argued for a greater focus on study of subjects that are in demand by employers, but it is important not to misunderstand this and think that all aspects of a qualification should be directly vocational. This is underlined in the Wolf Report,[64] which emphasises the importance of more general skills within the vocational suite of qualifications, both for employability (which is underlined by the CBI head, John Cridland) and for potential progression to higher learning. All qualifications should aim to develop critical thinking, and ideally quantitative and communication skills too. Qualifications that require these skills provide more employable individuals, who are 'future proofed' – in a changing world, vocation-specific training has the potential to become outdated quickly. Students must be pointed towards qualifications that provide a financial return, but we must make sure that such qualifications develop more than just job-specific skills.

PART TWO

The Economics
of the Big Issues

CHAPTER 5

We're All in It Together – Some of Us Up to Our Necks

T HE LABOUR MARKET is where government policy has the most
influence on levels of equality and inequality. As we shall see in
this chapter, most of the key measures of inequality are based on
differences in incomes. The situation in countries such as Brazil is thought
to be particularly worrying, as the proportion of household income going
to the top 1 per cent of earners (which translates into about two million
people) is about the same as that going to the bottom 50 per cent of earners (eighty million people). Half the people of Brazil share a piece of their
'national economic cake' that is the same size as the richest 1 per cent.[1]

It is not a static picture. While the situation in Brazil has seen some
improvement since the turn of the millennium, countries such as China,

starting with a much more equal income distribution, have become less so over the last twenty years.

The UK is somewhere in between these extremes, but it is both more unequal in its distribution of income than other industrialised economies and less equal than it was at the end of the 1970s. The big increase in UK earnings inequality occurred during the 1980s, when radical changes to economic policy were initiated by Thatcher's successive Conservative governments. Even in this very brief discussion, there are a variety of issues that need to be taken into account alongside indicators of inequality. For example, since 1978 China's growing inequality has been accompanied by economic growth that has lifted an astonishing half a billion people out of poverty, according to the World Bank. The National Equality Panel (NEP) report of 2010[2] does a good job of summarising the two sides of a philosophical argument around inequality:

- 'Some might argue that inequalities … are inevitable in a modern economy, or are functional in creating incentives that promote overall economic growth.'

- 'However, comparisons … with other equally or more economically successful countries, but with lower inequality, undermine arguments about the inevitability or functionality of the extent of the inequalities in the UK.'

This chapter considers the two sides to this argument, to arm voters with the information they need to make their own informed decisions.

Neo-liberals at one end and socialists at the other

What does the NEP report mean when it suggests some commentators argue that inequalities are inevitable as a way of creating economic incentives? Essentially, when we consider a more free market economic approach to policy we may expect a much less equal distribution of earnings as one of the outcomes. Individuals are born unequal. Each of us is born with a differing genetic, social and financial inheritance. Even birth weight has significance in predicting earnings and other social and economic outcomes in later life.[3] If we pursue policies that allow individuals to keep a greater proportion of what they earn, and pass it on to their kids (implying lower taxes, lower benefit payments and less government spending generally), then we will expect to see increasing inequality, because these inherited differences remain, as government does not intervene to make things more equal.

This approach of leaving individuals with a greater proportion of what they earn is often characterised as a 'free market' or 'neo-liberal' economic approach. It is said to be 'individualistic', as the government intervenes in people's lives much less frequently and does not force individuals to give up a portion of their income to others. This is an approach most closely associated with the United States, which has one of the lowest levels of government spending among industrialised nations[4] and large inequalities in earnings, health and other socio-economic outcomes. In Britain these 'free market' or 'neo-liberal' policy approaches are most closely associated with the Thatcher governments of the 1980s.

In the US there is not much of a 'safety net': if you find yourself on hard times, for whatever reason, you will face an amount of hardship that we often only see in much poorer countries. However, the US is considered to be one of the most efficient economies in the world. The US has continually outstripped the countries of Europe in terms of productivity, with the average US worker producing much more than the average EU worker. As work by Robert Gordon in the US suggests, the reasons for this are complicated, and many of the standard responses (that EU workers simply take longer holidays) can go only some way towards explaining the differences. Commentators will argue over the details, but at its most basic level we might expect that a rather harsh free market approach results in greater efficiency, because we leave people with more of the fruits of their labour. But there is also research, particularly more recently, using larger datasets, that suggests that these effects relate only to the extremes. For example, a February 2014 IMF research paper concludes:

> On average, across countries and over time, the things that governments have typically done to redistribute do not seem to have led to bad growth outcomes, unless they were extreme. And the resulting narrowing of inequality helped support faster and more durable growth, apart from ethical, political, or broader social considerations.[5]

So it is important to note that in countries such as the UK, this is nearly always a question of degree. Towards one end of an extreme we have the US, which adopts a more free market approach, where the talented keep more of what they earn and can expect to have a quality of life much better than those in society who struggle to find a job and whose skills and abilities are not so highly valued. Towards the other end of the spectrum, we can consider societies such as those of the old Soviet Union, where no matter how hard you tried, how talented or untalented you were, your income[6] was almost identical to everybody else's.

Somewhere in the middle are most Western countries, where between birth and death people experience a number of policies that try to rectify any initial inequalities. We can clearly see the problems associated with a pure free market approach, as it does not accommodate the compassionate side to human nature, where we care what happens to other human beings. In contrast, systems that have a very strong redistributive element cater to this compassionate side, but moving too far along this continuum may weaken economic incentives. If those who work hard and bring to bear an immense talent see no relative gain at all, compared to somebody alongside them working half as hard with little talent, then we may expect a fall in the overall size of the economic cake – reducing shares for all. Between the extremes, things are much less certain.

Do we need the UK to be more economically efficient but less equitable, or have we gone too far and do we need to reduce inequality, perhaps even at the cost of some efficiency? Do we really have to reduce the size of the economic cake if we want to make the slices that everybody receives more equal? What is the best balance to be achieved and are we anywhere near it? Let us start by considering some of the detail on earnings in the UK and figuring out where you are in the grand scheme of things.

What has been happening to earnings in the UK?

We often measure the 'middle point' of the earnings distribution (or what the 'representative' person earns) using the 'median', as this is less easily influenced by a few very high earners at the top of the distribution. It is almost the same as not including in our measure of the average the earnings of those who get paid salaries of £1 million+ each a year, as this would give a distorted picture of the 'average'. Taking this into account, if you are a full-time employee and in 2013 you earned around £517 a week (gross pay), you are the average worker.[7] This translates into an income of about £26,500 per annum (a figure that rises to around £32,000 a year for the average London worker). However, if you have been in work since the mid-1990s, you will be aware that a period of feast up to 2008 has been followed by famine.

Depending on the specific profession that you work in and exactly what is sold by the company you work for, different workers will have experienced different fortunes, but on average between 1997 and 2008 the average person will have seen their earnings grow by approximately 4 per cent a year. Average weekly earnings for full-time employees in 1997 were £321, so this resulted in weekly earnings rising by about £160 up to 2008, resulting in an average wage per worker of approximately £480 per week in 2008. However, from 2009 onwards earnings have only grown by about 2 per cent and, as many readers will be aware, this has not been enough to keep up with inflation.

Between 1997 and 2008 the growth of average earnings increased the amount you could buy, because your earnings were growing faster than prices of things you were buying. In contrast, since 2009 the rise of about 2 per cent per annum has meant that although the amount of money in your pocket has increased, it actually buys a lot less. In fact, by 2013 the average person earned a weekly wage that only allowed them to buy the same amount as they could in 2002 – the present recession has cost us about a decade of earnings growth.

These figures allow us to place ourselves on a point either side of the average, but these averages hide variation that is particularly pronounced in the UK and leads to a high level of inequality. Keeping our focus on full-time employees,[8] if we were to line up everybody in the UK according to how much they earn, starting from the person earning the lowest (which, for those aged twenty-one or over, cannot drop lower than £6.50 an hour by law) to the person earning the most, we would see the first two million people earning less than £287 per week and the last two million on more than £1,020 per week. Since 1997 this ratio has stayed about the same, with the top two million earning about three-and-a-half times as much as the bottom two million; and both have seen their earnings since 2009 rise less than prices.

So how does the situation in the UK compare to other industrialised economies and how has our relative position changed over time? Figure 12 considers the period from the start of the 1980s to the point just before the present downturn, during which time the economic policies made in the 1980s have been assumed to widen UK inequalities. As already suggested, we can see that the ratio of earnings of the top 10 per cent of earners (approximately two million) compared to the earnings of the bottom 10 per cent has most recently been around the 3.5 mark. This is an increase from 1980, when the ratio in the UK (the black 'bar' in Figure 12) was 3. On this measure, the UK was still one of the most unequal among OECD countries in 1980, with only France and the United States being more unequal – but with Germany and Australia coming close. Since this point in 1980 (or 1984 for Germany) all countries apart from France have become less equal, particularly the US and New Zealand.

FIGURE 12: INTERNATIONAL TRENDS IN WAGE DIFFERENTIALS SINCE 1980

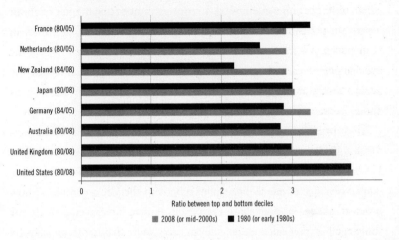

Source: Reproduced from 'An Anatomy of Economic Inequality in the UK: Report of the National Equality Panel' (2010).
Original source: OECD 'Decile Ratios of Gross Earnings'

The UK has clearly become more unequal, but so have most other countries at a similar stage of development and so it would be hard to argue that the relative position of the UK has worsened significantly. To understand the potential pros and cons of various policies that will be presented to voters during the forthcoming election, we need to consider what has been driving increasing inequality in the UK and elsewhere.

Have policies been driving inequality across the world?

First, it is important to note that the Thatcherism of 1980s Britain was accompanied by similar policy agendas in many other countries and we may expect some general increase in inequality across these countries. Older readers may remember Reaganomics in 1980s America and a wider pick-up in 'neo-liberal' agendas across countries such as Australia and New Zealand, imposed to some extent on developing economies from 1989 as part of the Washington Consensus.[9] More generally, from the 1990s a wider range of countries engaged in some amount of free market reforms. A raft of measures are included among these neo-liberal, free market agendas and they are generally seen to be associated with an expected increase in inequality. These policies may bear some responsibility for the rise in inequality across the countries in Figure 12. They were introduced because of concerns over efficiency – but what exactly do these policies entail?

As Nigel Lawson underlines in his political memoirs,[10] two core policies of the Conservative governments of 1979 to 1990 were to reduce the tax burden and to reduce the level of government spending. The assumption was that this was needed to realign economic incentives as discussed above. In Chapter 4 we tracked the history of government expenditure and receipts (taxes and other income) from 1979 to the present day. While the Thatcher administrations did not manage to reduce the tax burden in the way they wished, there was quite a substantial impact on government spending.

However, this reduction in spending arguably had less of an impact on inequality than the changes to British workplaces initiated by the Thatcher administrations of the 1980s, which started the long decline of unionism in the UK. A weakening of union power was a core aim of Thatcher administrations from 1979 onwards. The perception was that power had shifted from elected politicians to workers' representatives (mainly in the public sector and nationalised industries). The subsequent policies caused enormous social upheavals as we have moved from approximately 200,000 miners in the early 1980s to fewer than 10,000 today; from a situation in which one in four jobs were in manufacturing to a figure of only one in ten today; and during this period most of the nationalised industries have been transferred to private ownership.

FIGURE 13: LABOUR DISPUTES; UK; SIC 07; TOTAL WORKING DAYS LOST; ALL INDUSTRIES & SERVICES (000S): MONTHLY

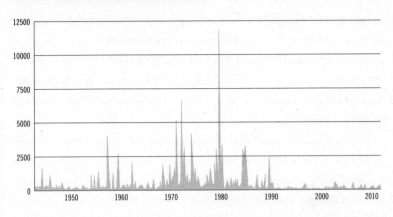

Source: Reproduced from timetric.com. Original source: Office for National Statistics

Figure 13 details the spikes in days lost to industrial action during the 1970s and in the subsequent industrial conflicts of the 1980s, when the Thatcher government took on the miners' leader Arthur Scargill and embarked on a programme of privatisation. The subsequent changes to the industrial structure of the UK would in themselves have caused some fall in unionisation, as the service sector employment that replaced heavy industry and extraction sectors (such as mining) has always been less heavily unionised. But if we look across most countries of the OECD, it is changes in government policy that seem to have had the most impact on union coverage.[11]

Specifically in Britain, the government banned the use of 'flying pickets', who would picket/blockade other companies where employees were still working, to 'persuade' them to join the strike; unions were forced to hold ballots before strike action could be taken; and 'closed shop' agreements were no longer permitted. These agreements had previously meant that workers joining a particular industry or company had to be a member of the union to be eligible for employment. The miners' refusal to adhere to the new legislation set up confrontations with the police that shocked TV viewers during the 1980s and came to define the terrible social upheavals of the decade.

As we can see from Figure 13, these changes achieved their aim. There have been very few years from 1990 onwards when days lost to union strikes have even scratched the surface. However, it is interesting to note that even at the peak of union power at the end of the 1970s in Figure 13, we still see the UK having one of the most unequal earnings distributions among OECD countries. When unions are strong we might expect workers from the middle of the earnings distribution and below to secure relatively better earnings, as union leaders use their power to secure a better deal for workers. Those higher up the occupational ladder and managers tend not to be so strongly unionised (though they have professional bodies which often serve the same purpose).

The fall in unionisation experienced in the UK can be seen across most countries of the OECD, mainly in response to policy changes, although relative industrial decline may also have contributed. Workers in the UK now rely for protection on a raft of individual rights, with the employment tribunal system used when they feel that these rights are contravened, in contrast to the collective action of the past.[12] However, while some of these individual rights relate to wages (e.g. equal pay), employment tribunals are not a forum in which individuals, or collections of individuals, can pressure employers to increase wages generally. We would expect the decline in collective action (as unions have become less powerful) to lead to a fall in the proportion of the economic cake secured by workers, and this brings us to an even wider trend that has caused a stir in recent years.

This wider trend has been popularised by the French economist Thomas Piketty, who suggests that when we look over the last century or more, we see the richest 1 per cent of the population securing more and more of the economic cake each year. Piketty's assertion is that those who own the factories, firms, bars, restaurants and other 'capital' that is needed to make the cake accumulate more and more of it, because the returns they make on their contribution to cake-making are higher than the overall rate of growth in the size of the cake. Because of the growing slice taken by the owners of capital, the workers get slightly less cake each year. We've gone a bit cake mad here, but Figure 14 underlines what has been happening in the UK, using data from the Paris School of Economics, where Piketty works.

FIGURE 14: TOP INCOME SHARES IN THE UK, 1937–2009

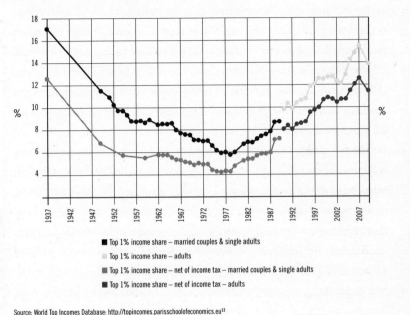

■ Top 1% income share – married couples & single adults
░ Top 1% income share – adults
■ Top 1% income share – net of income tax – married couples & single adults
■ Top 1% income share – net of income tax – adults

Source: World Top Incomes Database: http://topincomes.parisschoolofeconomics.eu[13]

While there are clearly problems with data in the UK (for instance, no data points between 1937 and 1947), the pattern in Figure 14 tends to be repeated across many countries of the OECD and Piketty's results seem to have been accepted by the academic community. The suggestion is that during the twentieth century, from the end of the Second World War onwards, high rates of taxation on wealth and top incomes stopped the richest 1 per cent accumulating a larger share of the cake, but then deregulation from the 1980s onwards across many countries, not just the UK, allowed the top 1 per cent to accumulate a growing proportion of the fruits from economic activity.

The richest top 1 per cent won't all be owners of businesses. Some will just be lucky enough to enjoy the growing fruits of unearned and earned wealth, having a mix of financial assets, pension assets and property assets. The greatest inequalities appear to be in financial and pension assets, which account for most of the differences in wealth; less so in property assets.

However, many of these people will be employed by the owners of these capital assets to manage their businesses and look after their wealth. Even if these top earners do not own the businesses, their earnings will often be directly linked to the increasing capital returns that Piketty identifies. In a world where the owners of capital are securing an increasing share of wealth, we can expect these owners to reward those who manage their assets, so that the managers' interest and incentives are fully aligned with their own: if I employ somebody to look after a firm, I want to make sure that as they do a good job and make more money for the company, so their wage goes up as well. If the returns to owners of capital have been going up, the returns to those who manage assets for them will have similarly risen.

When assets get destroyed, as they did in the wars of the twentieth century, inequality decreases. It happens again in periods of financial crisis and we saw that repeated after 2007/08. Of course a sustained period of low interest rates as at present and rising asset prices favours those rich already. The longer this continues and asset price increases outstrip GDP growth those inequalities will became more pronounced.

A number of economic studies have suggested that in order to get out of the present recession we need to reverse this trend.[14] Their argument is that growth is more likely to be driven by an increase in the spending power of those with wages below the stratospheric, and that this over-accumulation of wealth by the top 1 per cent may actually have sparked the present recession. Ultimately, the very free market policies implemented to improve economic performance may well have led to the sort of economic shock that we are still trying to pull ourselves out of!

The suggestion is that we now implement wealth taxes, improve the strength of unions and roll back many of the neo-liberal policies that have allowed the top 1 per cent to accumulate this wealth. The alternative argument is that the wealthy have a lower propensity to spend (they spend less as a percentage of their wealth and income than the less wealthy) and therefore accumulate savings which can be reinvested into productive capacity and this encourages innovation, productivity and growth. But this can be off-set if persistently high levels of inequality in a country lead to social unrest and a flight of capital and lessening in attractiveness to foreign investors.

Before discussing this, consider a group of people who have so far been absent from our consideration. The focus of our discussion has been on those in employment, but an important group who suffer enormous dis-advantage in the labour market are the unemployed. Many of the free market policies introduced in the 1980s were designed to alleviate the per-sistently high levels of unemployment that the UK and other European countries began to experience during the 1980s. The basic precept was that high levels of job protection and relatively 'generous' benefit levels com-bined with other institutional factors (such as strong unions) to make the transition from unemployment to employment particularly problematic. Insiders (those in work) are seen to be overly protected, at the expense of outsiders (those who are unemployed). The basic premise of free market reforms in this area is that a reduction in the protection afforded to insid-ers improves the prospects of outsiders (the unemployed).

In his memoirs, Nigel Lawson concedes that the Conservative gov-ernments of the 1980s massively underestimated the extent to which unemployment would remain persistently high as other economic indi-cators improved. With hindsight, this is something that should have been expected, as those becoming unemployed at this time were largely older workers who had skills that were no longer needed in the UK. The 1980s and early 1990s saw a massive shift away from heavy industry, coal, steel and manufacturing to services; even if there had been extensive government sub-sidised retraining programmes we would have expected these (mainly male) workers to find it hard to return to employment. Without such investment in retraining from the government of the day, lives were destroyed and many men in their early fifties found themselves unemployable.

In Chapter 4 we have considered the modern-day situation and asked,

IT'S THE ECONOMY, STUPID

twenty years later, how the reforms of the '80s might be influencing levels of unemployment and the experiences of the employed in the downturn of the late noughties. More detailed consideration of the evidence suggests that increased protection of those in employment reduces the job opportunities of the unemployed; for some, this may be considered a price worth paying for reduced earnings inequality.

The trends during the recession should give us further pause for thought. Those who fared better in terms of real wages were those who managed to keep their jobs during the recession. Nevertheless compared to 2007 the average worker, across the private and public sectors in the UK, has seen an 8 per cent decline in real weekly earnings. On the other hand the estimate is that the self-employed have seen a decline of 20 per cent in real incomes over the same period. That suggests a widening gulf in pay depending on the type of contract one has managed to agree with one's employer.

Yet the overall picture through the recession and its aftermath is not that depressing. According to the Institute for Fiscal Studies[15] there has been a significant fall in income inequality between 2007/08 and 2012/13, with the Gini coefficient that measures inequality falling from 0.36 to 0.34, which is lower than it was back in 1990. This reflects the fact that while benefit entitlements remained more or less stable, there was a sharp fall in real earnings for people in work, which means that the median income for pensioners and non-working households in fact increased from 60 per cent of median income before the recession to 67 per cent now. The IFS calculates that this relative improvement in equality is unlikely to last for long as medium and higher earners begin to benefit from higher wages and cuts to benefits and tax credits already in the system begin to have an effect.

Globalisation and new technology

In all of our discussions in this chapter, we have considered the situation of countries that are industrialised, within the OECD or other similar 'rich-country' clubs. The only hint that a neo-liberal agenda has spread wider is in our reference to the Washington Consensus, a free market prescription for developing nations that experience crises, based on the neo-liberal policies. It includes an aspect that we have not yet touched upon: that is, the requirement that economies should open up to trade and investment from other countries. The driving force behind this aspect of the prescription (which was a central component of the general neo-liberal agenda we have been discussing) is the core economic theory of comparative advantage. Without going into details, it is simply an extension of Adam Smith's argument that, if we all specialise in one thing and then trade between each other, we all gain.

We all do a bit of DIY now and again, but as economists the authors are aware that somebody trained to do the work would do a much better job, usually in less than half the time. The reason we do DIY might be that the job is perhaps too small to contract out; some people are genuine DIY enthusiasts (they get a kick from it); or, more often than not, we are skint and can't afford to pay somebody. In this last situation, if you could work an extra two days in your own job, rather than spending two days attempting to lay laminate in the kids' bedroom, you would likely earn enough to pay somebody else to do it and have some earnings to spare. By specialising in those things that we are better at, we all gain and the cake gets bigger – this has been a fundamental driver of our move from agrarian economies, where we all had to do a variety of tasks to survive, to modern economic systems where we all specialise in a single area. Just as this argument applies to individuals, it also applies to countries – one of Adam Smith's insights in his remarkable book *The Wealth of Nations*, published as long ago as 1776.

Is openness a good thing?

A number of the policies we have discussed have been taken up by countries such as India from 1991 (led by Manmohan Singh in response to the crisis of the late 1980s), Brazil and, perhaps most famously, China. Over the last two decades these countries have liberalised in the way that we have discussed, and have opened up to the rest of the world, allowing foreign companies to establish themselves in their economies, and also growing their own industrial giants, who have gone on acquisition sprees outside their own countries (for instance, India's Tata now owns Jaguar Land Rover). The basic rationale for this is the same as the one driving us to spend less time on DIY and more time working at what we are good at, and to pay a specialist to mend our houses. If we, as a country, increasingly specialise in high-value-added services such as banking, marketing, media and business services, it makes sense for us to trade with China and India, who specialise in production of manufactured goods that don't require such a high skill input. These countries' (comparative) advantage derives from the fact that they have millions of workers who earn much lower wages and so can produce these goods much more cheaply.

That seems excellent – we all gain? Well, we all gain as consumers, but some of us lose out as workers. If you are working in an area of the UK economy that faces direct competition from low-waged workers in India and China, any benefit you get from a reduction in the price of clothes, electrical instruments and other consumption goods will be far outweighed by the negative impact on your job opportunities – unless you are able to retrain and move into another sector.

Generally, the opening up of economies to trade – or increased globalisation, as it is also known – has generally been accepted to widen the gulf in earnings between the top, middle and bottom of the wage distribution. The extent to which this has happened to you will depend on whether the goods and services you work to provide are seen as 'tradable'. Take the example of haircuts, which are much cheaper in India than identical ones in the UK. This difference can persist because haircuts are not tradable. I cannot, without going to India, take advantage of cheap Indian haircuts. Indian haircuts will remain a lot cheaper than British haircuts and, most importantly if you are a British hairdresser, you will not feel downward pressure on your wages. The same can be said of plumbers, electricians and childcare assistants. However, if you are in a clerical job, working as a paralegal, an account technician or in another job that has a large element of routine, and which can be carried out by somebody at a distance (in India, for instance), we may expect your wages to be pushed downwards as companies outsource these functions to lower-wage countries, because these services are tradable.[16]

The question of what happens if a significant number of Indian hairdressers moved to the UK and competed with British hairdressers is a question for our chapter on immigration (Chapter 8), but for now we can perhaps see how those in more 'routine' jobs have faced downward wage pressure, even in the absence of other neo-liberal policy changes. By contrast, at the very top of the earnings distribution this opening up of economies is generally seen to have increased wages, as the support services that these workers rely on have become cheaper and this has supplemented their productivity. To see this, consider an example that also draws in an important additional component of this phenomenon, i.e. the advent of information and communications technology (ICT).

In recent years there has been a move to outsource more routine searches of legal documents to India and other countries where more educated labour is increasingly available but wages are still relatively low. In these instances we have a senior lawyer in the UK who must put together a legal case based on prior legal precedent. The lawyer's earnings are based on the rate at which they can put together sound legal arguments for multiple cases, taking the relevant legal precedents and knitting them together to produce a systematic legal case. The outsourcing of the legal search functions that act as inputs into the senior lawyer's deliberations increases the productivity (and therefore wages) of this senior lawyer,[17] at the very same time that it reduces wages and job opportunities for those less skilled staff in the UK who had previously carried out this function.

Even without a range of other neo-liberal policy prescriptions, we may expect this opening up of economies to result in increasing inequality between those who gain and those who lose from such globalisation. Ultimately, we may argue that policies such as a UK national minimum wage place a lower bound on how far the wages of those at the bottom of the earnings distribution can go, but once expected earnings are pushed below this level, these jobs simply disappear abroad. The loss of manufacturing over the past three decades in the UK is an example of this phenomenon, as 'goods' (rather than 'services') tend to be more tradable. Those working in services are experiencing something that has been driving the loss of heavy industry in the UK for many years – it is just that the advent of new technology (ICTs) has now made the process viable for many service sector jobs.

It is important to note that the opening up of markets has certainly benefited workers from countries that are much poorer than the UK. We may see our own widening distribution of earnings as only one small part of a wider distribution of earnings across rich and poor countries. If we take such a perspective, the earnings of those at the very bottom of such a distribution (in these poorer countries) have been dragged up by the very same factors that have hurt UK workers in more routine occupations. Taking this perspective, we may consider that the gap between the richest and poorest in the world may be reduced by globalisation.

Of course, it has to be accepted that cross-country data does not provide us with a bullet-proof case linking inequality and growth overall in the economy. We can't tell whether on average a country does better overall in terms of measured economic growth if it is more or less equal. But there is evidence that inequality can make a difference on how long a country can sustain growth once the recovery starts. An IMF study in 2011 found 'a large and statistically significant association between low-income inequality and growth duration' and described income inequality as 'among the variables with the economically strongest effect on predicted (growth) spell duration'.[18]

So inequality matters and therefore looking at the causes is a worthwhile pursuit. Of course the factors contributing to that inequality differ markedly between countries, and the corrective measures inevitably need to be adapted accordingly. But there are a few clear patterns. First, according to an OECD 2011 study, issues such as greater access to 'social capital' for those who need it are important. According to the OECD, non-cash payments such as, for example, education, health and social care play a crucial role – in the UK they were contributing to reducing inequality by about a fifth from what they would otherwise have been.[19] Second, the widening gap between high earners and middle to low, if left unchecked, is a main determinant of increased inequality. On 9 December 2014, the same day the *FT* reported that pay of FTSE 100 CEOs jumped by 50 per cent over the previous year, mainly because of increases in bonuses and stock options,[20] a new OECD working paper reported that in the UK the richest 10 per cent now earn 9.5 times more than the incomes of the bottom 10 per cent, compared to 7 times more in the 1980s.[21]

Why has upward mobility come to an end?

One solution often put forward as an answer to many of the issues we have raised – whether you believe in neo-liberalism or Piketty – is education, education, education! On an individual level this seems pretty straightforward. If you are sitting there wondering how to protect yourself against the forces of globalisation, make sure you are one of the high-skilled top earners, who benefit from it. More generally, education is one of the characteristics that is most likely to predict whether you are at the top or the bottom of the earnings distribution.

This brings us to an issue in the UK that has sparked debate for many years, and which has echoes of the American dream. The argument is that, while the levels of inequality are important, it is just as important (and, some would argue, more so) that even if you are born to parents a long way down the earnings distribution, during your lifetime you have a high chance of climbing to the top if you are smart. This is not just an issue of equity, but one of efficiency too. If we have lots of very talented people being born to poor parents, and they do not have the opportunity to do jobs that would best use this talent, this is highly inefficient. Similarly, if many sons and daughters of wealthy parents are only in top jobs because of their financial and social inheritance, rather than having the intellect to do a good job, then we face similar problems of inefficiency. A key question in this literature is the extent to which education acts as a ladder for those who make this journey.

Unfortunately, while there are examples of education providing a ladder up for some, recent research[22] suggests that education is simply reinforcing existing inequalities: the middle classes are still using the ladder to protect their position (whether their children are smart or dumb), and the children of poor families find it hard to take the necessary steps up that ladder. This is not to suggest that we stop spending on education, but clearly the money we are spending is not helping those most in need enough. In our previous chapter we have emphasised the need for spending on early years education and suggest that more focus on further education – as opposed to just higher education – would be a step in the right direction.

Conclusion

This question of how we best ensure that education spending best reaches those in need is an entire book of its own. What are we to conclude from a – relatively brief – discussion of inequality that has ranged from consideration of neo-liberal policies to globalisation and the ICT revolution? There are clearly certain types of inequality that we feel are wholly unacceptable. In the discrimination chapter we will look at the inequality that exists between men and women, white and black, able-bodied and disabled, and other groups. This kind of discrimination is unacceptable because it stems from these groups being judged by something other than the strength of their character and it is socially divisive.

The groups we have considered in this chapter who face inequality are potentially more fluid, as many have the opportunity to move up the income ladder (though clearly, the route through education has become more problematic). But we face the same risks in discriminating against these groups based on biased and inaccurate perceptions, often perpetuated by politicians. The majority who find themselves in situations of disadvantage are there because of economic experiences that are well beyond their control. For instance, adopting a rhetoric that emphasises the minuscule number of 'dole scroungers' among those who are on some form of benefit is unpalatable and discriminatory.

No individual should be consigned to suffer life choices that fluctuate between poor pay and stingy benefits. If we follow politicians who suggest that an apparent 'lack of moral fibre' among those at the bottom of the pile is the reason they are dependent, we pigeonhole the disadvantaged and risk social unrest. There should be constant opportunities for disadvantaged individuals to take up training and education to improve their situation, and we should observe much more movement up and out of any 'precariate' – expanding HE to the detriment of the FE sector is doing nothing to help, as disadvantage begins to limit opportunities from a very early age. The amount of 'dependency' is affected by the way the economy and institutions within it are run overall, rather than by any lack of moral fibre among the majority who find themselves in dependency. We need to renew the generosity of support to those who find themselves at the bottom of the ladder and one of the ways we can afford this is through a more efficient management of our competitive market economy. The two are not mutually exclusive!

Accepting that the 'poor will always be with us' was too fatalistic in the past and delayed progress on social reforms that alleviated much poverty. However, many people work in (relatively well-paid) jobs that they genuinely detest – all of you will have some friends for whom this is the case. If there is a core of people who will never work because they simply cannot access the education to raise them up the ladder, we should be wary of leaving them with only a stingy means of support, lest they become more desperate. In contrast, the political reality is that social welfare systems have to be supported by a (more advantaged) majority who work and will benefit only indirectly from unemployment insurance. The more advantaged will always insist on some limit to the benefits paid to those at the bottom of the income distribution, but the current rhetoric is poisoning social cohesion and has already pushed us too far down this road.

We need to embrace free markets, but alongside this we need generous safety nets. In such a system, we can expect a continued level of inequality, as this is the natural downside of creating environments that generate job opportunities for those most needing help – the destitute in other countries and unemployed/inactive in this country. Once in employment, some of these workers will have precarious situations, because of a lack of skills and relatively low earnings. However, once on this ladder, they should be able to tap into extensive (government-funded) education and training opportunities (which need to be more focused on those at the bottom of the social ladder in poorer communities). For those who fall off the ladder, we need generous benefit systems that provide an acceptable level of income, but for a limited period of time – social cohesion requires that the incentives must always be to climb up the ladder, but those who can't climb need to be supported properly.

Even if we lived in a meritocracy, would it be a society worth living in at all if we let our weakest members suffer from deprivation?

Some would argue that if disadvantage reflects decisions and choices made by an individual then we might wish to extend less help. But what 'choice' does an individual have if they are born poor, stupid, ugly and rubbish at games, no matter how industrious they are? If life chances depend on early advantages in education, parental attitudes and support, domestic stability, the cultures we are raised in, having the means to delay earnings in favour of study and having social networks, then how much talent must be wasted and how much social justice can there be? Whatever the case, before voting, reflect on the view of Associate Justice of the Supreme

Court of the United States Clarence Thomas when considering prisoners arriving to face his judgment: 'But for the grace of God, there go I.'

CHAPTER 6

The Three Ds:
Diversity, Discrimination
and Disadvantage

TODAY, BRITAIN HAS laws that prohibit discrimination on the grounds of sex (gender), race (ethnicity), disability, sexual orientation, religion or belief, and age. In 1968 the Race Relations Act[1] introduced protection for workers from the Commonwealth who came to help Britain rebuild after the Second World War. Workers from the Caribbean had been subjected to increasing discrimination during the 1950s, culminating in the 1958 Notting Hill Riots, and the Bristol Bus Boycott of 1963 reflected a wider refusal of many companies to employ black or Asian workers. The Equal Pay Act of 1970 (which came into force in

1975, along with the Sex Discrimination Act) prohibited, in law, the less favourable treatment of women, relative to men, in terms of pay, holiday entitlement, pension rights and other conditions of employment.

While the Stonewall riots in New York during the summer of 1969 marked an important turning point for movements determined to combat homophobia, it was not until 2003 that UK legislation prohibited discrimination on the grounds of sexual orientation. Similarly, while the US introduced the Age Discrimination in Employment Act in 1967, it was nearly forty years before the UK created something similar. People with disabilities have had recourse to the law since 1995 and religious belief has been protected since 2003.

In this chapter, we consider all these strands of discrimination, but much of the focus is on women and ethnic minorities. This is not to suggest that other areas are less important. It is simply that gender and ethnicity have been protected for a much longer period of time than the other four discrimination strands. As a result, economists know more about the situation of women and ethnic minorities, and we are able to gauge the possible impact of legislation over a period of forty years or more. Besides this, in the run-up to the 2015 election, the situation of women and ethnic minorities will come under particular scrutiny.

A lot has been achieved since the introduction of legislation to protect women and ethnic minorities, but these groups face much continuing disadvantage in the UK. More needs to be done and the call for action is likely to intensify in the run-up to an election. As we will see in Chapter 8, the immigration debate risks being dominated by those whose views discriminate against ethnic minorities. More generally, we are likely to see renewed pressure to consider socio-economic group (or 'class') as a characteristic that should be protected against discrimination. Groups pressing legislators to 'do more' often push for further regulation, legislation or even quotas. The flip side to this is the concern voiced by employers that such increases in legislation and regulation raise their administrative and cost burdens, a factor that has been important in driving the introduction of fees in employment tribunals (ETs).

Black women have it tougher than white men!

Looking at the changing situation of British women over recent decades, the main way that economists have attempted to measure the extent of discrimination is by measuring the wage gap: that is, the gap between the average woman's earnings and those of the average man. Figure 15 tells a story of significant improvement in the situation of women between 1975 and 2006 but still much less than parity. In 1975 men earned wages that were on average 29 per cent higher than the average for women; by 2006 this had fallen to only 12 per cent (and, more recently, to just under 10 per cent). Some readers will take heart from this as evidence of progress, while others will note that at this rate it will take another twenty years for women to reach anything like equality on this measure. There is something to both of these viewpoints, but let's dig down a little deeper.

FIGURE 15: MEDIAN GENDER PAY GAP OF FULL-TIME EMPLOYEES OF WORKING AGE

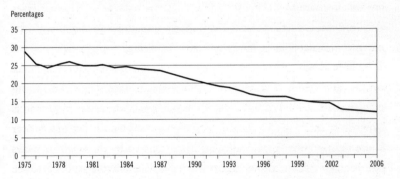

Source: New Earnings Survey Panel Dataset, taken from 'The gender pay gap in the UK', Office for National Statistics (2008)

British men and women have increasingly similar labour market profiles, but significant differences remain. Nowadays, about 67 per cent of working-age women are in a job, compared to only 53 per cent in 1971. By contrast, the proportion of men in work has fallen from 92 per cent to 76 per cent over the same period. There are a variety of explanations for this, including the decline of (male-dominated) manufacturing and the rise of (female-dominated) service sector employment. Similarly, an increasing number of men are now working part-time, but the 12 per cent of working men in 2013 who were adopting this form of employment is still low compared to the 42 per cent of working women who do so.[2]

Because of these differences, statistics on the gender pay gap often restrict earnings comparisons to only full-time men and women (as in Figure 15), in order to compare 'like with like'. This better ensures that any difference between the wages of men and women are due to their gender, rather than other factors that reflect differing patterns of employment. However, even restricting gender comparisons to only full-time workers still leaves many differences between men and women that could explain the gender pay gap. As a result, economists ask the question: what would women earn if they were remunerated in exactly the same way as men? This approach removes (or controls for) many of the differences between men and women,[3] and if there is still a significant gender pay gap left, we can be more confident that this is due to some form of discrimination.

Using this approach, economists and statisticians find that the gender pay gap does become smaller, but is still (statistically) a significant difference. This suggests that women with the same characteristics as men are not remunerated in the same way. Many studies suggest that any gender pay gap that remains after controlling for these differences is predominantly a result of discrimination (by men of women, or more generally of women by employers), but many also suggest alternative explanations that may result from differences in the behaviours of men and women.

For instance, an increasing number of studies identify the potential for differences in the extent to which 'women shy away from competition and men embrace it'[4] and other work[5] suggests that these differential attitudes towards risk-taking are further moderated, with 'girls found to be as competitive and risk-taking as boys when surrounded by only girls'. Studies that identify the apparent poorer performance of women in mixed-sex competitive tournaments may provide some explanation of

gender pay differences, especially in higher-paid jobs, where men dominate at present.[6]

Of course, there is a big jump from the notion that women may be less
keen on overtly competitive, risk-taking, environments and the suggestion
that this could explain some amount of the gender pay gap. The differences
in competitive behaviours between men and women are not that large and,
anyway, risky strategies are not always 'winning': with hindsight we might
have wished that testosterone-fuelled risk-taking behaviours among (predominantly male) bankers had been proscribed earlier than 2008.

These implied differences in men and women's attitudes to risk and competition are interesting, and perhaps they chime with your own experiences.
However, the most important and insightful findings from economists are
summarised in Figure 16. This chart shows how the age-earnings profiles
of men and women have changed between 1975 and 2013. For instance,
the black line at the top of the chart shows a 'textbook' age-earnings profile. The suggestion is that sixteen-year-old men earned an average £5 an
hour in 2013, and as we move along to the right from this point we see
older age groups being paid steadily more until the age of thirty-seven or
thirty-eight. After this point there is some minimal increase, but generally
average earnings flatten out into one's forties and then experience some fall
up to retirement (as people take partial retirement or move to jobs that
are less demanding and therefore less well remunerated).

FIGURE 16: REAL MEDIAN HOURLY EARNINGS FOR MEN AND WOMEN, BY AGE IN 1975 AND 2013

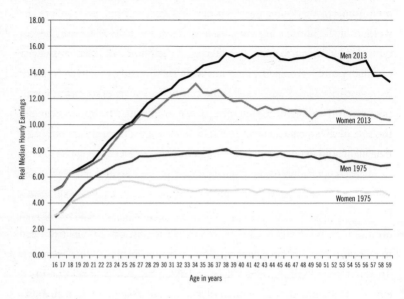

Source: New Earnings Survey Panel Dataset, Annual Survey of Hours and Earnings, Office for National Statistics (2014)

Comparison of this male age-earnings profile with that of women in 2013 highlights a particularly important aspect of the gender earnings gap. Even using these earnings figures, which don't take account of the differences in the employment patterns of men and women (e.g. the very different proportions of men and women working part-time), we see no discernible difference between the earnings of men and women up to the age of twenty-seven; a small gap opens up between twenty-eight and thirty-four and after this the wages of men and women diverge quite dramatically. This pattern of divergence is very different from the figures for men and women from 1975, where we see a divergence in the earnings of men and women from the very start of the chart, from age eighteen onwards.

There are many possible explanations for this, but perhaps the most compelling is the theory of household specialisation, which predicts that the spouse with the lowest potential wage will spend less time in the labour market. For many decades, tradition determined gender roles, with most men going to work and most women staying at home, even where the woman of the house was much smarter. This tradition reinforced stereotypical views that a woman's 'place' was in the home, and as a result their earnings power remained much lower. Even very smart women found it hard to earn a decent wage that would justify their partner staying at home, because of the discriminatory attitudes of employers. In 1975 we can see the sort of divergence in women's and men's wages, from a very early age, that we would expect in such circumstances.

However, women under the age of thirty no longer appear to suffer significant disadvantage in the labour market, but at the point of household formation and beyond, there is still a tendency for women to take on more responsibility for household or caring responsibilities (reflected in the much higher proportion of part-time working among women). This manifests itself in lower wages and again becomes self-reinforcing if employers assume that all women of a certain age have a high probability of making this decision in their career. In a situation in which many more women than men take on caring responsibilities in later life, discriminatory employers may consider the average female job candidate to be less worthy of human capital investment (training) and promotion, even in the face of rising wages for women and their continued outperformance of men in education.[7] Given the very strong association of women with domestic caring roles, it may be a very long time before we see convergence of men's and women's earnings in later career.

We'll leave the question of gender discrimination for the moment. As shall become apparent later in the chapter, we have arrived at something of a recurring theme in the consideration of discrimination. The long-term prospects for, in this case, gender equality seem relatively favourable, because the economics is on our side (not least because educational attainment among women outstrips that of men) and social viewpoints seem to be changing.[8] However, there are brakes on progress because of a continued perception that women are less likely to fully 'commit' later in their career; this suggests the 'long-term' may be more long-term than we are willing to countenance.

While the explanations for any ethnic earnings gap are very different from those for the gender pay gap, we see a similar story of progress, but with questions over the pace of change. Research suggests[9] that 'Britain's non-white ethnic minorities still do not appear to face a level playing field in the UK labour market and their relative position does not appear to have improved since the 1970s, reporting percentage earnings differentials between white and non-white workers[10] that actually worsen over time, from 7 per cent in the 1970s to 12 per cent in the 1980s and 10 per cent in the 1990s. While we must be cautious in comparing findings from different datasets, analysis of Labour Force Survey (LFS) data suggests that between 2002 and 2005, this wage gap remained at around 11 per cent.

The approach of researchers in this area is very similar to those who consider the gender wage gap, that is, attempting to control for all differences between white and non-white workers and then seeing what is not explained; the assumption being that what is not explained is discrimination (or at least a large part of it is discrimination). The majority of the differences in earnings described above cannot be explained by characteristics captured in the data.

It is not just in wages that we see a large gap between white and black workers in the UK: there have also been substantial employment gaps generally between ethnic minorities and the overall working-age population in Great Britain for several decades.[11] In the noughties, around three-quarters of the British working-age population were in employment compared with only just over 60 per cent of the equivalent ethnic minority population (Labour Force Survey). Since the mid-1990s there has been a slow but steady decline in the ethnic minority employment gap, but substantial differences remain.

This overall employment gap conceals considerable differences in employment rates across ethnic groups. For example, black Caribbeans and Indians have employment rates that are similar to those for the British working-age population as a whole, whereas Bangladeshis and Pakistanis have rates that are considerably lower, a fact that is partly explained by the very low rates of employment among women in these two ethnic groups.

Many studies attempt to identify the extent to which any apparent systematic disadvantage observed for certain ethnic groups, or ethnic minorities as a whole, can be attributed to differences in their characteristics which reduce their employability, as opposed to discriminatory behaviour. Some studies underline the high levels of concentration of ethnic minorities in poor inner-city areas. While analysis of these areas suggests less pronounced differences in employment rates between the local white and ethnic minority populations, the predominance of ethnic minorities in these areas translates to a higher level of disadvantage on a national level.

From even this brief review of the extensive economic research on gender and ethnic diversity, we see a story of improvement, but at a pace that has slowed to a crawl in recent decades. This lack of recent progress on earnings gaps has caused frustration among campaigners, and the debate is increasingly focused around worryingly low levels of ethnic minority and female representation at the very top of most career ladders. Statistics on the gender and ethnic pay gaps may suggest some progress, but consideration of the data on representation at the top of career ladders suggests there is still a very long way to go.

Women on boards: is that the only debate to have?

The last few years have seen a high-profile debate across Europe around the issue of gender representation at executive level in large, usually publicly quoted, firms. The 2012 Female FTSE Board Report suggests that only 15 per cent of FTSE 100 board members are female.[12] According to the GMI Ratings' 2012 Women on Boards Survey, the percentage of women on US boards in 2009–11 was 12.6 per cent. The same survey suggests that this US proportion was somewhere below the figure for France at 16.6 per cent and very close to the 12.9 per cent of female directors on supervisory boards in Germany. A number of studies have identified similarly low levels of ethnic minority representation on the boards of many companies.[13]

In many countries, including the UK, there is particular concern over the lack of women and ethnic minorities at the very top of the legal profession, as this is such an important institution of civilised society. Baroness Hale of Richmond, the only female UK Supreme Court justice, has suggested that 'unconscious sexism' is to blame for the lack of women in top jobs across the UK legal profession. Law Society and Bar Council statistics show a continued upward trend in gender diversity among senior staff, but with year-on-year improvement that is painfully slow. Women still make up only 12 per cent of Queen's Counsel (QCs) in British chambers and only 27 per cent of partners in law firms, even though they constitute a much larger proportion of workers (41 per cent and 60 per cent) in more junior roles. Similarly, only 5 per cent of QCs and 8 per cent of law firm partners are from an ethnic minority background, even though the proportions at more junior levels are 13 per cent and 23 per cent respectively.

The message from a recent OECD Global Forum[14] confirms that this pyramid structure exists across a large number of private and public sector institutions. It is typical of many areas: despite recent trends, men continue to be overrepresented in senior leadership roles in schools in all phases.[15] There is a particularly pronounced 'last-step barrier' for women who wish to get to the top of many professions. For instance, in British chambers and law firms, women make up approximately one-third of barristers in practice and 60 per cent of (more junior) associates across firms, suggesting that the 'pipeline' is not particularly 'leaky' at these earlier stages of career. Rather, it is the last step up the ladder to QC and partner where we see representation plummet. The pyramid is more Aztec than Egyptian.[16]

While the educational situation of women may be improving and other economic fundamentals are working in the right direction, many employers and decision makers, male and female, still seem to consider women of a certain age to be higher risk than an equivalent man – because they assume that childcare responsibilities will fall upon the woman. At the highest level there is perhaps an assumption that the job demands too much to make that viable. As Ms Laurel Bellows (immediate past president, American Bar Association) has underlined, there is immense pressure to book billable hours in large firms and an 'eat what you kill' culture in small law firms. Not an environment that seems conducive for primary carers.

Another strand of the academic literature considers the 'occupational segregation' that arises from these pressures being more apparent in some occupations than others.[17] Of all individuals studying a Full Level 2 qualification in Construction at English further education institutions, 98.5 per cent are men, while 97 per cent of those studying Child Development and Well-being at the same level are women.[18] We have talked of the pyramid structure within many occupations, but we also see some occupations dominated by women; unfortunately these tend to be lower paid and even at the top of these professions we often see men. The classic case is in HR, where the vast majority of workers are women but senior group HR directors tend to be men.

These concerns over representation have come to dominate recent debates on discrimination (though debate over the 'glass ceiling' has been around for a very long time), and, as Baroness Hale suggests, there is increasing concern over 'unconscious bias'. Similarly, these debates have begun to consider new issues such as 'inclusion', and the concept of 'diversity' has come to dominate; most people in employment over the past decade will have experienced some form of diversity training. Discrimination is still at the heart of these issues, but alongside the expansion of protected characteristics[19] there has been an increasing realisation that social and economic trends have combined to increase diversity, most importantly, in the workplace. Over time this increased diversity has come to be seen as an important strength of the UK economy and society. The celebration of diversity is in some contrast to concerns over discrimination – what has brought this about?

The business case for diversity

First, consideration of diversity is simply an adaptation to the new reality. Immigration since the 1950s has increased cultural diversity and fundamentally changed what it is to be British. Similarly, women have taken on a greater diversity of roles in society, outside of the home. Ageing populations, lowering of international barriers to trade, increased movement of capital and labour across borders, together with technological innovation, have all contributed to further increases in diversity in UK workplaces across a range of characteristics. This increased ethnic, gender, age and religious diversity has been accompanied by an increased willingness among politicians to legislate to ensure equal treatment on other characteristics such as disability, sexual orientation and transgender identities.

Whether you're responsible for a large firm, small firm, school, charity, university or coffee chain, if you do not accommodate the increased diversity of the UK population you will have problems. All of your consumers, pupils and workers will come from an increasingly diverse range of backgrounds. If you do not have workers from a similar range of backgrounds as your customers you are going to lose out, as they are unlikely to have the required insights; this argument holds particularly for marketing teams, where this diversity of insight is essential. If you are not attuned to the diversity of potential employees, you are not going to be able to attract and retain the best people, as you will not draw from all sections of British society. These are all quite compelling arguments, and they are summarised in a varied literature that considers the business benefits of diversity.[20] To understand what we mean by a 'business case for diversity', consider the high costs of investment in training that many firms incur for junior staff. Then think of the statistics we have just set out on the gaps in representation of women and ethnic minorities at the top of many career ladders. Many firms are losing millions of pounds by investing in the training and education of women and ethnic minority employees who aren't motivated to remain with the firm because they see limited opportunities for progress beyond a junior level.

Analysis of UK law firms provides interesting insights into the strategic winners and losers in this scenario. Many law firms have diversity profiles that are pyramid-shaped, in that they have relatively high levels of gender and ethnic diversity at more junior levels but then experience a precipitous decline when we jump to consideration of diversity among their senior partners. In contrast, we also observe firms with high levels of diversity among partners, but this is not underpinned by particularly large numbers of ethnic minorities and women in more junior roles.

There is a clear business case for some employers to take advantage by attracting talented female and ethnic minority employees, who are frustrated by their lack of promotion prospects in other firms. Even if there were no institutional barriers to attaining the top positions in a particular firm, a lack of female and ethnic minority representation at the top can give the impression to more junior staff that they do not have realistic promotion prospects, pushing them to consider their options elsewhere.

Firms that poach talented women and ethnic minority employees secure competitive advantage from a clear diversity strategy. However, even considering this basic example, we can see why Urwin et al. suggest that 'single-threaded diversity solutions, such as reliance on recruitment or requiring every employee to take diversity training, are not sufficient to create lasting change or sustainable advantage'.[21] Firms could not poach and retain talented employees if they were not able to provide the sort of opportunities denied them elsewhere. Any approach that emphasises the poaching of disillusioned talent from elsewhere must be 'threaded' with other strategies that ensure progression of the poached staff.

We began by recognising that diversity encompasses a much wider array of characteristics than just gender and ethnicity. For instance, there are a number of firms who recognise the value of the 3.7 million people in Britain who are lesbian, gay or bisexual. As Stonewall suggests,[22] there are examples out there of 'pioneering campaigns from leading companies engaging this substantial and often affluent market'. In the Stonewall report we again see this reiteration of advice that firms must adopt holistic, rather than single-threaded approaches, as 'one common feature of many of those successful companies is that they have an organisational culture to back up their campaigns and have deployed the priceless resource of their own gay staff in developing and marketing their products and services'.

Disability bias – we have moved a long way

In the opening statements of the 2005 report 'Improving the life chances of disabled people', Tony Blair highlights the negative economic impact of not using the talents of disabled people to their full. However, when it comes to disability, arguments that there is a 'business case' may not be as well developed, understood and/or researched as in other areas. The business case for diversity in other areas often rests on the argument that 'difference' brings benefits – in the case of disability, this message has perhaps not been communicated as strongly in the past, partly due to fears that it may deflect attention from the severe disadvantage that often accompanies disability.

However, there are a number of changes to British society over recent years that have improved acceptance and inclusion,[23] and the recent London 2012 Paralympic Games seems to have been a particular turning point. When watching Paralympic swimming, there was an ongoing discussion by the commentators of how the various disabilities of the swimmers forced them to throw the book on 'technique' out of the window and innovate. The technologies that went into supporting the blade runners and wheelchair athletes are perhaps some of the most visible drivers of innovation. This is disability and disadvantage necessitating invention, innovation and fantastic achievement.

The Paralympic Games also underlined how sports like wheelchair basketball and wheelchair rugby are not just imitations of the versions played by able-bodied athletes. The superhuman disabled athletes portrayed in Channel 4's trailer for the Paralympics have become genuine cultural and sporting icons. In all of this, there are reasons to believe that we have witnessed a 'game-changing' moment, as disability has become difference, not just disadvantage.

Differentiation by religion

The more cynical will perhaps begin to feel that the diversity literature promotes too much of a 'good news' story, which is in stark contrast to the 'bad news' story of discrimination and disadvantage we began with. However, this is not always the case. For instance, the literature on age diversity has a strong focus on concerns that ageing populations will be increasingly costly in terms of pension arrangements and health-care spending. In the UK, as elsewhere, this has led to a number of policies that have sparked a debate over generational fairness, as they imply that future generations will receive fewer resources in their old age.[24]

However, at present one of the most challenging areas of diversity, for the UK and for governments across the world, is religion and belief. For instance, the European Court of Human Rights (ECHR) has recently upheld the French ban on Muslim women wearing a full-face veil (or niqab) in public. The case was brought by a young Muslim woman who felt that the ban violated her right to freedom of expression and religion. In a society where women and men are overtly sexualised, do we really feel the need to stop Muslim women making a stand against this and covering themselves? In contrast, many take the veil as a form of female repression; should we not be standing up to this as a society?

There are clearly no straightforward answers, but this example draws an important distinction between the French approach to culture and difference, which seems to say, 'This is the French way, you are French, do things this way', as opposed to the British, who suggest, 'This is what we do at the moment, what you do? Oh, I'm not sure about that, but let's see if we can find you a place'. The British multiculturalism that comes in for such stick is essential to our increasingly diverse British identity and represents a more fluid idea of exactly what it means to be British. However, for this approach to multiculturalism to be successful, we need to represent diversity at all levels of society – how well are Muslims represented among the seventeen judges of the Grand Chamber of the ECHR who handed down this judgment?

So, where do we go from here? Do we need more legislation and regulation to make the final push towards equality, however measured? Or would this prove counter-productive, if many employers view this as increasing the risks associated with employment of protected groups?

Conscious and unconscious bias

Some of the most important original theories of discrimination were primarily focused on behaviours arising from 'conscious' decisions of individuals to discriminate between groups.[25] One of the enduring economic frameworks for consideration of discrimination is the one developed by Gary Becker, where discriminating employers perceive the cost of hiring a worker of a different (minority) group as being higher than the actual cost. These approaches, particularly in economics, assume that individuals from certain groups have a conscious 'taste for discrimination', in that they purposefully and openly dislike individuals from other groups and act to avoid them in social and workplace settings. This is an assumption that seems particularly unpleasant but unfortunately, in many cases, accurate.

One of the most important developments in the years since Becker's work is the recognition of 'unconscious bias' – as opposed to the idea that individuals consciously dislike one or more groups within society. During the 1980s and 1990s, a series of high-profile cases changed the nature of the discrimination debate in the UK by alerting the public to the potential for institutions to have systems and processes in place that perpetuate discriminatory practices – even in situations where individuals may not necessarily have a conscious 'taste for discrimination'. The murder of Stephen Lawrence in 1993 following a racist attack and the subsequent public inquiry headed by Sir William Macpherson into the handling of the case by the police and the Crown Prosecution Service raised public awareness of the potential for such unconscious biases.

Individuals and institutions may be genuinely unaware that they are discriminating. They feel that they try very hard to overcome any personal bias when faced with job applicants from a variety of backgrounds; they treat all employees equally and use the same language with all. Macpherson and others showed that this is not enough, nor even appropriate. In diverse societies it is essential to recognise and value difference, rather than just treating everybody equally. Consider the manager who feels they are not discriminatory because 'everybody gets invited down the pub after work, no matter what colour, sex, age, religion…' Awareness that individuals of some faiths do not drink and that many workers have caring responsibilities is essential in the modern world.

The ability to recognise and celebrate diversity is often seen as an essential component of the business case, where the challenge is to make everybody feel valued and respected in the workplace. Whether discrimination and bias are conscious or unconscious, they are likely to impact negatively on the working lives of those who experience it and ultimately lead to negative impacts on performance and commitment at work. The arguments that the overcoming of such biases leads to more productive and harmonious societies are compelling.

Is there a role for legislation?

In Becker's model, discriminating employers will incur extra costs that make them less competitive and there will be an incentive for non-discriminating firms to enter and compete away the discriminating firms. The analysis becomes more complicated when we consider discriminatory consumers and co-workers, but we can see clear analogies here with the diversity business case. If there are business benefits from diversity, then the perceived benefit of hiring a minority group worker should actually be greater than those of hiring a majority group worker, up to the point where we have a more representative workplace.[26] If employers expected such business benefits, then they would be inclined towards profit-driven affirmative action, in contrast to the discrimination model. Becker's analysis of discrimination may seem many light years away from modern arguments over the business case for diversity, but they share one important implication: that competitive markets will act to drive out discrimination and bias, whether conscious or unconscious, even in the absence of other interventions.

Those who argue for affirmative action on ethical grounds suggest that firms (and society) should place a greater value on the promotion of individuals from groups that suffer disadvantage. In the discussion above, the suggestion is that any business case for diversity works in a similar way. We have a business case for diversity providing many employers with an incentive to improve the situation of disadvantaged groups; we have a number of economic fundamentals working to improve the situation of groups such as women; and, on top of this, we have a raft of legislation, recently amalgamated into the Equality Act – some of it going back forty years or more. Why do we still have groups who suffer systematic disadvantage and what more can we do?

There are many possible responses to this question and in reviewing the possible answers we get to the heart of questions that will be the focus of debate in the run-up to the election.

First, it is important to recognise the potential downsides to legislation and regulation. This is one of those areas of policy-making in which economists can provide important insights. Unfortunately, these insights are important because they are the kind of thing that most people do not want to hear and would prefer to ignore but are essential to recognise if we are truly focused on improving the situation of disadvantaged groups in society. All economists recognise the need for an extensive framework of regulations and legislation for individuals, firms and government to operate in a modern economy. One of the key factors holding back many countries in areas such as Africa, South America and the Middle East is the lack of such a framework.

Even the most ardent free market economist would agree that there is a role for government in regulating market transactions, for instance, at the most basic level ensuring clearly defined property rights; clarifying avenues to pursue conflicts when they arise; detailing the relative rights and responsibilities of any parties in the exchange of such rights; and arbitrating in cases of conflict. In addition, many would wish a government to impose limitations on its own powers, as the state clearly has an unequal power relationship with any individual member of the electorate. It is then only a short step to suggest that employment rights need to be in place to protect the interests of employees against 'overbearing' employers.

However, on the flip side of this argument there is also a balance to be achieved with increasing amounts of regulation and legislation imposing costs on employers and reducing their willingness to create more jobs. As the position of the employee becomes more protected, employers (particularly small employers) take on a greater risk when they employ somebody – and this may dampen employment creation. In a modern society, the idea of a legal system without laws banning discrimination is unacceptable, but even our brief discussion gives some idea of the potential unforeseen consequences of additional legislation to protect the interests of certain groups – unforeseen consequences that can potentially worsen the situation of the very groups we aim to protect.

Take the example of regulation and legislation that enshrines the right to paternity and maternity leave for men and women. While being available to both men and women, the vast majority of this allowance is taken up by women, and employers are well aware of this. Research by Catherine Hakim for the Centre for Policy Studies in 2011, looking at experiences in other countries that have legislated for shared parental leave, confirmed this.[27] If we think of the discussion on the gender pay gap, with women and men's wages diverging just at the point where families are formed, this seems a particularly important piece of legislation to overcome this problem. However, this regulation makes women who are likely to have children in the near future more costly to employ, on average. Governments legislate for more rights for certain groups of employees, but they fail to compensate employers fully for the increased costs that this implies. This directly undermines the very aim of the legislation. Furthermore, a disproportionate amount of this extra burden is borne by small firms, which are more likely to be creating job opportunities for disadvantaged groups.[28]

Women are statistically more likely to incur caring commitments later on in life and this now has the potential to cost the employer a lot more because they are extensively protected. If we believe that some employers still consider that the majority of women at a certain age will take a more caring role in the home, then the imposition of legislation to force employers to allow more maternity leave and the right to part-time working have the potential to make the situation of women worse, or at the very least, not make it better.[29] This is not something that anybody would condone, but ignoring uncomfortable truths doesn't help: voters should be asking whether it is a good idea that employers are not fully compensated. Similarly, if we accept the argument that a business case for diversity provides a positive incentive to provide employment to minority or disadvantaged groups, the potential negative financial and reputational impacts from employment tribunals may do the opposite. Firms could be put off employing ethnic minority workers, women, gay men and other protected groups if they feel that their workplaces are not diversity friendly: because the risk of a damaging ET case rises when individuals from different backgrounds join such a workplace. Again, this is wholly unacceptable, but to deny it as a possibility does not help us to understand the barriers we face on the journey towards greater inclusion in British workplaces. We can see where economics gets its reputation as the dismal science – these are not things that people want to hear. But it is important to recognise that legislation and regulation are not silver bullets.

Discrimination as a disadvantage

Discrimination is a specific form of disadvantage suffered by a number of groups in society, who are placed in situations where they are judged not by the 'content of their character', but by the colour of their skin, their sex, age, sexual orientation, religion or disability. However, because this discrimination has being going on for a very long time in Britain, even if we eradicated it entirely (and from this point on, nobody discriminated), ethnic minority groups, women and others would still be in a relatively disadvantaged situation.

Consider the long history of discrimination, and associated lack of opportunities, that is likely to account for a large component of the continued disadvantage among many ethnic minority groups in modern-day Britain. The fathers and mothers of modern-day second and third generation immigrants lived in a world where they were not allowed to fulfil their potential because of the colour of their skin and the tone of their accent. All the evidence suggests that if you are born to poor parents, you are more likely to remain poor yourself. Leaders of all the main political parties were born into dynasties that made it very likely that they could aspire to high office. The children of those who faced discrimination in the past carry a lot of the disadvantage into the present day, as many of their parents were barred from climbing the social ladder and they may also suffer from discrimination on the grounds of their social class.

We have arrived at a point in the debate where many commentators would argue that legislation and the incentives of a competitive market are inadequate, and to rectify the inequities that are driven by historical prejudices we need to consider *quotas*. The problem is that, when we consider the realities of quotas, there is a lot of resistance, because a) these historical prejudices are associated with a previous generation and the present generation are much less racist, sexist, homophobic etc.), b) a large proportion of ethnic minorities and women are against it, and c) it may make things worse, alienating those who are on the margins of acceptance. More fundamentally, some would argue that it is, by definition, favouritism and exactly the thing we wish to avoid.

However, while we must recognise the problems associated with their introduction, the evidence is that quotas work. While the authors do believe that economic fundamentals are working in the right direction, the present pace of change is unacceptable. It is perhaps time to threaten the 'nuclear action' of quotas in some areas, and gauge the response.

Coming back to the comments of Baroness Hale, one solution that she approves of, which would be 'positive' or 'affirmative' action of sorts, is the use of a 'tie-breaker' where candidates from less well-represented groups are favoured when candidates cannot be differentiated by ability. This seems in line with the extended scope for lawful voluntary positive action created by the Equality Act 2010.[30] But, while these developments suggest a greater freedom for organisations to take positive action, there remain questions of how EU law will affect interpretation of the new UK positive action provisions, depending on 'whether the extended scope for voluntary positive action is seen as going further than European Union equality legislation or as contravening it'.[31]

Why people discriminate

In all of this discussion we have not yet considered why people discriminate. Becker gives no reasons why some individuals have a 'taste for discrimination' and nowhere have we considered the drivers of unconscious bias. However, there would seem to be one answer to all of this, and that is: ignorance and fear. Groups such as the suffragettes, the members of the civil rights movement and those involved in the Stonewall riots were trying to overcome ignorance. When black Caribbeans started working in Britain after the war, the majority of the population had no experience of other cultures, and in such situations of ignorance many people attack what they do not know out of misplaced fears. The misconceptions that many had of gay men and women were based on ignorance, as these people had previously had to hide themselves away for fear of prosecution.

We have come a very long way on the path towards more enlightened approaches, but this journey has rarely been smooth. The movements promoting greater acceptance, equality and recognition have often been revolutionary in nature, and increasing diversity has often led to periods of conflict as dominant groups resist the demands for greater protection from less powerful groups. Sometimes, increasing diversity in one area of society can conflict with the demands of other groups. We are a society that celebrates John Barrowman's gay kiss during the Commonwealth Games opening ceremony, while hoping that a ban on the niqab never comes into force and wondering about the views of some in the extremities of the Christian Church – this is no easy task. The greater the diversity of views and expressions, the greater the potential that one set of views will conflict with those of another group.

But, as we have said, much of this is really about ignorance and fear. Figures show that those living in larger cities where ethnic minorities predominate are the least likely to hold discriminatory views, and the same is true of younger generations that have grown up in a more multicultural Britain. People who live together in close proximity, with an amount of economic success spread across communities, get on. It is the same as the immigration argument: people who live together and see at close hand the travails of their neighbours begin to consider them as neighbours, irrespective of gender, ethnicity, sexual orientation or other difference.

The argument at the election should be over how we move forward to incorporate diversity and overcome disadvantage – as this chapter has suggested, this is no easy task. There should be no consideration of whether we have 'gone too far' in changing *Britishness* to accommodate a more diverse range of identities. Britishness is now fundamentally changed for the better: we are no longer a faded nation of empire but a young, vibrant multicultural country and as a result British culture is one of the dominant forces in the world. Do we really think that if our institutions were dominated by white, middle-aged, heterosexual (or covertly gay) men, hiding and ashamed of any disabilities, and notionally Christian, we would be riding high in world league tables of cultural influence?

Clearly, this would not be the case. But across the main political parties at the moment, nobody is making this case forcefully. There is clearly a greater acceptance of difference in the UK and the rhetoric of the parties when discussing some aspects of diversity, such as sexual orientation, disability, age and gender, has improved. However, despite individuals on the fringes imploring their leaders not to follow UKIP in a race to the bottom, the debate over immigration is becoming more and more toxic. Similarly, discussion of religion is being poisoned by a lack of understanding and concern over a very small number of radicals and extremists, who we find in all walks of life, not just among certain religious groups. Britishness has changed fundamentally since the end of the Second World War and even before this we were a trading nation, open to influences from around the world. The first Indian restaurant in the UK was started in 1810; the first Chinese restaurant in 1908; British multiculturalism is a global brand that benefits us enormously as a nation – hopefully at least one of the parties will make this case more forcefully in the run-up to the election … and hopefully, you will vote for them!

CHAPTER 7

Here's to Our Health

NOW APPROACHING ITS 70th birthday, the NHS was created by the National Health Service Act 1946, passed by Clement Attlee's radical post-war Labour government. It has been the beloved jewel of our welfare state ever since; Britain's most cherished institution. The NHS beats even the army and the monarchy for making us proud to be British.[1] It's a national treasure that delivers us and lengthens our journey from cradle to grave. No wonder it featured in Danny Boyle's much admired opening ceremony to the London Olympics, though viewers from less fortunate countries might have wondered what there was to celebrate about seeing a load of kids in hospital beds. Over 70 per cent of us agree that '[the NHS is] a symbol of what is great about Britain and we must do everything we can to maintain it'. This is rather a frustrating sentiment for politicians on the right. They complain about the difficulty of breaking through with any rational debate on reforming the NHS – a frustration reflected by Nigel Lawson (him again) in his famous rueful description of the NHS as 'the closest thing the English have to a religion'. Reforms since its creation – some legislated, others brought about by stealth – have since reintroduced market mechanisms and even let in private providers. A surprising amount of the NHS has been quietly shifted out of universally provided health into means-tested social care provision.

Nevertheless, the deeply socialist principles of the NHS laid down by the deeply socialist 1945 Labour Health Minister Aneurin Bevan remain entrenched in the British psyche. Bevan's three core principles for the NHS were:

- that it meet the needs of everyone;

- that it be free at the point of delivery;

- that it be based on clinical need, not ability to pay.

They are as left-wing as they are popular!

Why have an NHS?

As we have seen, most economists like markets. For good reasons, economists believe that markets usually work better than state bureaucracies. The economist's argument for the NHS is not that the poor can't afford health care; the poor struggle to afford food too, but we don't have a national food service. Food banks apart, markets, mainly supermarkets nowadays, deal pretty well with our food needs, so long as we bolster incomes enough to buy it. No one of any relevance to the debate is arguing to nationalise Tesco. The public may assert that the NHS is a basic right, but we need more than that as economists, so we use arguments for publicly financed and owned provision for the NHS based on 'market failures'. Without the presence of these market failures in health provision the easier option would be simply to redistribute income in order to provide for all health care needs through markets.

Extreme libertarians are still not convinced. They habitually argue that everything that could be bought and sold should be provided entirely by markets, including health. Not free but rather through free markets. It's still a popular view among those of the bellicose political right in the US, though in Europe it's seen as impolite to assert such a view in mixed company.

The world's remaining socialists may hold that public provision is a statement of a society's commitment to collective values. But it is more pragmatic to avoid getting ideologically hung up about the method of provision and concentrate on the outcomes instead. We suspect you will agree that if ever you are unlucky enough to be in a hospital bed you will be more in favour of a system based on experience of what works than of one designed to correspond with the dictates of a particular dogma.

One of the first recognitions of market failure in health was the result of germs not respecting social class. Long before germs and infection were understood, the rich could hardly ignore the fact that they could smell the doings of the poor. Sewage left in streets, overflowing the cesspits and dumped raw into rivers, caused unpleasant smells, then often thought, erroneously, to be the direct cause of illness. This is an example of a market failure caused by what economists call an 'externality'. An externality occurs when the actions of one party directly affect another party but the affected party has no recourse to affect the decisions of the first party. It's easiest just to think of it as an unintended 'spill-over' effect – in this case, the smell of poo got up everyone's noses, rich and poor.

The famous culmination of this lack of waste disposal was the 'Great Stink' in London, when the summer of 1858 warmed all this sewage and it stunk out even the House of Commons, situated of course next to the then 'as high as heaven' stinking Thames. This smell was associated, again wrongly, with outbreaks of cholera; the belief was that the disease was due to airborne 'miasma', when it is actually caused by a waterborne bacterium. MPs were so disgusted – and afraid of cholera – that they directed huge sums of public monies to build vast sewers that still flow under the London Embankment. These huge Victorian sewers were built by Joseph William Bazalgette, and although the theory of miasma was wrong, in removing the contaminated water his sewers did the trick. The smell and the cholera both disappeared. It is a vivid example of market failure that was sorted out through collective action; sorting it out by getting everyone to cough up individually for hygienic poo disposal would not have worked. It is also a good lesson to note early on in this chapter: the health of the nation depends on much more than what we directly spend on the health service.

Such externalities go beyond hygiene. Being surrounded by unhealthy people is a risk to your own health. For example, polio, diphtheria, measles and other contagious diseases did and would thrive unless the population was inoculated. People whose immune systems are depressed by illness can become incubators for nasty bugs. It is good for other people if treatments for sexually transmitted diseases are freely available. Thus, free-at-the-point-of-delivery health service can protect even those who do not use it. That is, by contrast with the negative externality of poo lying in the street, an NHS keeping all of us, whether rich or poor, healthy bestows positive externalities for us all.

Another important reason markets might not work well for health is that efficient markets rely on consumers making the right choices. That is unlikely for consumers of health care services, who go to the doctor largely because they lack the expertise to diagnose themselves. They have to rely on the doctor's advice. As treatments are not usually repeat purchases patients may have little knowledge of what treatments should cost. Even if they did know of the fees charged by a range of different providers, they may not know if the cheaper ones were better value or poorer quality.

We also know that patients are not only ignorant of the best treatment options but also differ in their ability to be assertive with doctors.

Profit-seeking health providers may actually have an incentive to allow you to get ill. That does not, hopefully, imply that they will actually sabotage your health, but they may have little to no incentive to provide preventative education and care that, if effective, would decrease the demand for their services. It is said that in ancient China doctors were paid only when their patients were well and they stopped paying when they were ill. This story is probably apocryphal, but it illustrates the potential for perverse incentives in private health care providers. Equally worrying is imagining contracting an illness you were unlikely to recover from. In a market-driven system based on payment by results the doctor's incentive is to waste no further time on you. Conversely, if payment is by treatment the most profit is to be had by selling you as many futile treatments as possible before you shake off your mortals! Unscrupulous medical providers, keen to provide treatments, have considerable scope to do so for profit rather than medical reasons. The book *Freakonomics* noted that when medical revenues from other treatments fall, the number of caesarean births 'mysteriously' increases! A for-profit system could well lead to unnecessary and more expensive treatments, and there is strong evidence that this is indeed the case: life expectancy is lower in the US than in the UK and yet the US spends almost twice the proportion of its GDP on health compared to the UK.

Private medicine is overwhelmingly financed through insurance. So for a wholly private market to work well, medical insurance would have to work well too. It doesn't. Firstly, a private sector, hence profit-seeking, insurance company will only sell you insurance if you are not very likely to get ill. If you already have a condition that will require treatment then the company will only sell you insurance at a price equal to the treatment. That is not insurance at all! Insurance for medical conditions is also dogged by asymmetric information between the insurer and the insured. People may well have 'insider' knowledge of their likelihood of becoming ill, or more ill, for reasons and symptoms that it would be difficult for insurance companies to know about. A person seeking insurance may well know they have been having chest pains but 'forget' to declare this to the policy provider when taking out the policy before visiting a doctor. Many of us lie about the precise details of our health regime even to NHS doctors, and we may be put off by the requirement for insurance company medicals, which might reveal a condition that could prevent us buying medical insurance from anyone.

This means that health insurance suffers from market failures associated with markets for 'lemons'. No, not the yellow ones, but what Americans call unreliable second-hand cars. Cars are more likely to be sold if they are lemons and so the price of second-hand cars will fall below the value of good cars to their owners. That in turn means that good cars don't get sold unless there is a reliable means for the buyer of identifying them as a non-lemon, and so the market for good second-hand cars is likely to fail to meet either the sellers' or buyers' needs. Similarly, medical insurance will tend to disproportionately attract those who will actually need treatments, while those who feel they are unlikely to need treatments may opt out or take only partial cover. This 'distortion' of the pooling of risk that is so vital for insurance to work erodes the ability of companies to provide insurance – so much so that in the US, even governments averse to anything at all that smacks of 'socialism' have had to provide free or subsidised medical care for the over-65s.

Of course, as with the second-hand car market, there might be ways around this problem. For example, to avoid the distortion of asymmetry we could all have insurance taken out on our behalf before we are born, or the state might act to make the insurance risk-pooling market work by making insurance compulsory for all. But then a simpler way of doing this might simply be to collectively fund a free-at-the-point-of-access NHS through general taxation!

This is an important point that is often misunderstood. A national health system as we have it here in the UK achieves economies of scale and avoids the resource costs and complexity of 'middle-men' private insurance companies taking a cut from health care, and of supporting an army of insurance regulators. Some estimates put administration costs in the US insurance finance system alone at almost a third of health care spending. A largely state financed system and the economies of scale associated with universal state health coverage is a major reason why the NHS spends well under less than half that of the US per head but still has a very much better overall performance.[2]

Another form of asymmetric information that is well known by economists to cause market failure is called 'moral hazard'. This type of asymmetric information occurs because insurance companies cannot know how you will behave *after* you have insurance. When you have the reassurance of a health insurance policy behind you, you may begin to take greater risks with your health, such as taking up hang-gliding; riding a motorbike; eating, drinking and smoking more; and generally indulging your vices more than you did before! Indeed, people planning to become more reckless with their health will actively seek out medical insurance. As they are no longer paying for treatments, they may also pester their doctors more and urge them to recommend more expensive treatments. All this raises the cost of insurance premiums, even for those people who would behave more cautiously and so now may view the payments as excessive, and so again the risk pool is no longer a pooling of risk but a subsidy of reckless lifestyles by the cautious. This similarly distorts and impedes the working of insurance, and the moral hazard problem extends to the doctor too. Doctors no longer have to worry about the income constraints of their patients; they can earn extra income by draining insurance covers to their limits. Again, there may be complicated ways to make the market work, such as trying to specify in advance the cost of a specific treatment, but funding from taxation is again simpler and less resource intensive. It's important to note, though, that the NHS does not completely remove the problem of moral hazard: for example, the nation might consume less alcohol if there were no NHS!

The state may also be in a better position to detect and address inequality in the consumption of health care, whether paid for or freely provided. For example, it is well known that the middle classes get more from the NHS than those lower in the socio-economic scale. This is for a variety of reasons, including the fact that poorer patients may be put off by travel costs and lower car ownership, and they are also more likely to lose pay when taking time off to visit a doctor than those with salaried occupations. A big factor is the difference in social status between a lower socio-economic group patient and a doctor. The middle class are likely to feel more on a level footing with professionals and so have the confidence and ability for articulate communication and persuasion with their doctors. These can be key factors in inducing GPs to make onward referral to specialists. Doctors may also suspect that a middle-class patient will have the wherewithal to make effective protests over any shortcomings in their treatment, whether real or perceived. Such socio-economic differences are also likely to cause differential access for the children of richer and poorer parents. In fact, the average difference in disability-free life expectancy is a massive seventeen years between the richest and poorest neighbourhoods.[3] Again, the state, by understanding social behaviours, implementing preventative health measures, tackling inequality between genders and social classes, increasing social care and support, introducing redistribution policies, making educational interventions and generally looking across its wider remit of services, will be in a better position to take action, directing resources toward achieving greater equality. And as we shall see below, seeing the big picture is also vital for efficiency.

It has been suggested that there could be tax relief to encourage the take-up of private medical insurance. This adds another dimension to the problems with private insurance. There is evidence that those who hold private medical insurance are less willing to pay taxes to support the NHS, when a key strength of the NHS is that it operates as a giant compulsory insurance pool. Having articulate middle-class patients using the NHS also helps protect its quality. This much seems to be recognised by

David Cameron: 'We should not use taxpayers' money to encourage the better-off to opt out, when rising expectations demanded a better NHS for everyone.'[4]

Even outsourcing ancillary services to private sector providers can have its perils. Replacing cleaners directly employed by a hospital may look good on the balance sheet, as costs are reduced through competitive tendering, but it might be costly in terms of the consequences for health. It is just about impossible to create a complete contract that covers all aspects of hygiene and even harder to monitor closely how well the stipulations of existing contracts are met. The contract cleaning staff, often working on lower wages and poorer conditions, do not report to the hospital but to their own company. That makes monitoring and control harder for those in the hospital who used to be directly responsible for standards of hygiene. The seemingly over-meticulous matron, who took great pride in the condition of her ward and insisted on the scrupulous cleaning of every nook and cranny, may well have been the best long-term defence against the bugs that now breed in hospitals and have become a costly and dangerous problem.

Private companies can also go out of business. It is still rather unclear what would happen if an NHS Health Trust went bust: many are in deficit, but the evidence is that they could dump their patients and leave other health providers to sort out the mess. To avoid going out of business, private providers may start – most do already – to cherry-pick the treatments they provide. That is, they seek to provide profitable ones and leave the unprofitable ones to the NHS, hence increasing the financial difficulties of NHS providers. To hide their lemon-dumping and cherry-picking private providers can plead 'commercial confidentiality' to avoid scrutiny; even the redoubtable Labour MP Margaret Hodge, chair of the House of Commons Public Accounts Committee, has complained of the difficulty of breaking through their wall of secrecy.

For all these reasons and more, a programme of radical privatisation for the health service would be a very bad prescription. An unrestricted profit-seeking health service would not only be unjust, it wouldn't work well either. That said, all the main parties are committed to reducing the fiscal deficit, and the ever growing cost of the health service doesn't help much in that respect. For a range of very valid reasons that we look at below, health costs persistently outstrip inflation. These cost increases and the pursuit of a reduced Budget deficit mean that an ossified approach that attempts to preserve the NHS in formaldehyde will lead to a poor prognosis.

Health and efficiency?

Economists know that efficiency requires the returns to all inputs to be 'equalised at the margin'. That is, the return to an extra pound spent here should equal the return to an extra pound spent there. Why is this? Take a *reductio ad absurdum*: if the entire NHS budget were spent on medical equipment alone, capital in economics, then there would be no one to apply it, so it would be better to cut back on the expenditure on equipment and train and employ some staff instead. The return in health benefits, the measurement of which we discuss later, to an extra £1,000 spent on NHS staff would be greater than from spending another £1,000 on yet more equipment that has no one to use it. Continuing that train of thought, whenever spending more on staff yields more 'units of health benefits' than spending this extra amount on equipment it would be best to spend the extra on staff. Obviously going to the other extreme, where we have staff lacking the equipment they need, is not optimal either. The optimum balance is when £1,000 spent on staff or capital yields the same return in health benefits. If capital spend were in one budget and staffing spend were in another, this balance might be missed, but a good accountant, i.e. one trained in economics, will check across for efficiency.

The point of this quick lesson in the efficiency of marginal returns becomes more apparent when we consider that medical treatments are only part of what affects our health, and perhaps not even the most important part. Our health depends on a wide range of factors beyond the treatment of medical conditions. For example, our lifestyle, our diet, our exercise regime (or lack of it!), the environment, personal circumstances such as marriage and employment, health and safety at work and in the home and, crucially as it turns out, our independence and ability to look after ourselves, and so especially our mental health and infirmities. The astute reader will see that efficient spending on health would have to equalise the health returns across all of these factors, and perhaps one day genetic composition as well as any other emerging new approaches. There could be diminishing returns to repeatedly sending out health advice, but for maximum health returns the available health budget should be allocated across all the things that affect health, including better management, until the returns at the margins are equalised. Money spent on better management and lifestyle and dietary advice is not wasted money unless there would be greater returns to diverting this money to treatments. Of course, judging when that point is reached is not so easy. What is clear is that, because of the strong complementarities with health and well-being, there should be much more attention paid to comparing the marginal returns to social care and health spending. Ever since the health and social care systems were created by Beveridge and Bevan, the two have been unhelpfully separate. This dichotomy is especially spurious today as the two services have come to overlap more and more for people's needs. Another interesting result from considering marginal returns is that if health budgets are distributed by area then the composition of the spending across locations may depend on the characteristics of the local population. Imagine a population that is mainly female: it would be sensible to spend more on provision for screening and treating breast cancer for that population than on testicular cancer. If heart disease is a particular problem in an area then it may be optimal not to make provision for much rarer illnesses so as to better prepare for coping with the number of heart treatments. In short, the so-called postcode lottery in health provision, whereby the availability of certain treatments varies across the country, could be optimal if each area has been allocated a pre-set budget. Treatments which have seen significant 'postcode lottery' variation across locations have included certain cancer drugs, surgery for cataracts, fertility treatment, hernia repair, hip and knee replacements and psychiatric drugs, and of course there are well-publicised variations in waiting times and in the availability of screening programmes. Differences in the availability of treatments across areas could actually be the most efficient outcome of giving GPs a fixed budget that they then allocate across their particular cohort of patients for non-urgent treatments, as was done from the 1990s. But was this variation by area the result of the efficient allocation of fixed budgets that reflected differing local populations? No, of course not! It was much more likely to be the result of GPs' own perceptions of need, based largely on who could persuade their GP to fund what – and there was an awful lot of lobbying to influence GPs.

The principle of marginal returns works in allocating funds across areas, too. That is, if £1 spent in one area can do more good than £1 spent in another area then it is efficient to spend it in the area where there is the highest marginal return. Variations in treatments by area can be efficient if local autonomy is given by first allocating a budget which the local GP then dispenses. Obviously, though, if the overall budget were not so fragmented in the first place, but rather integrated, then it could be spent so as to equalise marginal returns across the whole country. The point is that there is a conflict in practice in allocating the available NHS budget across the nation to achieve efficiency, and the bestowing of local autonomy. In 2008, Gordon Brown pledged to end the NHS postcode lottery, but it continued to be a bone of contention and so the coalition's 2012 Health and Social Care Act allowed for more generic commissioning policies aimed at reducing the impact of the postcode lottery by making treatments available to all, regardless of where they live.

These anomalies arise from allocating finite health budgets to areas, but you might well be thinking that it is immoral to have a finite health budget at all. Surely if someone needs medical help the state should be obligated to provide it, as human life and health is too precious to be denied. The truth is that we could easily sink the whole of GDP into the NHS, but it wouldn't be optimal. Few of us would sacrifice all our material possessions to guarantee against bad health; we all make trade-offs to some extent. We could pay enormous taxes to build the best health screening centres, clinics and hospitals that technology allows; we could sink everything into health. There would be no jobs outside the NHS, of course, so we would all sit cold and starving, waiting for the NHS to collapse as there would be no incomes and therefore tax revenues to pay for it!

The uncomfortable truth is that we are prepared to trade off with risks to our health. We personally trade off health risks for other pleasures all the time: we do it when we over-indulge, when we cross a road where we shouldn't, when we drive a car or especially a motorbike, when we put salt on our food, as well as implicitly whenever we spend any money at all that might otherwise have gone to health care. We have as individuals a high discount rate – in other words we opt for pleasure now against possible pain in the future. Again, the optimal allocation of resources is not to spend all of GDP on health but only to spend on health until our expected health benefits are valued equally at the margin to all the many other things that we value.

The saying that 'health is the most important thing' is no doubt true, but we don't want only protection from ill health. We want many other things too, and when we spend on these other things we are in effect reducing what we could spend on health. Economists call this 'opportunity cost' and it applies to just about everything we spend on; it makes economists seem real party-poopers, forever reminding people who are enthusiastic about something to look at all the alternatives. Buying other things reduces the resources that could be used for health and so increases the risks from the consequences of us, and others, getting ill or having accidents.

Is NICE as good as its name?

If we accept that we will have a finite budget for health care, then maximising the return from this budget requires equalising the marginal returns to spending across all of the things that affect our health, so long as they can be improved by putting money into them, of course. The organisation that gets nearest to doing this in the UK is called NICE. The acronym is because when it was set up in 1999 it was the National Institute for Clinical Excellence. Then it looked only at medical treatments, but in recognition of the argument above that our health depends on a lot more than just medical treatments, its remit was extended in the 2012 Health and Social Care Act to cover aspects of social care too. So in April 2013 it was renamed the National Institute for Health and Care Excellence, but NIHCE just isn't as nice an acronym as NICE, so it is still known as NICE. This is sadly appropriate, for it is very limited in what it can do outside the NHS, as social care is overwhelmingly in the hands of local authorities.

NICE was set up to take the politics out of health care, and, in effect, override the local autonomy that had created the postcode lottery. The experts at NICE make their recommendations for what treatments the NHS should fund on the basis of their careful evaluation of all the available evidence, and since January 2005 the NHS in England and Wales has been legally obliged to provide funding for all medicines and treatments recommended by NICE. This is a good thing. Politics is never a good way to allocate health care: decisions that reflect public pressure or politicians striving to be popular will inevitably be emotive and parochial, and therefore much less than optimal in getting the largest health benefits from a finite budget. For example, if a dying child is denied a particular treatment because it is expensive and very unlikely to help much, the headlines would no doubt scream 'Little Johnny Left to Rot'. There would most likely be a popular campaign to put pressure on the authorities to relent and 'Save Little Johnny'. The local MP might well meet with Johnny and his family for a poignant photo-call.

If the campaign succeeds, the headlines are unlikely to scream, 'Misallocation of NHS budget results in net loss of lives'. The press may follow up the story if Johnny's organs are transplanted, but there will not be coverage of the treatments that were forgone by futile expenditure on poor Johnny.

NICE is there to conduct a calm, dispassionate review of the evidence and assess the cost effectiveness of the many different ways in which the NHS budget can be spent. This has included such unpopular measures as providing free syringes to prevent cross-infections between drug users. Although it actually saves lives, NICE was likened to a 'death panel' by some Republicans campaigning against ObamaCare, so it has to be thick-skinned, particularly as it is constantly lobbied by giant pharmaceutical companies. NICE is still subjected to the most emotive campaigns while those whose lives are saved or improved by NICE probably know nothing of its existence. It remains an outstanding innovation for evidence-based policy, rising above the clamour and, too often, irresponsible populism of the democratic process. If it does not recommend a drug it is because the expected benefits from spending on it are less than from the drugs it does recommend. Politicians challenging its adjudications through ignorance of economics are not to be admired; those who wish to distort health spending for their own popularity are not heroes.

As you will readily accept, the job of NICE is not an easy one. It's a nasty job but someone has to do it; rather than abuse, NICE should be given more resources and powers. NICE would be the first to admit that it is very difficult to define and measure the benefits of health care, but unless we do that, we can't compare the 'cost–benefit ratios' – that is, how many bangs to the buck we get from each of the different ways we use up the health budget – to see if we are getting the most from our money. Apart from checking for a pulse, just how do we compare how healthy someone is compared with someone else? Can we say someone is 'twice' as healthy as someone else? If they get better after a treatment, do we know that was actually down to the treatment? Perhaps they would have got better anyway, or they may have changed their lifestyle. If someone has a positive attitude and enjoys life and health to the full, should we prioritise them over someone who is a misery guts both in sickness and in health?

There is no perfect measure. Even if we were solely concerned with ensuring equality, there would be problems. For example, should the standard for equality be equal spending on each patient, or should the aim be to produce equality of health? Equal health for everybody would require differential spending and would not be achievable anyway. So the general rule used by NICE is that, more or less, each person with the same medical condition has access to the same medical provision. The word 'access' is significant, for equality of access does not guarantee equality of take-up. The evidence is that some people are far more likely to avail themselves of treatments than others. In short, measuring benefits and equality is not straightforward, but even an imperfect NICE is very much better than leaving health to politics.

Whose life is it anyway?

Accepting that there is never going to be a perfect measure of the benefits of health interventions, NICE has opted for a composite measure that uses estimates of life expectancy combined with a subjective measure for the quality of life. This necessarily constructed unit of measurement for the benefits of health intervention is known as a 'Quality-Adjusted Life Year', or usually just 'QALY'. NICE defines the QALY as

> a measure of the state of health of a person or group in which the benefits, in terms of length of life, are adjusted to reflect the quality of life. One QALY is equal to one year of life in perfect health. QALYs are calculated by estimating the years of life remaining for a patient following a particular treatment or intervention and weighting each year with a quality-of-life score (on a zero to 1 scale). It is often measured in terms

of the person's ability to perform the activities of daily life, freedom from pain and mental disturbance.[5]

'Alive or dead' is usually the easy bit, and so pretty binary at 1 for alive and 0 for dead. If alive (hooray!), how do we weight for quality of life? Obviously the prospective patients are not the ones who are asked to put a subjective valuation on their own quality of life – that might be very biased if you know the higher value you put the more likely you are to get the treatment! Instead, samples of respondents are used where disinterested people place weights according to their assessments of various health states.

Absence of health problems is set at 1, so ten years of healthy life is 10 x 1 = 10 QALYs, and then various combinations of detractions from perfect health are weighted in relation to the benchmark 'no health problems'. These include problems with walking, with self-care, pain, anxiety etc. So, 'some problems walking about; some problems washing or dressing self; some problems with performing usual activities; moderate pain or discomfort; moderately anxious or depressed' comes in at 0.516. So ten years of life like this 'earns' 10 x 0.516 = 5.16 QALYs. As QALYs focus on the quality of life, and how much medical conditions are judged to detract from feelings of well-being, they are known in the trade as a 'cost–utility' measure, i.e. how much QALY you get per pound spent.

The scale of QALYs extends right down to negative values where living is, implicitly, judged to be worse than death. So, 'confined to bed; unable to wash or dress oneself; unable to perform usual activities; extreme pain or discomfort; moderately anxious or depressed' is scored at –0.429 – yes, minus.[6] So, to the extent that denying life-saving treatment because of the poor quality of life of a patient can be considered the equivalent of assisted death, then it is clear that assisted death because of chronically distressing conditions is already here.

To equalise returns at the margin there should in principle be a threshold set for the cost of QALYs that determine if a treatment will be recommended by NICE or not. NICE does not actually publish this threshold cost, but it is in the region of £30,000 a QALY. That is, it is worth spending up to £30,000 to give you a year of healthy life, or two years of half a healthy life etc. In practice, the evidence is that there are also clear exceptions to this made by NICE. This valuation of a year of healthy life is not consistently followed by local NHS providers either. Where NICE does not recommend a particular drug or treatment, patients can either accept the standard NHS treatment or go private. Private is, of course, beyond the remit of an NHS that eschews ability to pay as the criterion for treatment, but the Lib Dems successfully campaigned to allow NHS cancer patients to pay top-up charges to get some drugs not recommended by NICE because of their prohibitive cost. This was opposed by those who see patients on the NHS using money to get different treatments as a breach of the core principles of the NHS. Where NICE has approved a treatment, the NHS must fund it, but not all treatments have been assessed by NICE and so access through the NHS to these treatments is still often dependent on local NHS decision making.

The aim of the health service should therefore be to maximise the output of QALYs from the resource envelope that the government decides to give it. Put like that, the issue is to choose the types and patterns of provision that produce this maximisation. Whether the health service is privately owned or publicly owned seems secondary, but we have seen that there are very good reasons why the state should be heavily involved for reasons of both efficiency and equality. For example, we noted that our health depends on a lot of things beyond just medical treatments. Extensive research now shows that one of these factors is inequality itself (see Chapter 11). You've probably guessed which way round it works: on average, poorer people have poorer health and shorter lives. This is not just about absolute poverty, i.e. living at or near subsistence levels; relative poverty kills too.

Among rich countries it is not the very richest ones that have the best health but those with the most equal societies.[7] Inequality kills! Stress, low self-esteem, dysfunctional social relations and habits, boredom and diet are all contributors. Unemployment also tends to be very bad for health.

Though these are all very real influences on health, they are way beyond the narrow remit of a private health provider. The state, however, is in a position to have an overview, to look across all its policy initiatives and services, including social care, and to shift resources across the different causes of ill health, including mental health, to get nearer to equal marginal returns for wider health spend, i.e. greater efficiency.

As things like social care and support are both important contributors to health, care and health can be seen as 'joint products' – or, if it's easier to think about it this way, one can be seen in many respects as the by-product of the other. In assessing the return on the production of joint products we should add up all the returns from the products produced. Often the separation between care and health is manifestly artificial. Why is cancer regarded as a medical condition that is the responsibility of the NHS but dementia is regarded as a social care issue that falls to local authority budgets? For dementia, more spend on social care might well greatly reduce subsequent costs for the NHS. An integrated public sector should be more alert to these complementarities than fragmented private providers, but unfortunately the public sector in practice remains far from integrated on this.

The divide between care and health stretches back hundreds of years, perhaps to seventeenth-century Poor Laws. The post-Second World War Labour government entrenched the dichotomy. Bevan created the NHS as a nationally run service funded out of general taxation and Beveridge led the National Assistance Act, abolishing the Poor Law that since 1601 had been administered by local councils, but this left the new social care services in the hands of local authorities. This new social care service retained the Poor Law principles that assistance should be means-tested and subject to tests of eligibility: that is, it had to be established that individuals had 'need' before they received publicly funded help. Given the huge overlap between health and care that demography, social changes and technology have now brought, the dichotomy, if it ever was sensible, is now a huge obstacle to efficiency.

What should be done to improve our health service?

Sir David Nicholson, Chief Executive of NHS England, has warned that

> if we continue with the current model of care and expected funding
> levels, we could have a funding gap of £30 billion between 2013/14 and
> 2020/21,which will continue to grow and grow quickly if action isn't taken.
> This is on top of the £20 billion of efficiency savings already being met.
> This gap cannot be solved from the public purse but by freeing up NHS
> services and staff from old-style practices and buildings.[8]

Like it or not, we will need some major transformations in social and
health care in order for the NHS to remain a world-beating service. No
party can ignore this. There are clearly indicators that the NHS is in crisis. Targets such as waiting times are not met in many instances and there
have been some serious scandals in health care in a number of hospitals,
which has shaken public confidence. Resources are stretched, not helped
by an ageing population and increased cost of drug treatments. The financial pressures have been compounded by expensive PFI contracts used to
build hospitals and new facilities, and a large increase in pay to doctors
and GPs under Labour, which has eaten much of the budget. Demand
for A&E and normal GP services has also increased as more immigrants
come into the country and the population has risen faster than had been
anticipated. At the same time, pressure on hospitals has intensified due to
cuts in mental and social care in the community that have swollen GP visits and the demand for hospital beds. The reorganisation started by Andy
Burnham and then continued by Andrew Lansley until he was reshuffled and replaced by Jeremy Hunt has added to confusion and suspicion
between the government and the medical and nursing professions, which
see the coalition as attempting to privatise the NHS through the back door.

The financial and other pressures that are already weighing on the NHS
can be seen in the reports of Monitor, the organisation set up to assess the

performance and finances of NHS Foundation Trusts. Foundation Trusts were initiated by the last Labour government to afford well-run NHS Trusts more local autonomy from the Department of Health. It seemed a good idea at the time, as local decision making would be closer to the ground and so better informed. Foundation Trusts are still obliged to heed the recommendations of NICE, which is again sensible in terms of the economic principles we have explained. The coalition's infamous Health and Social Care Bill 2011 proposed a target that all NHS Trusts should achieve NHS Foundation Trust status or become part of an existing NHS Foundation Trust by April 2014, but this is yet another provision of the Act that has failed, as around a third of Trusts failed to make it and about a quarter of the 147 Foundation Trusts were in deficit at the end of 2013/14.

Given the Conservatives' vulnerability on looking after such a social-ist institution, Labour is hoping the NHS will become a major issue in the forthcoming election, and is trying to make it so. Given the experi-ence of the coalition, it is unlikely that any party that is likely to form a government, or even part of one, will be advocating yet more disruptive top-down reorganisations of the health service, but all are aware of the enormous pressures that will be placed on the NHS in the next fiscally restrained parliament. A dyed-in-the-wool socialist will want whatever funding is necessary to keep the NHS as it is, or better, improve it and make it entirely free. That is not an indefensible position. They could point out that the NHS was created when the national debt was much higher than it is today and, after all, we are now much richer, or that, even on the government's own conservative figures, the tax that is avoided by large corporations is more than sufficient to plug the funding gap.[9] And it is true that the ageing population does not put as much pressure on the NHS as was once expected (it turns out that it is dying that costs most, whenever you do it!).

The alternative argument is that the 'spend whatever-it-takes' lobby are ignoring the 'opportunity cost' of an unreformed NHS. That is, the benefits that could be had from not spending so much on it, for example, as we have seen, providing more for social care and mental health. Most of all of course, it just ain't gonna happen! Any party that could conceivably be in the next government will feel obliged to tackle the issue on the grounds that the NHS in its current form is unaffordable. Of course there can be efficiency savings but they can only take us so far. So the effort that must be made is not to resist the inevitable but to look at the evidence and ensure that whatever is done is well judged and keeps our still largely free-at-the-point-of-delivery health service a world-beating service, as it is today.[10]

What the next government will have to do must involve some selection from and combination of: improved productivity; a change in the way resources are spent; an increase in taxation; new or higher charges – and perhaps other forms of rationing. These will be uncomfortable choices, but our health and social care systems are currently structured and funded in a way that is both inequitable and financially unsustainable in the face of the growing pressures on them. It's no wonder that the parties are reluctant to be too specific before an election on what they would do if they were elected – with the notable exceptions perhaps of UKIP and the Green Party, who won't be elected anyway! The Green Party pledge is simply to 'restore the NHS to public ownership' and introduce free personal care for older people. UKIP says it has no plans to fundamentally change the NHS, but Paul Nuttall, the UKIP deputy leader, has said, 'The very existence of the NHS stifles competition,'[11] and UKIP leader Nigel Farage has argued for a US style insurance system.[12] It makes you wonder if UKIP voters ever get past the word 'immigration' – and that of course is their main focus: making sure that if there is to be an NHS it is not open to any 'health tourists'. In fact cracking down on health tourism could contribute only a tiny amount in terms of the NHS budget and might well cost more to administer than it collects.[13] As usual, UKIP is busy blowing up the problem of foreigners out of all proportion (see Chapter 8).

The forthcoming election should also see the new 'National Health Action Party' (NHAP) field up to fifty candidates. They obviously won't be having a say in power either, but they do raise concerns that all voters should heed. Their basic message is that privatisation is bad for your health and that public health and well-being should be prioritised in all policy decisions. We shall argue that the first argument is too blanket a condemnation of the role of private providers and we have already argued that the second assertion should not be taken to extremes. NHAP rightly point out, however, that a privatised health care service is generally more expensive than a publicly organised one.

For example, a marketised system, necessary for privatisation, greatly adds to the administrative and legal costs required to manage the contracting of health services. Money ends up in the pockets of lawyers and accountants and is taken away from frontline care. Administration costs in the NHS have indeed risen, from around 5 per cent to 15 per cent since the introduction of the market, although the NHS confederation states that the management costs of the NHS had fallen from 5 per cent in 1997/98 to 3 per cent in 2008/09, but NHAP notes that in the US system such non-clinical staff overheads are higher, at around a third of all health costs. As might be expected, NHAP opposes the austerity argument being used to starve the NHS of funds. Incidentally, they also remind us that what has not featured much in public debate are the possible consequences of the EU/US Transatlantic Trade and Investment Partnership (TTIP), which could potentially make a more privatised health care system irreversible.

Bad economics can be politically attractive

The political parties might try to woo the electorate, again, by extending the gimmick of 'ring-fencing' the NHS budget. That might be good politics, as it impresses a deceived public, but it is very bad economics for several reasons. Firstly, ring-fencing in cash, or even with the usual inflation measures, is largely meaningless. It is simply another popular myth that the coalition has ring-fenced the NHS in real terms. By historic standards, it has been and is being severely cut. Since 1950, health spending has grown at an average annual rate of 4 per cent; the current so-called ring-fencing will see an average rise of just 0.5 per cent. That is not nearly enough to keep up with the demands upon the NHS and to meet its own higher-than-inflation cost increases, so there has actually been an effective cut of about £16 billion. If the NHS receives similar flat real cash settlements in the next parliament, this real cut will increase to £34 billion, or 23 per cent over the first three years. So recent pledges of more for an NHS ring-fenced budget have been little more than catch-up and a political exploitation of the public's lack of understanding of the relevant economics.

Secondly, as we have seen, our health depends on a lot more than just NHS medical treatments: to ring-fence just part of the spend that supports our health will take us further away from equalising marginal returns, and so make health and social care spending more inefficient, especially if the health bit is preserved at the expense of social care. In fact, the last Labour government did significantly increase spending on the NHS to bring it up to a European average, and NHS net expenditure (resource plus capital, minus depreciation) increased from £57 billion in 2002/03 to £105 billion in 2012/13, but any economist will tell you that the best place to look for waste is in the areas that were previously expanded most rapidly.

Equally, setting targets for waiting times is another populist gimmick that is usually bad economics. Labour did it and Jeremy Hunt, the current Health Minister, has recently announced £250 million to focus on 'long-waiters',[14] even though it will mean the NHS will miss eighteen-week waiting-time targets over the coming months. In practice, such targets tend to distort what should be left to clinical decisions on priorities and they often create perverse incentives. For example, the easiest way for a GP to reduce the waiting time for appointments is to simply refuse to let anyone book an appointment more than a few days in advance! Hunt blamed the former Labour administration for imposing 'perverse' incentives, which he said had led hospitals to prioritise those who had not been waiting long over those who had; his arbitrary imposition of a limit will invariably create anomalies where the target overrides a clinical priority. Unacceptable waiting times are a symptom, not the disease.

The solutions to the funding gap are easiest for those who don't much approve of the NHS in the first place. Predictably, they advocate taking the NHS further towards a free market 'solution'. The free market-oriented think tank Reform calls for at least a £10 charge for GP consultations, £10 fines for missed appointments, a means-tested system for end-of-life care (that expensive bit), and a further hike in prescription charges from £8.05 to £10. Reform estimates that these measures would raise around £3 billion a year. Their research director, Thomas Cawston, argues: 'Few will want to debate higher NHS charges but the funding outlook for the service makes it unavoidable. Prescription charges are the easiest route to new revenue, with exemptions for people on low incomes built in.'[15] We could easily extend this approach of charging for all but the poor to the whole of the NHS; the problems are that it can often turn out to be impractically expensive to administer and enforce and takes us nearer to the private system that we wish to avoid. And the more the average person has to pay for the NHS, the more they might just as well take out private health insurance, so the NHS could become less of a political 'no-go area' for right-wing politicians as the middle-income earners drop out of it. Eventually, we probably arrive at something not unlike the traditional US system: that is, a world-class service for those with incomes to pay and a pretty crappy 'charity' service for everyone else.

Other changes may well be overdue; approaches that were appropriate in 1948 can be anachronistic in the twenty-first century. For example, Sir David Nicholson mentions 'buildings', as the emphasis in the NHS is still on hospitals, but hospitals are very expensive to build and to run, and may not be so important now that technology means that, increasingly, health care and monitoring can be provided at the patient's home. Better social and primary care can prevent admissions in the first place. This is especially important when you consider the changing patterns of health care users. Over fifteen million people in England have a chronic condition or 'long-term condition' (LTC), as it is called in the health service. Although LTCs make up a quarter of the population, they account for 50 per cent of all GP appointments, 70 per cent of all hospital bed days and 70 per cent of the total health and care spend in England. Nearly two-thirds of people admitted to hospital are over sixty-five years old and health care costs are concentrated in the last eighteen months or so of life.[16] Tailoring care to specific needs and finding alternatives to hospital wards is likely to be far more efficient as new technologies increasingly blur the distinction between health and social care, and more nurses visiting care for the elderly homes might actually reduce the load on hospitals.

Not just health care, but health and care

We know how loath politicians are to publicise the uncomfortable health choices they would have to make after the election, but Labour has proposed to go much further along the route of integrating health and social care. The policy economist Dame Kate Barker, Chair of the King's Fund Commission on the Future of Health and Social Care in England, says, 'A health service with a ring-fenced budget and free at the point of use is not likely to work well with a social care system funded through local authorities and heavily means-tested.' Our principle of marginal returns, and that of looking at all the benefits of a particular spend, even when they show up under someone else's remit, means that a fragmented health and care system is just about certain to be inefficient.

To be fair, these very significant overlaps were acknowledged by the coalition when setting up a £3.8 billion 'Better Care Fund' in June 2013. Its intention is to ensure a 'transformation in integrated health and social care' and a local single pooled budget to incentivise the NHS and local government to work more 'closely together around people, placing their well-being as the focus of health and care services'. This is laudable but the imbalance between health and care is now actually widening. We now fund health care to a similar extent to other rich EU neighbours, but spending on social care lags behind. So much so that our underfunded social care system now relies very heavily on unpaid carers who have been largely neglected by politicians, an aspect that the Lib Dems, to their credit, say they would do something about.

The draconian cuts in social care we have seen and will see are unprecedented in the history of adult social care. In 2012/13, 26 per cent fewer people aged over sixty-five were receiving publicly funded social care and 24 per cent fewer younger disabled people, compared to 2008/09. The decline has been sharpest, 30 per cent, for those receiving care in their own home, precisely the care most likely to reduce the demand on the NHS and residential nursing homes. There are many other such examples of the costs of this lack of integration and cooperation. For example, 123,081 bed days were used up in June 2014 alone because of people being stuck in hospital waiting for further health and social care assessments, arguments over who should fund continuing care or simply a lack of social care provision such as housing. Cuts in social care are in effect often simply being passed back to the NHS, a long-term and arbitrary trend that will only accelerate as social spending per head is again cut massively in the next parliament.

Public opposition to these huge reductions in social care may be muted by the fact that many people simply do not understand that they could be personally liable to pay for much of their care should they themselves need it. Nearly half of those in care homes have to meet the entire cost from their own pocket until their assets are run down to £23,250. The Dilnot reforms, due to take effect in 2017, will lift that threshold to £118,000, but even then, those with sufficient assets will still have to fork out up to £72,000 for 'eligible' care; non-eligible care will of course be charged in whole, and none of this includes the costs of accommodation if they enter a nursing or residential home, up to a £12,000 a year limit. Yet still up to 50 per cent of the population believe that this care will be free in the same way as the NHS is free. It is perhaps also odd that there is so much popular support for a cap on social care liability that protects the windfall gains of those that inherit these preserved savings, rather than for using them to support care for those that really need support. Although the same argument could also be used to means-test NHS care for the elderly and so prevent it being used as a subsidy to inheritance.

At a time when health and social care should be converging to better meet the demands upon them, the two systems are diverging, with publicly funded social care becoming a residual service available to those with only the very greatest needs. The NHS is still largely free at the point of use so almost no one has to worry about medical bills. Social care, by contrast, may take large amounts of an individual's or family's income and savings.

Rationing

A completely free 'whatever is wanted for whosoever wants it' service suffers from a condition endemic to any free service: that is, the likelihood that it will be abused. Some estimates suggest that around 50 million unnecessary trips are made to GPs each year, accounting for nearly one-fifth of GPs' workload.[17] This may cost the health service about £2 billion a year. Often these visits are for minor aches and pains, colds, coughs and even dandruff! Even a modest charge, with exemptions for low incomes and chronic conditions, could reduce this abuse. Similarly unnecessary visits to accident and emergency units might be deterred by a small charge. But you need to be careful of taking this pricing deterrent argument too far. In 2013, Sir Bruce Keogh, former NHS medical director, endorsed the closure of A&E departments largely on the argument that '40 per cent of patients who attend accident and emergency departments are discharged requiring no treatment'.[18] Backed by stats like this, Jeremy Hunt, the Health Secretary, has also called for several A&E departments to be closed. But subsequent research, admittedly commissioned by the Royal College of Emergency Medicine, found Sir Bruce's figure was an 'urban myth'. The researchers found that more than 80 per cent of accident and emergency patients were there legitimately, that only 15 per cent of patients could have been seen by a GP without the need for assessment by an emergency department, and that many of these were visits by parents worried about their children's symptoms.[19]

A welfare support service that can reach the parts it has to reach without leaving open some scope for abuse is a holy grail. The tabloid press delights in tracking down extreme examples and then blasting us with screaming headlines to 'prove' that social benefits are way too generous. The real issue on this type of abuse is whether, having done everything to prevent it, putting up with the inevitable abuse is worth it because of the overall support it brings to those who need it. Such big-picture overviews do not excite those who want to believe that most of their hard-earned tax goes to loafers and spongers. It usually turns out that the notion of abuse is not so straightforward anyway. For example, in health care, a patient may not know that their complaint is trivial. The doctor may be irritated but the caller may have been genuine. Chronic tiredness can be caused by a host of things, some serious. A persistent cough may be just a cough, or it may be an early symptom of lung cancer. Deterring 'trivial' visits to doctors may mean that early detection of some serious conditions is reduced, perhaps leading to much more expense later. It is certainly an exaggeration to claim that modest charging would lead to the 'survival of the richest', but that hasn't stopped Labour overstating the case and cutting short its own more considered assessment with the party political jibe 'the government must come clean on any plans to charge for NHS care'. In any case, under the new commissioning arrangements, doctors probably already find it difficult enough to spare the time to be good accountants; adding the duties of a tax collector would be unlikely to increase their attention to things medical. Other methods of deterring unnecessary loadings on doctors also have their pitfalls. For example, a recent study found that introducing telephone calls in place of visits to the GP actually increased the loading on GPs![20]

Another real worry is over the nature of the huge political lobby, often backed by providers of private medical care, that doesn't want the NHS to exist in its current form because a) it shows that socialism can be popular, b) because it requires taxation, or c) simply because they can't make as much money from health care while the NHS exists! Knowing the less than disinterested backgrounds of many of the proponents, the 'thin end of the wedge' argument becomes a worry. That is, once charging breaches the 'free' principle, fees could be successively raised to close the gap between NHS and private providers and so drive the NHS further down the road to privatisation. Some historic battles were fought in the Labour Party over this free principle when Labour reintroduced prescription charges. The father of the NHS, Aneurin Bevan, resigned over their introduction for spectacles and dental treatment, as did Harold Wilson, the future Labour Prime Minister. In October 1952, a Conservative government set the charge at one shilling per prescription. Three years later this went up to two shillings per item. The 1965 Labour government, under Harold Wilson, abolished the charges again, but the NHS drugs bill soared, partly because people stopped buying their own over-the-counter treatments, and so in 1968 the Labour government felt forced to reintroduce prescription charges, at a higher rate but with exemptions for the old, young, those on benefits and those with chronic conditions.

Prescription charges have subsequently been abolished in Scotland, Wales and Northern Ireland, but today a prescription in England costs over £8 – that is, if you are not in one of the vast majority of groups that enjoy exemptions. These include: anyone over sixty; anyone under sixteen; anyone aged sixteen to eighteen in full-time education; anyone pregnant, or anyone who has had a baby in the previous twelve months; anyone who has a listed chronic medical condition; anyone who is an NHS inpatient; anyone who gets Universal Credit, Income Support, Income-based Jobseeker's Allowance, Income-related Employment and Support Allowance or Pension Credit Guarantee – and anyone whose partner receives any of these. This means that almost 90 per cent of prescriptions in England are free,[21] but then again about 80 per cent of people aged 18–59 did have to pay for their medicines. Dr James Cave, the GP who edits the *Drug and Therapeutics Bulletin* journal, has argued that exemptions linked to features such as age and pregnancy seem arbitrary, and some qualifying patients are allowed free prescriptions for illnesses that are unrelated to their main condition. He concludes that 'many such exemptions appear illogical and unfair, adding to our belief that the prescription charge is a poorly conceived, manifestly unfair tax'.[22]

Today, prescription charges are 'supplemented' by other controversial ways of raising revenue, such as parking fees. Fifteen years ago most NHS hospitals provided free car parking, but over the last decade charges have escalated so that they now cost patients and hospital visitors at least £100 million a year. Telephones and TVs are another new money spinner. From 1995, the commercial Patientline payphone and TV service was introduced into NHS hospitals, despite an Office of Fair Trading investigation. The annual cost to patients is around £43 million, while claims to recover costs from road traffic accident compensation are now running at about another £200 million. It does not seem unreasonable to charge for meals in hospitals – we would be eating anyway – and it seems preferable to hiking up non-means-tested parking charges as a means of extracting revenue from concerned relatives. Another suggestion, criticised by libertarians as state nannyism, is to kill two birds with one stone by introducing hypothecated (i.e. the revenues go only to the health service) inflation-proofed 'sin taxes', say on alcohol, tobacco, fat and sugary foods.

Is socialism still best for the NHS?

Yes, for the most part. GPs can behave like private firms on occasion, but the NHS is still overwhelmingly financed out of public money and still mostly delivered by publicly owned institutions. The private sector in the UK is very small in comparison, partly perhaps because of the public's general confidence in the quality of the NHS (see below). Although

Scandinavian countries also have an overwhelmingly publicly financed and provided health service, this is not the norm internationally. In France, health is similarly largely publicly funded, but health care providers are much more of a mix of both publicly and privately owned organisations. Canada uses mainly public finance but health care is privately provided. The US is overwhelmingly private provision funded by private finance: that is, a system of for-profit medical providers funded overwhelmingly through medical insurance. This almost completely private sector health provision was unique among OECD countries. 'ObamaCare', or the 2010 Patient Protection and Affordable Care Act, as it is officially known, has very recently ensured that the vast majority of the US population is now able to buy, or at least contribute to, subsidised health insurance. As we saw earlier, in order to make the market work it also compels them to buy it.

So, which system is best? That is disputed and multi-dimensional, but in most surveys the NHS does pretty well, both on the quality of service and on efficiency. For example, in June 2014 the Commonwealth Fund, a Washington-based foundation which is respected around the world for its analysis of the performance of different countries' health systems, reported that the NHS is the best health-care system among the eleven leading developed countries examined. The NHS bested countries that spend far more per head on health. In fact, the UK spent the second lowest amount on health care among the eleven countries: just £2,008 per head, less than half the £5,017 in the US. Only New Zealand, at £1,876, spent less. The US, with the most privatised health-care provision, and despite the highest level of spend, was found to be the worst among the eleven countries. The report concluded: 'The United Kingdom ranks first overall, scoring highest on quality, access and efficiency.' This does not remotely mean that the NHS is perfect – it still compares badly for cancer survival, though there may be under-reporting in some countries, and for some other conditions and it has some curiously large regional variations in the quality of service, as the Mid-Staffordshire and Winterbourne View tragedies demonstrated. But it may be relevant that between 1990 and 2010, life expectancy in England increased by 4.2 years.[23]

Parties and the NHS

Given that it's a national treasure with a high international ranking, surely no politician would dare tamper with the NHS! Maybe that was why David Cameron was absolutely adamant in his pre-election promise of 2009 that he wouldn't: 'With the Conservatives there will be no more of the tiresome, meddlesome, top-down restructures that have dominated the last decade of the NHS.' A speech later conveniently erased from their party website.[24] Voters elected Cameron Prime Minister in 2010, partly because the Conservative Party had already cut into Labour's lead on health care, which Labour had enjoyed almost since it founded the NHS in 1948. This disillusionment in Labour's commitment to the NHS was in large part because Labour *had* tampered with the NHS, introducing more market mechanisms that included allowing more private providers to bid for contracts, and some atrociously bad value for money 'private finance initiatives', whereby private companies funded hospitals in return for leeching off the service ever after. All parties should be considering the best way out of these disastrous PFIs.

Once elected, Cameron must have been too busy to have remembered his solemn pledge, for he appointed Andrew Lansley as Conservative Health Minister to embark on some of the biggest NHS reforms ever. Not only just tiresome and meddlesome, they were intended to reshape the NHS from top to bottom. The massive Health and Social Care Act of 2012 was designed to increase competition, give the service more autonomy and give more power and responsibility to GPs to make decisions about the purchase of care for their patients. The departing head of the NHS, Sir David Nicholson, described the reforms as 'so big that they could be seen from space'. The reforms were not well received and have never had public support and so became a bigger headache for the coalition than even the Lib Dems reneging on student fees.[25]

The biggest change was the creation of 211 'Clinical Commissioning Groups' (CCGs) that put about 60 per cent of the NHS budget into the care of GPs and health workers. These then became responsible for procuring non-GP services such as hospitals and other specialists. Many doctors warned that the reforms would lead to more fragmentation and more privatisation. Many GPs complained that their time is better spent as doctors rather than as accountants. Others worried over GP competence for procuring the best value care and of a more 'commercial' basis to doctors' referrals. The new system of commissioning allowed 'creeping privatisation' as GPs could choose 'any qualified provider' of health services for their patients, including privately owned ones. Indeed, for larger commissioning it was made compulsory to tender across 'any qualified provider'. Concerns over the reforms grew, especially among those working in the NHS itself, who were concerned by the growth of private providers under the new commissioning arrangements. Cameron was alarmed by the backlash, but did not reverse the restructuring, which would have been a humiliating, costly and messy move, so he responded to the general disapproval by amputating Andrew Lansley from the Department of Health instead, less than six months after his reforms had been passed by Parliament. It was a big promotion for Jeremy Hunt, who replaced Lansley as Health Minister, though strangely Hunt hardly ever mentions these huge reforms, which about says it all.

Staff in the NHS, and a majority of the public too, fear that the NHS is slowly being privatised. The public have a mixture of reasons and emotions for opposing privatisation, empathy for our 'wonderful nurses' and the gratitude that so many of us owe to the NHS, but above all it's a lingering fear that health provision will revert back to being for 'profit rather than need'. Older people in particular have had memories passed down to them of just what a marvellous social revolution the NHS represented. As we have seen, economists have better reasons than these, but mostly they come to a similar conclusion that the NHS is needed. For the sake of stability and to reduce initiative fatigue within the NHS, Labour has also pledged not to instigate yet another large-scale restructuring.[26] They do propose, however, to curtail the extent of the 'internal market' by making it more difficult for private companies to compete in it through making NHS providers the 'preferred providers' in place of the current 'any qualified provider' approach. They will also repeal forced competition throughout the NHS in England. Private providers would only be used for novel or particularly specialised provision, or for when the NHS provision is judged inadequate or absent. Labour promotes this as a move back to re-establishing a national and integrated health service: in the words of Unison, Britain's largest public sector union, a health service 'in which cooperation and collaboration are reinstated as the guiding principles – in place of competition and fragmentation'.

A seamless integrated service, however, does not necessitate resurrecting a monolithic nationalised deliverer of all health care. It could involve a common system of commissioning but from many diverse providers, all within a better integration of health and care, perhaps through a greatly strengthened and expanded NICE and Better Care initiative. Economists largely agree that competition can be a good thing for keeping people on their toes and for increasing efficiency. In fact, competition is probably more important for the performance of an organisation than ownership, state or private. 'Competitive socialism' is when state-owned organisations compete with other organisations, not in the traditional way by arguing in Whitehall corridors of power, but in markets or quasi-markets. The concept was introduced into our health service by Conservative Health Minister Ken Clarke in the early '90s by his creation of the internal market within the NHS, whereby NHS hospitals competed with each other for patients. But the shadow Health Minister, Andy Burnham, might be being unnecessarily protective of NHS providers. He certainly seems to imply that they couldn't cope with the competition from private providers. Last year, £10 billion worth of NHS business went to private and other providers: that's only a small fraction of the £150 billion or so spent on health care. So a better approach could be to allow the continuance of privately owned competition but to investigate very quickly if the share of private providers starts to increase, as such a rise could indicate things are amiss in the NHS, or that the private versus public competition has become unfair, perhaps because of poor conditions and low-quality staff, and of course by cherry-picking the most profitable treatments. Having such comparisons available, and the innovations that private providers can bring, can yield a great deal of information on what works and what doesn't, and this experience could be used to improve a system that should remain overwhelmingly publicly owned.

A new settlement for health and social care?

It is good to know that there is a good economist on the job of considering the various options. Kate Barker is an excellent public policy economist working with other excellent policy economists, such as the massively experienced Julian Le Grand, to produce 'A New Settlement for Health and Social Care', a report funded by the King's Fund,[27] an independent charitable organisation that works to improve health care in the UK. The authors not only explain why we need a single budget for health and social care, but they also know all about the market failure and inequality problems of private health insurance, and about the international evidence that it just doesn't work well in practice either. So the commissioners have ruled out a wholesale switch to social insurance and/or tax relief on private medical insurance or a general switch to NHS charges. Their report deserves to be very influential for election manifestos, hopefully reducing the populist gimmicks too often used by politicians to entice voters by exploiting the public's reliance on the NHS and their poor grasp of the economics involved. The options examined in the New Settlement Report range from proposals to change taxation for everyone, such as a dedicated tax for health and social care, noting that national insurance is in effect a regressive and hence unfair tax, to ideas that would raise the tax burden on, or reduce the benefits available to, the elderly population. Other proposals include increasing user charges for aspects of health care that are currently provided by the public purse, but still leaving the NHS very largely free at the point of use, and they make it clear that they would only support higher user charges if these were linked to an improvement in entitlements and demonstrable improvements in the overall funding available for health and social care.

The report inevitably and sensibly suggests that at least some of the funding should come from a pensioner population that on average is now better off than its preceding cohorts. Pensioner poverty is at its lowest for decades according to the ONS, thanks to increased private sector pension provision, income from earnings, savings and investments, and due to the fact that pensioner benefits have risen faster than earnings over the past decade. By contrast with thirty years ago, when more than 40 per cent of pensioners were in the bottom fifth of the income distribution, today barely 10 per cent of pensioners are in the bottom fifth. The NHS has yet to adjust to this dramatically changed picture.[28]

In sum, the call for an integrated social care and health service makes sense. The New Settlement interim report opens by noting that the current division of services is

> leading to confusion and frustration for patients and their carers, and wasting resources on administration. Life expectancy, family structures, medical treatments and technologies are all quite different from when Beveridge and Bevan devised the 1948 settlement for health and social care. It is time to think afresh – and establish a new settlement fit for today's circumstances.

The report acknowledges that the social care and clinical commissioning groups are now 'tentatively linked' through nascent health and well-being boards but conclude that the 211 clinical commissioning groups that currently commission acute hospital and community health services, the social care that is the responsibility of 152 completely separate local authorities, and the NHS England commissioning of all primary care and specialist provision make up a disjointed and fragmented system, as the different parts of these systems have different funding, governance and accountability arrangements.

If you care about the NHS, and that's the vast majority of us, you should go beyond ideology and the smoke-and-mirrors rhetoric of party politics. The King's Fund Barker Commission on the Future of Health and Care is an eminently clear read which makes sensible and realistic suggestions; party manifestos should stop using the NHS as a political football and adopt or adapt the commission's twelve recommendations. These should be read in full to gain a full understanding of their considerations and realism, but in brief they are:

1. An end to the historic divide between health and social care.

2. A single, ring-fenced budget for health and social care, with a single commissioner.

3. Simpler access paths to health and social care based on personal budgets.

4. A greater parity by need in access to health and social care.

5. Health and welfare boards that evolve into a single commissioner.

6. No general switch to NHS charges, but a reduction in prescription charges with far fewer exemptions, and new recipients of NHS continuing health care should contribute to their accommodation costs on a means-tested basis.

7. Public spending on health and social care planned to reach between 11 per cent and 12 per cent of GDP by 2025. This will involve some significant tax increases but economic growth will assist their affordability.

8. The older generation should contribute more through reducing non-means-tested age benefits and by ending or reducing their exemption from employee national insurance contributions.

9. Free access for a wider range of social care needs to be phased in coupled with an additional one percentage point employee national insurance contribution for those aged over forty 'as a contribution towards the more generous settlement from which they and their parents will benefit'.

10. An increase to 3 per cent in the additional rate of national insurance for those above the upper earnings limit, again timed to match the recommended extensions of free social care.

11. A comprehensive review of wealth taxation including inheritance tax, wealth transfer tax, changes to capital gains and property taxation.

12. A regular review of the health and social care needs of the country and the spending and revenues required to meet them.

Conclusion

Politicians should to a large extent just butt out of health and leave it to the experts; they should certainly refrain from knee-jerk measures that get headlines but do little to improve the service. They should recognise that the NHS is a world-class service largely because it avoids the market failures and dysfunctions that beset private health systems elsewhere. It is high in the list of public spending priorities, but it needs careful reconsideration of its funding. The demographic strain turns out not to be as bad as was once thought, but the public purse cannot provide complete solutions to funding problems that are also exacerbated by expensive new treatments, high cost inflation in general and rising expectations. Any changes should note that the elderly are now, as a group, overly subsidised. Changes need not and should not further dilute the founding principles of our beloved NHS, but we must find very substantial efficiencies through exploiting new technologies that can reduce hospital overhead costs and do much more to integrate our social care and health care systems, to better acknowledge the contribution of social care and carers and to achieve the complementarities that are now more important than ever before. The King's Fund report should be central to manifesto plans.

CHAPTER 8

Bloody Foreigners:
They Come Over Here,
Creating Jobs and Paying Taxes

The truth about immigration

T HAT'S NOT A sentiment you'll often see in UK tabloids, but it's just as likely as the more common charge that immigrants steal jobs and overwhelm public services. As if enduring tired jokes about economists isn't enough, explaining the economics of immigration against a wall of common prejudices and a barrage of media vilification can be another social ordeal for economists. You are having a pleasant meal, the waiter has a charming accent and is diligent and pleasant, but your friend whispers, with no knowledge of the waiter's immigration status, 'It's wrong that foreigners are taking jobs away from young Brits.' Or, as Mrs Duffy famously implied in answering her own question to Gordon Brown: 'All these Eastern Europeans what are coming in, where are they flocking from?' When you reply, 'It is just as likely that immigration creates more jobs for British workers,' your now ex-friend gives you a look mixed with pity and scorn that you could be so misinformed.

The analysis and evidence shows that, most likely, immigration does not mean fewer jobs for British workers. But if you want to believe it does then it certainly looks as if it does, for people can see the evidence with their own eyes: 'That immigrant there has taken a British job.' Trying to tell some people that economics suggests otherwise is like trying to convince them that black is white. Much easier to keep schtum, don't rock the boat: life is easier if you let people believe what they want to believe, and a common dislike is great for bonding.[1] Maybe that is why so many people do so want to believe that foreigners are to blame for everything. Compared to other rich nations, the British tend to be particularly hostile to immigrants.[2] However, economists are much more likely to know that analysis and evidence just do not support the notion that immigrants make it harder for British incumbents to get jobs. It's hard for economists to resist the temptation to point this out, even when you know it might lead to a 'heated' discussion that is testimony to just how much some people really do want to believe that immigration is the cause of their problems.

It is self-evident to many a non-economist that if 'that foreigner there didn't have that job' then it could be done by a 'British' worker. The economist is asking them not to believe their own eyes; they can *see* that foreigners *have* 'taken' jobs in Britain, but they are not thinking about how immigration may also increase the number of jobs available. Putting aside the tricky job of actually defining a 'British worker', it just isn't so that if one person has a job then there is one less job for other people. Economists call this widespread belief that employment is a zero-sum game the 'lump of labour fallacy': that is, that there are a fixed number of jobs in the economy. Or, as Nigel Farage of UKIP put it, 'With two and a half million people unemployed in the UK, of which 958,000 are under twenty-five, every job vacancy counts.'

We've seen it before

The lump of labour fallacy is a very old one. In the nineteenth century the Luddites went about bashing machines on the assumption that if a machine does work then there must be less work left for humans. Of course, it is true that new technologies can displace workers – mechanical looms did replace the handloom weavers who previously were the 'aristocracy' of the working class – but mechanisation overall enabled the industrial revolution that created millions *more* jobs for humans. In the middle decades of the twentieth century it was women working who were blamed for taking men's jobs and so leaving 'fewer jobs for men', the widespread sentiment being that a married women, who presumably has a husband to provide for her, should not 'steal' a job from a 'bread-winning' man. Of course, women working actually led to millions more jobs too: indeed, today a lack of women working is often cited as part of Japan's recent economic doldrums.

This resentment towards 'women taking men's jobs' was strikingly similar to today's resentment of immigrants. Many married women were working through necessity rather than choice, but there was still much hostility towards them. The resentment, as with immigrants, was increased by economic downturns and so rose sharply during the Great Depression of the 1930s. In the US, twenty-six federal state legislatures were still considering laws limiting married women's work. In the same way as many established immigrants themselves now support less immigration, a US Gallup poll in 1936 reported that 82 per cent of respondents believed that wives with employed husbands should not work outside the home, and three-quarters of the women polled agreed!

Of course, the Second World War inevitably sucked women into the labour force, and after the war the vast majority of these working women wanted to keep working. So in the 1950s, media depictions of 'greedy selfish women' neglecting their homes and families were commonplace. It wasn't just that they were stealing jobs: these selfish irresponsible women were apparently responsible for everything from child neglect through juvenile delinquency to creating homosexuality! Similarly, immigrants today are still blamed by many for a host of assorted ills. As with immigrants today, the influx of women into the workforce was blamed for tearing apart the – no-doubt similarly nostalgic rose-tinted-specs-coloured – social fabric. Whereas such vilifications of working women are now rare today, and no one really argues any more that more women working means fewer jobs for men, it is very common to see similar, or even worse, derogatory depictions of immigrants in our media today.

Public perception is not a reliable guide to the facts on immigration

The eagerness of sections of our press to feed xenophobic and racist myths about immigrants, broken here and there by a few warm-hearted stories to show they are not just xenophobic rags, has a strong connection with public perceptions. As a whole, the public massively overestimates the things commonly associated with the supposed negative aspects of immigration.[3] Opinion polls show that if you ask the public what percentage of people in Britain today are immigrants (that is, born outside the UK) they say 31 per cent when the actual figure is 13 per cent. Their average response is that the percentage of the UK population that is Muslim is a quarter, when the actual figure is just 5 per cent. The average estimate is that 'black and Asian people' make up 30 per cent of the population, when it is actually only 11 per cent. Incredibly, 5 per cent of people even think that over half of the British population is Muslim!

Similarly, the public believes that about a quarter of benefits are claimed fraudulently, and benefit fraud is often associated with immigrants even though immigrants are actually less likely to claim benefits; the actual figure for all fraudulent claims is less than 1 per cent. When asked whether capping benefits at £26,000 per household would save more money compared with raising the pension age to sixty-six for both men and women, the yes camp outweighed the no by two to one. In fact, capping household benefits is estimated to save £290 million compared with the £5 billion that would be saved by raising the pension age! In short, the public has a grossly distorted image of foreigners taking a big slice of a national pie that should be reserved for the British.

Resentment towards immigrants has been more resilient to changing attitudes than for women working. It is simply a myth that the current high level of public opinion that there are 'too many immigrants' is a new phenomenon that has been caused by recent high levels of immigration. Britain introduced its first immigration controls in 1905: the Prime Minister, Arthur James Balfour, argued that without such controls, 'though the Britain of the future may have the same laws, the same institutions and constitution … nationality would not be the same and would not be the nationality we would desire to be our heirs through the ages yet to come'. Two years earlier, a Royal Commission on 'Alien Immigration' expressed concern that newcomers were inclined to live 'according to their traditions, usages and customs' and hence there might be 'grafted onto the English stock … the debilitated sickly and vicious products of Europe'. There's nothing new about UKIP!

In fact, since opinion polling on this issue began in the 1960s, the overwhelming majority of people in Britain have always agreed with the sentiment that there are 'too many immigrants'. The percentage of those feeling this may even have fallen since the '60s.[4] Certainly a major reason for the introduction of immigration controls in 1962 was the popular hostility to black immigration that manifested itself in racial discrimination and occasional outbursts of violence. By far the worst incidents of violence were the riots in Notting Hill and Nottingham in 1958, a clear contrast with the equally unwelcome but manifestly multi-ethnic riots of 2011!

Even when it's really about hatred of foreigners and racial prejudice, there are usually attempts to 'justify' this hostility. As with women working, the resentment towards immigrants through the decades has often been justified by a cocktail of declared ancillary 'reasons'. These have at times included: foreigners crowd an already crowded Britain, they have dirty habits, their cooking smells, they smell, they commit crime, they are excessively libidinal, they will breed like rabbits, they are not Christians, they will take over, they harbour terrorists, they swamp our services, they are genetically inferior (and win at sports only because they have genetic advantages), they will interbreed and pollute our 'British blood lines' and, apparently, they simultaneously both live off benefits and take our jobs.

As this is a book about economics, we do not have space to dispel all of these 'non-racist' rationales, so let's focus on the most common and least personal derogatory economic 'justification', that immigrants supposedly steal our jobs, before nipping back to examine some of the other charges against them.

Economic analysis does not suggest that immigration is much of a problem, and it's likely to have benefits too

It takes only a moment's calm reflection to see that the notion that the total amount of jobs in the UK is a constant is nonsense. For example, in 1900 the UK population was about 36 million, and today it is about 63 million, but there are 'only' around two million unemployed today, not tens of millions. The UK today has the highest ever number of jobs: why? Because the UK population today is the highest it has ever been: economies consist of people, and the economy arises from the interactions of these people, so the more people there are, the bigger the economy is too. That's why there are no vacancies on desert islands and why shrinking populations are associated with higher, not lower, unemployment.

By contrast, if migrant labour prevents bottlenecks in production, this may disproportionately contribute to economic growth by providing skills and effort when and where it is needed. It may also contribute to job creation by bringing in entrepreneurship, increasing domestic demand for goods and services, raising the productivity even of non-immigrants and improving the efficiency of labour markets, for example, by increasing overall labour mobility. Unlike simplistic supply and demand diagrams drawn by economic novices, which misleadingly show an increased labour supply but a static demand curve, such increased productivity and enterprise in a dynamically expanding economy could actually increase the demand for *all* labour, including so-called British jobs. And of course, immigrants are only employed in the private sector if they produce more than they are paid, so this 'surplus' productivity flows back into the rest of the economy.

Believing that deporting immigrants will increase your chance of getting a job is like believing that murdering a millionaire increases your chances of becoming a millionaire. In the same way that banning women from working is not the answer to male unemployment, it is how the economy responds *overall* to changes in immigration that matters. For example, if you tried to buy up all the baked beans from supermarkets you would find on your next visit that there are more, not fewer, cans of beans on the shelves. What looks like common sense as a little picture is not necessarily so in the bigger picture. If there were fewer immigrants there could well be fewer, not more, jobs for British workers.

Stoking up fear of foreigners is no longer the preserve of fringe right-wing parties. For a long time politicians exercised caution following Enoch Powell's 1968 'rivers of blood' speech. Of course, Powell's predictions of mass ethnic conflict are in stark contrast to the reality of multicultural Britain's modern ethnic integration, as highlighted by, say, the London Olympics. But more recently many MPs have again sought popularity by engaging in more subtle 'dog-whistle' messages to certain sections of the electorate. 'Dog-whistle' messages are ones that are not necessarily racist or xenophobic per se, but are designed to appeal to those seeking a 'cover story' for their true feelings. The call for an 'honest debate on immigration' is often followed by trotting off such cover stories, consisting of extremely misleading assertions and statistics, such as '90 per cent of all new jobs go to immigrants', despite the clear data showing that most vacancies are, of course, taken by British workers.

The '90 per cent of new jobs' statistic, for example, is misleading as there is no definition of a 'new job' – there are simply vacancies. Obviously if you were to take the net increase in jobs and compare this with the number of immigrants taking jobs then the percentage of net jobs taken by immigrants is bound to be high. To see this, use simple numbers: if 100 jobs are lost and then 101 more jobs are created, then the net increase in jobs is one. In real economies large numbers of jobs are lost and created all the time, but if the net increase is just one, and there is just one new worker who is an immigrant, then a mischievous commentator might say that 100 per cent of all 'new' jobs were taken by immigrants, even if that job is just 1 per cent, or much less, of the total new jobs. If a British worker had dropped out of the labour force and been replaced by another immigrant then similarly we might claim the daft result that 200 per cent of new jobs had been taken by immigrants!

If we only look at first entrants to the labour force, it is of course still the case that groups whose share in the labour force is increasing, be it immigrants or those in a particular age group or hair colour, will inevitably constitute a disproportionate share of any net change in employment. When the UK working population is falling we can very easily construct meaningless figures showing astronomically high percentages of foreigners taking over 'British jobs'. Migration Watch, an organisation that campaigns against immigration and is often cited in the press, highlighted that between 2004 and 2011 an extra 600,000 Eastern European workers entered the UK labour force, and then explicitly linked this to UK youth unemployment rising by 400,000. Migration Watch used this negative correlation to mock more rigorous research findings by challenging them with the rhetorical question 'Is this just a remarkable coincidence?' But on closer examination it turns out that the vast majority of the rise in youth unemployment was during 2008 and 2009, when the number of Eastern European workers actually fell slightly!

Even if they had got the correlation right, no serious economist or statistician would suggest, as Migration Watch did, that correlation demonstrates causation. In fact, ignoring such silly statistics, foreign-born people tend to fill vacancies roughly in proportion to their representation in the population, as we might reasonably expect, a little higher as they tend to be younger and so more likely to be of working age. Of course, this is all a red herring: the real question is not what such percentages are but whether the presence of foreign-born workers makes it harder for British-born workers to gain employment. Overall, the evidence suggests that it does not.

The basic analysis of immigration is pretty easy to understand, though as we have just seen, collecting and interpreting the evidence is more problematic. For a simplification of the analysis, just imagine an economy in which the population doubles through time. If the new population has the same characteristics as the old then our first guess at what will happen must be that output will double too. Twice as many people will be working and spending as before. But wouldn't labour productivity have fallen due to diminishing returns? No, not if the capital goods, machines and materials used in production have also doubled. We can expect more capital investment too, as a doubling of labour supply will increase the return on capital and hence encourage investment until the balance of labour and capital inputs is the same as it was before. This is provided that interest rates and some other things are the same as before – but there is no reason to suppose they won't be. If the increase in population came from immigrants that are on average younger and better-educated than the rest of the population, as is usually the case, then the size of the economy, jobs and output, will more than double.

Of course, a sudden change in population with a slow movement of capital is a different matter. Economics does predict that if there are employment effects from immigration then these will tend to be in the short run, during the adjustment period. The question is how long is this adjustment period? That of course is an empirical question, and the evidence is that the effects are surprisingly slight and short lived. Why is that so? In sectors where new immigrants are most concentrated there is expansion of those sectors made possible by a better labour supply. So overall there may be little decrease in the overall demand for labour, and in some sectors the evidence is that there is scant direct competition between immigrants and the incumbent workers in any case. But again, economic interactions are complex, and so even if wages appear to be kept down for one section of labour it is still possible for the economy to be stimulated overall, with gains in productivity and international competitiveness, so that all wages end up higher than they would otherwise be.

The evidence is that immigration tends to increase average UK wages, though that is not very surprising as immigrants tend to earn more on average. What may be more surprising is that the average wage of incumbent workers is also raised, as immigrants often complement the skills of existing workers. A genuine concern is that the evidence suggests that immigration may adversely affect specific wage ranges and occupations. Worse, these adverse wage effects are found for the lowest-paid workers. For each 1 per cent increase in the share of migrants in the UK-born working-age population there might be around a 0.5 per cent to 0.6 per cent decline in the wages of the 5 per cent lowest-paid workers, even though there is an increase in the wages of higher-paid workers.

One thing to note is that the adverse wage effects are small, and even Migration Watch felt obliged to point out that 'even large-scale immigration is relatively small compared to a workforce of thirty million'. A House of Lords Committee in 2008 reported that 'the available evidence suggests that immigration has had a small negative impact on the lowest-paid workers in the UK and a small positive impact on the earnings of higher-paid workers'.[5] These effects are much smaller than the impacts of other changes in the economy, such as technology, loss of union membership and structural changes in the jobs markets. Of course, any adverse wage effects of immigration are likely to be greatest for other immigrants, as the skills of new migrants are closer substitutes for the skills of migrants already employed in the UK than for those of UK-born workers. The research bears this out: the main impact of increased immigration is on the wages of migrants already in the UK. Economists also point out that even if restricting migration could raise pre-tax wages in the short run, after a time, overall post-tax wages and benefits could be lower because of the higher tax rate that would result – more on immigrants' fiscal contributions later.

Low pay is a problem, but immigration is far from being its main cause. Enforcing minimum wages, paying a living wage, providing training, creating new jobs and providing support where needed are far more important for the low-paid than reducing immigration. Inequality is the responsibility of us all; we can't absolve ourselves by scapegoating immigrants.

In any case, economically, any adverse effects on pay would be little different from workers who are in UK sectors exposed to international competition. It is rather odd to allow competition for UK workers in general by allowing imports but protecting, say, UK builders, whose products are not so portable. Of course, to be consistent, those who wish for protectionist immigration policy might also advocate protectionist import controls. Most parties, including UKIP, ignore the economic inconsistency of advocating both restrictions on the movement of people and open borders for goods. The BNP is more consistent and calls for import controls as well, ignoring the history that protectionism leads to retaliation and the economics of protectionism that depresses world trade and output and prolongs recessions, and hence unemployment.

Most of those advocating immigration controls also seem to ignore the fact that, in a globalised world, capital goes where it wants to go. Restrictions on labour movement may simply mean that investment goes to the labour that is overseas, meaning fewer, not more, employment opportunities for UK workers. Lack of investment and capital will then depress the economy and hence further decrease the UK's international competitiveness. It is a fallacy that immigration controls are necessarily a way to protect jobs in the UK: they may simply lead to the UK being left behind, with all the undesirable economic consequences that follow from a declining economy in a fast moving globalised world. The point here is not that this is provable in a definitive way, but only that the 'common sense' and commonplace reasoning that abounds that more immigration *must* mean fewer jobs and lower wages for the incumbent population simply does not follow.

Evidence does not suggest that immigration is a problem either

Analysis and theory alone cannot settle such questions, but empirical studies are dogged by what are called 'endogeneity' problems. For example, if an area of the economy is expanding it will tend to have increased job vacancies and higher wages. Most fluctuations in migration levels are economic, and so such an area will tend to attract both more immigrants and more incumbent labour. As the employment of incumbent labour and their wages are increasing, the negative effects of immigration on incumbents may not be detected and hence be underestimated. Conversely, the dynamic positive effects of immigration are notoriously difficult to model, and so any apparent negative effects may be overestimated. Economists have to be careful to try to take these endogenous effects into account. Other problems also arise from using different definitions of the variables. Should we look at unemployment or employment? How long is it before an immigrant becomes an incumbent etc.? It can all become very conditional.

Although the bulk of research suggests that immigrants do not steal jobs from British workers, because of such empirical problems, the respected Migration Observatory unit at Oxford University warned:

While this creates a headache for news headline writers, and lots of space for politically motivated misuse of research results, the latest contributions to the research on the labour market effects of immigration in the UK strongly suggest that there can be no 'absolute' answers to this question. Anybody who argues that it is 'obvious' or 'clear' that immigration does or does not create unemployment in the UK needs to think again.

So, if you hear someone stating that immigrants steal British jobs, and particularly if you know that they are probably better informed than that, then you should be very suspicious indeed as to their real motivations.

'Natural experiments' can help avoid these endogeneity problems. These natural experiments occur when a sudden and large change in immigration occurs for non-economic reasons. The advantage of these events is that they isolate what economists call a 'supply shock' to the labour market: that is, the sharp increase in labour occurs for reasons unrelated to other factors in the economy. That makes it easier to have confidence in what the effects of this shock are. Two significant studies of such events were David Card's study of the Mariel boatlift, which brought upwards of 100,000 immigrants allowed to leave Cuba in 1980, and Rachel Friedberg's study of the effects of early 1990s Russian Jewish migration to Israel. Both the Cuba and Israeli immigrations were very big labour supply shocks indeed: the boatlift increased Miami's population by 7 per cent and the working population by about 20 per cent, and the Russian migration increased Israel's population by 12 per cent.

The surprising conclusion, even perhaps for many economists, was that even in these unusual and large-scale immigrations there was no decrease in native employment or wages. As with most things in economics, these results are not entirely uncontested, but the near-consensus view among economists is that the effects were, at least, negligible. These case studies, and others, are dramatic confirmations of an economy's capacity to adjust and a falsification of the commonplace notion that immigration must impact adversely on incumbents.

It may suit some politicians to portray immigration as a problem

Although econometric evidence is inevitably less certain than such natural experiments, it does largely flow in one direction. Firstly, that immigration probably has no effects on the employment levels of incumbent workers. Secondly, it increases the average wage of British workers and has only slightly depressing effects on unskilled wages (and these may, as we have seen, be better addressed in other ways). This weight of evidence didn't stop the Home Secretary, Theresa May, at the end of 2012, using an inflammatory descriptor of a very tentative finding from the Migratory Advisory Committee.[6] In her efforts to justify the Conservative Party's policies for a supposed crack-down on immigration, she announced:

> We asked the Migration Advisory Committee to look at the effects of immigration on jobs, and their conclusions were stark. They found a clear association between non-European immigration and employment in the UK. Between 1995 and 2010, the committee found an associated displacement of 160,000 British workers. For every additional 100 immigrants, they estimated that twenty-three British workers would not be employed.

So just how 'stark' were MAC's conclusions? Theresa May's own commissioned report was at pains not to use descriptors like 'stark' or to suggest that the possible relationship was causal: 'In particular, any link between immigration and employment of British-born people cannot be proved to be causal. Rather, it should be thought of as an association.'

Also note that, unlike Mrs Duffy, the MAC report found *no* significant association of negative impacts from immigration on British-born workers from EU immigrants and *no* significant negative effects from *any* immigrants at all when the economy is growing, as it usually does.

And yet in the run-up to the 2014 European elections UKIP posters ran the slogan '26 million unemployed people in Europe are looking for work. And whose job are they after?' This question was answered by a huge finger pointing directly at the reader. Putting aside the strange assertion that all the unemployed of Europe wish to work in the UK, or are likely to affect the reader's job in any way, this is clearly a repeat of the lump of labour fallacy. It has no foundation in rigorous evidence.

What of the MAC report's finding of an association between non-EU labour and UK employment when the economy is depressed? The first thing to note is the oddness of a conclusion that finds that EU migrants have no effect but that non-EU migrants do. The second thing to note is that this finding is inconsistent with similar research. The National Institute for Economic and Social Research published its own findings on the same day as the MAC report. Using more disaggregated data, the NIESR report was in line with other studies and found no association at all between immigration and UK unemployment.

Nevertheless, the MAC report remains the main evidence for the wide-spread claim that immigration causes UK unemployment, apart from a lot of completely spurious statistics bandied around by anti-immigration campaigners. The reliance on this isolated finding was implicitly admitted in the later report by analysts from the Home Office and the Department for Business, Innovation and Skills' 'Impacts of Migration on UK Native Employment: An Analytical Review of the Evidence'.[7] This report states that its findings were discussed by chief economists from BIS, the Department for Work and Pensions and the Home Office, as well as by senior analysts from HM Treasury in September 2012. So one can only speculate why the paper wasn't published until March 2014! Some cynical souls have even suggested that it was because the findings did not provide a firm foundation for the Conservatives' immigration controls.

This later report highlights the unusualness of the MAC report:

> This report considers a broad range of literature examining the impact of migration on the UK labour market, as well as the most relevant international studies. Until recently, the bulk of the UK literature did not

identify statistically significant impacts of migration on the employment rates of natives (for example, Dustmann et al., 2005; Lemos and Portes, 2008). The Migration Advisory Committee (2012) study provides a more recent example suggesting a statistically significant displacement effect, particularly linked to non-EU migration. But similarly recent research by Lucchino et al. (2012) failed to identify any statistically significant impacts of net migration on claimant count rates.

As it has been a main plank of anti-immigration claims, the MAC finding is crucial. The MAC report itself points out, however, that 'the results are statistically insignificant when outliers are removed from the data'. An 'outlier' is when a few observed data points are a long way away from the rest of the data points. So whereas the main mass of the data suggests there is no relationship at all, it is the nature of econometric analysis that just these few very untypical data points can drive the estimated results. Social researchers know that when the overall statistical result is down to 'odd' outliers, the results should be viewed with suspicion, and that is what the MAC report was dutifully pointing out. The MAC report also pointed out the fragility of the non-EU result in other ways. For example, making reasonable changes to the specifications that produced the result eliminated the association, and they also warned that 'our results may not be robust to endogeneity bias'. It was also telling that when the results for just 2010 were dropped the overall results again became insignificant.

Jonathan Portes of NIESR concluded: 'In other words, tweak the data just a little, and the result is no longer statistically significant. Most economists would place rather little weight on estimates which seemed to fail these fairly standard tests.'[8]

In short, even the strongest evidence that some immigrants, and then only in some downturns, might reduce UK incumbents' employment turns out to be weak. Given the weight of evidence that is contrary to the association described by MAC, the least that can be said is that there is no strong evidence to support the view that immigration causes unemployment. Economists who understand how the wider economy works easily see through the fallacies and common myths about migration that pervade our media, so none of the above will surprise them, but for good measure the Centre for Research and Analysis of Migration (CReAM), an independent and interdisciplinary research centre located in the Department of Economics at University College London, has recently provided a succinct summary of the available research evidence in their publication 'What do we know about migration?'. CReAM confirms:

- Immigration improves innovation, trade and entrepreneurship.

- Recent immigrants tend to claim less in benefits than native-born British and contribute more in taxes than is spent on them.

- Not all immigrants are entitled to claim all benefits and there is no or limited evidence that immigration is driven by welfare generosity.

- Most research into the impact of immigration upon wage rates or levels of employment suggests that there is little impact.

- Immigrants in effect provide the UK with billions of pounds of free education – that is, education, skills and training that immigrants bring with them that has cost the UK nothing.

- One in five health professionals are immigrants. Immigrants use health and GP services about as much as the native-born population. On arrival they are typically healthier than the native-born population.

- There were about 435,000 international students in UK universities bringing over £10 billion to the UK economy in 2011. In 2012/13 the number of overseas students dropped for the first time in twenty-nine years.

- There is no evidence that economically motivated immigration has any impact on rates of crime.

- Migration is a very important means through which individuals can lift themselves out of poverty.

- The percentage of British residents born overseas is 13 per cent. This compares to France and Germany (12 per cent) and the US and Spain (14 per cent), Ireland (16 per cent), Canada (21 per cent), Australia (28 per cent) and Switzerland (29 per cent).

Of course, some observers will always persist in refusing to be influenced by evidence come what may. For example, another recent CReAM report's main thrust is again that immigration overall adds, not detracts, from public coffers.[9] The salient finding is clearly that recent migration, since 2001, has made a positive contribution to public finances even at a time when incumbents' own fiscal contribution has been strongly negative. But sections of our press, and Migration Watch of course, still hunt for any negative spin on immigration. So they misrepresent the report's own example, which it used merely to demonstrate its own rigour, that is possible to construct a negative fiscal contribution for non-EU immigrants living in Britain between 1995 and 2011. What the negative spinners failed to report is that the report explicitly explains why this figure is *not* comparable with the positive contribution since 2001. For example, it ignores the contributions of immigrants now returned to their homeland and the earlier contributions of migrants now retired.

What might be the benefits from immigration?

The analysis and the empirics suggest that mostly all immigration does is increase the size of the economy more or less proportionately with the size of the population. But as that suggests per capita income will be unchanged, we might ask, 'What is the point of that anyway?' This is more or less the conclusion and question posed by the 2008 House of Lords Select Committee on the Economic Impact of Immigration.[10]

Putting aside the important fact that immigration usually has large advantages for the immigrant, there are good reasons to believe that there may also be economic benefits for the incumbent population too, even though, as explained, these are often difficult to capture as hard evidence. Overall, it should be clear that the free movement of labour can be expected to increase world output by allowing labour to move to where it is most productive. If world output is increased then there is simply more output overall to share out, though who gets this extra output is not as straightforward, but host nations are at least likely to benefit from a wider variety of goods and services and lower prices.

Labour shortages reflect unmet demand for the particular things that a particular type of labour produces, and so the free movement of labour towards the higher wages that follow from this will lead to more output of the things that people want most. That is, the value of world output is increased by the international mobility of labour. Across the world incomes vary much more than prices, and so labour movement towards countries with higher incomes will raise average world income. The real worry may be that rich countries gain too much from the inputs of effort and talent from immigrants, perhaps at the expense of the poorer countries they come from.

One benefit that has been clearly quantified is how much immigration can help the UK to pay off its deficit. Various studies confirm that immigration brings a net contribution to government funds, but the Office for Budget Responsibility, set up by George Osborne to be an independent forecaster of public finances, has linked immigration to the relief of that much discussed economic burden, the fiscal deficit. The 2013 Office for Budget Responsibility's Fiscal Sustainability Report had an annex on 'the impact of inward migration in the long-term projections'. This showed that if the UK had zero net migration, instead of the OBR's assumption of net migration of around 140,000 per year, then the debt-to-GDP ratio would rise by 40 per cent. That would make it a whole lot harder to pay down the deficit as a percentage of GDP, which is supposed to be the UK's number one economic priority.

The considerable size of this contribution to UK finances follows from the fact that immigrants tend to arrive as adults but are on average younger than the incumbent population. They are more likely to be of working age and to use public services less, and, contrary to yet more popular myths, be less likely to claim welfare benefits. So the OBR simply adds up what follows from the assumption that immigrants will make the same contributions to tax revenues, and impose the same costs on public services, as incumbents of the same age.

The OBR concludes:

> Given this pattern, it seems probable that immigrants will make a more positive contribution to the UK public finances over their lifetimes than natives. They are relatively more likely to arrive as adults, so the UK will receive the positive contribution from their work without having to pay for their education, although their children will require support. It is also the case that upon arrival, if unemployed, they are not immediately entitled to – or are not eligible for – unemployment benefits, and they will contribute to tax receipts as soon as they start working. Those who spend enough years working in the UK will be eligible for state pensions once they retire, but to the extent that they leave the UK in later years, they will not require access to health and long-term care support.

Critics of these findings say that it is a type of Ponzi scheme – that is, a scheme that can only be sustained by adding new members – as the immigrants will one day grow old themselves and hence become an added burden to the fiscal balance. But as we can see in the OBR's quote they did factor this in, and they take their projections out as far as 2062, which is a very long time in economics. Also, the evidence from the Office for

National Statistics is that over half of immigrants intend to stay for less than three years, and only a quarter for more than four years. Much of so-called immigration is really a form of temporary international commuting, but a continued flow of these younger immigrants will assist the UK in paying for the effects of her own ageing population. There are also other good reasons to think that the OBR estimate is an underestimate of the size of the fiscal contribution. The OBR refrained from factoring in additional factors such as the increased productivity of the labour force as a whole, because the evidence is so difficult to capture. If they had done, the estimated contribution to public finances could have been much higher.

The Conservative Party has been claiming that it is prioritising both paying off the deficit and getting immigration down. This is clearly an oxymoron as immigration helps pay down the deficit. The fact that immigrants contribute more to government coffers than they take out also shows the fallacy of the idea that immigration is the cause of overloading on public services. Not only have immigrants provided much of the additional staffing for our services and hence made their provision more feasible, but they also as a group provide the funding to invest in those services. Of course, better planning and provision for contingency funds than in the past could also be used to relieve any temporary overloading from unexpected local population changes.

The Bank of England has also explained how migration may also smooth out supply shortages at the macroeconomic level, by providing more elasticity of output change in response to fluctuations in overall demand in the economy. A reservoir of capacity provided by immigration, rising and falling with the state of the economy, reduces the chances of unintentionally injecting inflation into the economy. This in turn may have made it easier to control inflation and hence, before the financial crisis obliged the Bank of England to push them near to the floor anyway, could have resulted in lower interest rates. 'Immigrants reduce your mortgage' is not a headline you will often see in tabloids, and perhaps that is right, as it is a possibility rather than a proven fact, but then it has more analysis and evidence to support it than the scare stories that we do so often see in the press.

It is another oxymoron for David Cameron to take a message that 'Britain is open for business' when Indian and British business leaders are urging him to reform the visa rules they say are hindering trade between the two countries. He cannot credibly argue for a less protectionist, less regulatory, more economically liberal Europe that is 'open for business' when at the same time calling for new restrictions to labour mobility. It is an oxymoron for George Osborne to say he wants a rebalanced economy when immigration and visa controls are severely hitting one of our major export industries: higher education. Several universities are now reporting over 50 per cent falls in Indian student numbers that they attribute directly to changes to student visas and the perception among overseas students that they are not welcome in the UK. The 2012–13 academic year saw an overall fall in the number of international students studying in the UK, the first ever recorded.[11] Britain is in real danger of irreversibly damaging one of its major export industries, currently bringing in £13 billion a year, and that together with a more positive marketing positioning could increase on that sum greatly in the light of a rapidly increasing global demand for high-quality university education – a provision that Britain should otherwise be particularly well placed to provide to students from overseas.

But what of all the other, non-economic, reasons for cracking down on immigration?

As we saw, a host of reasons have been, and still are, given to justify unwarranted hostility towards immigration. They are largely as spurious as the economic excuses, but even spurious prejudices can be genuinely felt. Indeed, Nigel Farage candidly admitted in January 2014 that he actually thinks that 'the social side of this matters more than pure market economics' and that he would rather fewer people moved here in the future even if it left the country worse off! Which he still maintains would not be the case.[12]

Another non-economic argument used against immigration is that 'no one voted for it', or for that matter for a multicultural Britain. Well, no one voted for most changes that have shaped modern Britain. Ken Clarke, the veteran senior Conservative minister, once said that to stop immigration we would have to 'uninvent the jet engine', and there are a host of other unelected inventions that have profoundly changed our lives and cultures. The notion that civil society and culture is unchanging without immigration is nonsense. Cars and telephones were not voted on either, but despite exasperating traffic congestion and the inconsiderate use of mobile phones on trains, most people strive to balance the irritations with the benefits. No one voted for the internet or the loss of community from the proliferation of personalised entertainment devices that have replaced social and community intercourse. No one voted for the creation of teenage culture, more varied family structures, the decline in village pubs or the demise of the local high street and the rise of impersonal shopping malls.

Today we have supermarkets where lonely old ladies desperately try to strike up conversations with strangers in impatient queues. Once they knew and chatted with most of the other customers. Mr Smith who owned the corner shop always had a cheery hello for them when asking, 'What would you like today, Mrs Ross?' Life, technology and cultures are not constants: changes have been happening all down the centuries. Perhaps the changes that affect all our lives seem more rapid today but that's not all down to immigrants, and it is easy to be nostalgic for Britain's closer communities of the '50s and '60s, conveniently forgetting their many unpleasant aspects. So perhaps there is a reason why immigrants are particularly often singled out for special blame? Especially as many immigrants have valued 'traditional' British customs more than the children of Britain, and the variety of foods they have brought have been literally gobbled up by the British!

'I'm not a racist but we are an overcrowded island, we simply can't take any more!' is another common phrase used by anti-immigrationists.

Population increase should, as always for England, be forecast and planned for, but, again, it is easy to concoct misleading statistics. One example is to look only at England and exclude Scotland, Wales and Northern Ireland and then compare us with, say, Japan, including Japan's many smaller islands. Actually England is less populated than Japan's mainland. The UK population density is about the same as Vietnam's, and about 400 fewer people per square mile than in the Netherlands, and about half that of South Korea. The overall population density of the UK is about 680 people per square mile, not particularly world beating, about 50th in a ranking of countries and dependencies, and about 20th in terms of countries. Over a quarter of the world's population live in more 'cramped' conditions than us. The real point, though, is that such statistics are pretty meaningless.

By limiting the statistics to just England, as is usually done by those wishing to raise fears about immigration, the population density rises to a little over 1,000 people per square mile. Now that *is* high in world terms. That is, if we are prepared to accept that comparing just a portion of Britain is sensible. If so, why stop there? Let's take just the most populous bit, London (ignoring Gibraltar, with a population density of over sixteen times that of the UK). In fact, London is the most populous city and metropolitan area of the European Union: its population density is ten times that of any other UK region (London counts as its own region). By restricting our chosen area to just London we can get up to nearly 12,500 people per square mile, or if we take just Islington in London, up to near 14,000 – a statistic that doesn't seem to reduce the popularity of the borough! Again, it's all pretty meaningless: the truth is that high population densities arise from us bunching together in cities. Cities, by their nature, would still be crowded if there were fewer immigrants or even if there were far fewer people in the UK, as turn-of-the-twentieth-century footage of London's horse-carriage filled streets shows.

An IPPR report of 2012 notes:

> Today's figures show that some local authorities, particularly in the north, are struggling with the opposite problem. The fundamental driver is

economics, rather than migration or birth rates, and the issues it raises – of planning for infrastructure, housing, and services, and more fundamentally, our attitude to urbanisation, resource scarcity, emissions and other related questions – would remain even in the hypothetical scenario of zero net immigration.[13]

If our anti-immigrant dining partner is still there, we might by now hear, 'But they overwhelm our services until they just can't cope.' Well, yes, if the population increased and we did not invest in expanding our services that must certainly happen. Luckily, as we have seen, immigrants not only provide extra staffing, they also provide the funds for this, and being younger on average, but already educated at another country's expense, they tend to use public services less. As a last ditch the protesting diner might throw in, 'But all these foreign languages mean that our schools can't cope.' Damian Green, when he was the Minister for Immigration, would have agreed: 'The number of pupils with English as a second language makes life difficult for teachers, parents and pupils. Whether or not they can speak English, everyone suffers when it's more difficult for teachers in the classroom.'[14]

As with the other 'common sense' anti-immigration justifications, it appears that people so want to believe them, or to appeal to those who do believe them, that they don't bother to check out the evidence – even when they're Immigration Ministers. The data actually shows that immigrants have a positive effect on school performance. It is now well established that the performance of schools with higher proportions of pupils with English as an additional language has in fact been better than for other schools, when matched with equivalent levels of disadvantage. And, as many head teachers reporting on the vibrancy of their schools attest, immigrants tend to boost the school performance of all kids, immigrant or native English speaker. In 'stark' contrast to the anti-immigrant rumour that Damian Green endorsed, English native speakers actually do somewhat better, not worse, where there are more English as an additional language pupils.

NIESR adds that if deprivation levels for this research were accounted for then the apparent positive 'spill-over' effect would increase substantially.[15]

We could go on exposing more and more of the many myths that those who wish to have a 'reasoned debate' on immigration have in mind. Crime, benefits, training for Brits, terrorism, disease, social housing – no, they don't get preferential treatment[16] – there is still a long list of rumours, all designed to instil fear of foreigners. Of course the UK needs effective checks on who passes across its borders, no one is disagreeing with that, and that is what we should be doing instead of wasting effort on attempting to meet arbitrary net migration targets that can be 'fiddled' by discouraging vital overseas students and encouraging the British themselves to emigrate!

The point is that the economic arguments put forward for drastically cutting immigration turn out to be plain wrong, silly or massive exaggerations. As said, evidence in social science is seldom conclusive. We cannot say that there are no negatives: there are certainly social issues, but, considering the likely positives, we would need *much* better reasons for even the current immigration restrictions.

Hardly a warm welcome[17]

The government's efforts to bring down migration have largely failed to reduce net migration but have had significant impacts on migrants in the UK and on those seeking to come to the UK, particularly from outside the European Economic Area (EEA). The government has introduced a series of rule changes across visa categories for non-EEA nationals that now present a formidable set of hurdles for those wishing to come here to work, study or reunite with family members. As we have seen, the rules for international students have acted as a deterrent. Universities and colleges, like employers, are now also required to register with the Home Office as 'sponsors' to take on non-EEA students from outside the EEA. The language requirement was raised and the Post-Study Work route was closed:

this had previously allowed graduates a two-year period within which to find a job in the UK.

Economic migration from outside the European Union was the first area of major reform: the immigration route for highly skilled non-EEA migrants was closed and a cap on visas to skilled migrants, even with a job offer, was introduced. The minimum skills level for non-EEA migrants coming to work in the UK was raised from National Qualifications Framework level 4 to level 6 (degree-level), and a new requirement for earnings of at least £35,000 per year will be set from April 2016 for workers wishing to apply for settlement. Employers now have to register with the Home Office as official 'sponsors' to take on non-EEA migrants, a bureaucratic process that acts as a considerable deterrent.

Economic and student migration have not been the only visa categories subject to higher requirements. New rules for family migration have introduced an income requirement of £18,600 for British citizens and permanent residents seeking to bring their non-EU spouses to live with them in the UK. It is estimated by the government that it will affect up to 17,800 lower-paid families. These new rules have met with legal challenge on human rights grounds and are on course to go for a hearing at the Supreme Court in 2015.

The 2014 Immigration Act requires new immigration document checks for private landlords and introduces similar checks for banks, building societies and the DVLA and other services. This is bound to result in wider racial discrimination, if only for convenience's sake, and will affect all migrants, regardless of immigration status. The Act also denies a right of appeal for the majority of immigration and nationality applications, thereby greatly reducing the opportunity to challenge poor Home Office decision making. The deterrents are increased by ongoing cuts to legal aid for immigration cases, and this makes it harder for many applicants to secure good quality advice in the first place. An ongoing series of local enforcement initiatives continue to take place and some of these have been accused of leading in effect to racial profiling.

In contrast to Canada, which has a Ministry for Immigration dedicated to making immigrants feel welcome, Operation Vaken, in the summer of 2013, did little to improve the negative impression given to the UK's minority ethnic communities. Despite its futility as a deterrent, the Home Office sent vans with huge posters telling illegal immigrants to 'go home' to drive round six ethnically mixed London boroughs. This blatant echoing of an infamous racist chant caused huge offence, not only in those boroughs but across the UK, but it was defended by Tory Immigration Minister Mark Harper, who feigned surprise that anyone would find the posters offensive. By contrast, it was roundly condemned by the Lib Dems and after threats of legal action the Home Office decided not to carry on with the project.

In their eagerness to ward off UKIP and engage voter prejudices, the parties have tended to overlook the effect of all this on the views of migrant communities themselves. A substantial number of migrants and the established ethnic minority population will be eligible to cast a vote in the 2015 general election, and anti-immigration measures and rhetoric do not necessarily endear politicians to Britain's minority communities. Ruth Grove-White, the Policy Director at Migrants' Rights Network, warns those politicians:

> Migrants and those with migrant heritage are more positive about immigration and its impacts on the UK, and that anti-immigration messaging and policies can play badly with some minority communities ... It would be wise for politicians to consider more deeply how the impacts of the current policy approach look to the UK's migrant populations, which could have more of an influence next May than is currently realised. In this light, treating immigration as a numbers game, to be dealt with through increasingly tough measures felt at the community level, looks increasingly like a short-sighted approach from our political leaders. They may find it makes sense to have a rethink.[18]

An image makeover? Political integrity and responsible leadership

Immigration is not an economic problem but it is a social issue. We might expect that overall the young are much less prone to worry, so it is no surprise to find that UKIP draws its support disproportionately from older people: whereas 46 per cent of all voters are over fifty, and 38 per cent under forty, the figures for UKIP are 71 per cent and 15 per cent respectively.[19] It wouldn't do any harm to point out that many Brits are themselves immigrants, having emigrated to foreign countries (ex-pats living in other countries in Europe number some two million). But if immigrants are persistently and overwhelmingly portrayed as a problem then it is going to be difficult for any amount of real evidence or reason to cut through the fear and prejudice. It was always thus. A Gallup poll at the time of the infamous Enoch Powell 'rivers of blood' speech in 1968 showed that 74 per cent of the public agreed with Powell – about the same as the percentage of people today who think immigration is too high – but still Edward Heath, the Conservative Prime Minister, personally explained on television that 'I dismissed Mr Powell [from the shadow Cabinet] because I believed his speech was inflammatory and liable to damage race relations'.

So if we want to engage in warm nostalgia it might be heartening to see more being similarly said today to fight the ignorance and fears around immigration. That is not a hopeless task but it seems that many of today's major politicians, even in the main parties, with some notable exceptions such as Vince Cable, are all too willing to pander to ignorance and prejudice in their pursuit of power. This may well be a tactical error: instead of countering the gross misrepresentation by UKIP the main parties have seemed to fall over each other to repeat and hence amplify them, all to UKIP's further advantage as it further inflames xenophobic fears. For example, in July 2014 Cameron announced, for the second time, to a repeat chorus of approving headlines that he was cracking down on immigrants claiming benefits. Despite the clear evidence that immigrants are least likely to claim benefits and more than cover the costs of those that do, Yvette Cooper in a speech she emphasised had nothing to do with inflaming irrational fears, also announced in November that a Labour government would further restrict access to social benefits. Edward Heath was driven by his fear of ethnic tensions to introduce stricter and racially biased immigration rules, but he never demonised immigrants as scroungers.

CHAPTER 9

What Has Europe Ever Done for Us?

The folly of nation states

THREE MONTHS OUT from the general election, Europe looks set to dominate the campaign – despite the fact that when voters are asked to enumerate the issues that are at the top of their concerns, Europe tends to be way down their list. However, it has become very tangled up in the discussion about immigration that has been fuelled by UKIP's anti-EU and anti-immigration stance that resulted in them coming first in the European elections in May 2014. The Conservatives, Labour and to a lesser extent the Lib Dems have tightened their own positions on migration, particularly in relation to the availability of welfare benefits to EU migrants, mindful of the forthcoming elections (see previous chapter).

Background

European integration has been more or less ongoing since the end of the Second World War. After the war we had the establishment of the European Coal and Steel Community in 1952, followed in 1957 by the Treaties of Rome to establish the European Economic Community (EEC) and the European Atomic Energy Community (Euratom) signed between France, Germany, Italy, the Netherlands, Belgium and Luxembourg. This treaty, which has been of great significance, had the immortal phrase in it, calling for 'an ever closer union among the peoples of Europe'. The phrase has long galvanised anti-Europeans, fuelling their fear that national sovereignty would disappear and calling for the phrase to be removed in any renegotiation. Unfortunately for them, there is very little appetite from the Europeans to renegotiate the Treaty of Rome but the phrase has become a poisoned chalice and infiltrates any sensible discussion about Europe and the way forward for the UK. As Hugo Dixon says in his book *The In/Out Question*,[1] if we ever manage to get to the point of renegotiating the Treaty of Rome, maybe a better phrase would be to call for 'ever closer relations between the peoples of Europe'.

The Treaty of Rome was followed by the 1962 agreement on a Common Agricultural Policy (CAP), which was a French device to keep its agricultural sector going by providing subsidies. The French are the main beneficiaries but the UK farming community has also done rather well as prices have been kept higher than they otherwise would have been if they had been exposed to open competition. The UK applied to join the treaty in 1963 but President de Gaulle of France turned it down, and then turned it down again when the UK re-applied in 1967. That same year a Merger Treaty brought together the executives of the European Coal and Steel Community, the European Economic Community and the Euratom and ended up with a single executive (the European Commission) and a single Council. A custom union came into effect on 1 July 1968 and then Denmark, Ireland and the United Kingdom also formally joined the European Communities on 1 January 1973. Although Norway had also signed the treaty, a referendum in September 1972 resulted in a 'no' vote, so Norway did not join. The country is still outside the EU but a member of the European Economic Area, which allows it access to the market but no influence, and it has to accept the EU's social and product rules. (This is slightly different from Switzerland: the latter is not an EEA member but has negotiated access to the single market, which doesn't include much of the financial sector but at least is not subject to the EU's social rules.)

A closer economic union was attempted through the signing by the twelve EEC members of the Single European Act in 1986 that came into effect on 1 July 1987 and which set a deadline of 31 December 1992 to establish a single market in Europe. The Cecchini report in 1988 under the auspices of Professor Paulo Cecchini, subtitled 'The Cost of Non-Europe', estimated the benefits to Europe from removing tariffs to be significant – mainly felt in the first instance through lower prices to consumers. Extra spending by consumers, who would also see their real incomes improve, would then be translated into increased demand, and companies would then respond by investing more, leading to a larger impact than the original boost to demand from lower prices alone. What the exact benefits have actually been is difficult to tell because the counterfactual – in other words, what would have happened if the single market had not been created – is genuinely difficult to estimate. But there was widespread acceptance at the time that this was worthwhile and the countries moved forward, helped by the European Commission, to attempt to integrate their economies further.

Understanding Britain's Euroscepticism

Understanding the current debate about Europe requires that we better comprehend Britain's current Euroscepticism. In a memo to the Cabinet in 1942 when Europe was still at war, Churchill wrote:

> Hard as it is to say now, I trust that the European family may act unitedly as one under a Council of Europe. I look forward to a United States of Europe in which the barriers between nations will be greatly minimised and unrestricted travel will be possible.

You could argue that much of Churchill's vision has broadly been met. Barriers to trade have been progressively removed, and travel is indeed almost unrestricted between the various countries, though the UK still insists on checking passengers from Europe entering its territory, not having signed the open borders agreement known as Schengen which has eliminated the need to show passports as you move around Europe. But the free movement principle, with some checks to ensure that people are genuinely allowed to be in the EU, remains. The 'wall' separating Eastern Europe from the rest, a sad remnant of the incredibly divisive Second World War, has also come down and there has been peace, with some sad exceptions such as the Yugoslav wars of the 1990s. Russia's intervention in the Ukraine and the effective annexation of Crimea have certainly muddied the waters recently, but overall Europe has been at peace with itself. But the concept of a 'United Europe' going further than the progress we have seen already has been anathema for the British politicians for a while now.

Why is that? Well, as this book has tried to demonstrate throughout, one of the main reasons is economics, though this is not the only reason. Charles Grant of the Centre for European Reform, talking to one of the authors of this book, pointed to four reasons for Britain's Euroscepticism:

> First, history: Britain had a very honourable war while most other European countries didn't and that set us apart. Second, geography: Britain is at the edge of Europe and that, combined with its history, means that it has traditionally had more global trade flows, investment flows and

migration flows than any other country in Europe. Third, economics: from the mid-1990s to 2008 Britain had the most successful economy of any big country in Europe, And fourth, the role of the British media: of all newspapers sold in Britain, 75 per cent preach Euroscepticism and many proprietors don't allow their journalists to deviate from that line.[2]

So economics matters. In fact, you can trace this love–hate relationship with Europe with the relative economic performance of the UK and the large countries in the Continent. In the years after the 1957 Treaty of Rome, which established the European Economic Community, or the common market as we know it, and up to the mid-1980s, by and large Europe grew much faster than the UK. But the coming down of the Berlin Wall in 1990 and the agreement to let West Germany merge with its former communist Eastern part was a heavy burden for that country to bear, costing West Germany some €1.3 trillion over a ten-year period to properly bring West and East together. And in many ways the process is still going on, with persisting inequalities between the two parts of the country. This has certainly held the country back. Only a decade and a half ago Germany was still referred to by *The Economist* as 'the sick man of Europe'. Other countries in Europe had similar issues, including Italy, which has had long periods of stagnant growth. In contrast, the Thatcher 'revolution' in the UK in the '80s, taken further by the Conservative leaders who followed her in the 1990s, set in train a long period of catch-up, and certainly until the financial crash of 2008, as Charles Grant pointed out, the UK has performed better on average than its large European neighbours.

The impact of the euro

The advent of the euro was a hugely divisive issue. The UK's ignominious Exchange Rate Mechanism exit in 1992 still rankles, and when the euro project was contemplated after the Labour government came to power in 1997 the decision was taken not to join the single currency in the first instance but to base a future decision on assessing the UK's readiness to join through performing five economic tests. Rumour has it that the idea for the five tests the UK used finally in 2003 to decide whether to join the euro was devised in five minutes in the back of a taxi shared between Gordon Brown and his then economic adviser, Ed Balls. It was really a clever political ruse to allow the then Chancellor Gordon Brown, who was instinctively hostile to the idea of a single currency as it would take away the UK's control over its own economic affairs, to at least be able to present some economic evidence for any decision. However, it was clear to everyone that the choice would ultimately be a political one.

Nevertheless the tests themselves were devised and carried out rigorously with a number of departments working with the Treasury and with the contribution of many distinguished external academic economists. The five tests looked at:

- Whether the UK cycles were compatible with the ones in the Continent (the convergence test);

- Whether there would be enough flexibility in the system to deal with any problems that may arise (the flexibility test);

- What impact entry would have on the City of London (the financial services test);

- Whether joining would encourage more long-term investment in the UK (the investment test);

- And whether joining the Eurozone would improve the climate for jobs and growth (the employment and growth criterion test).

The 2003 study concluded that if the convergence and flexibility tests were met then joining the euro would indeed lead to greater investment, employment and growth and would on balance be beneficial, especially to the financial service sector in the UK. But there were doubts about whether there was sufficient convergence with the cycles in the other countries in Europe and whether the system allowed for enough flexibility if it suffered an external shock. So the UK did not join.

When a few years later the world as a whole did indeed fall into the grip of a severe financial crisis the Eurozone institutions and its politicians proved incapable of swift solutions. Seven years on from the beginning of the crisis, the Eurozone as a whole is still struggling to see any sustained recovery. The UK, with its flexible exchange rate and fewer constraints on fiscal policy, has now belatedly begun to recover, albeit it has suffered a deeper and longer contraction due to the importance of the stricken financial sector for its economy. Though GDP per head is still below the 2008 level, the actual GDP level – and hence the size of the economy – now comfortably exceeds the level it had reached before the crisis and the economy is growing faster than any G7 country. In contrast, by mid-2014, Germany, Italy and France were still showing either contraction or stagnation and periphery countries like Greece had lost a quarter of their output and were finding it hard to get it back. For the UK, of course, a big question for its relatively strong performance is whether this is just a stronger but temporary rebound from the much lower point to which activity fell in the UK because of the importance of its financial sector, or whether recent data are the 'green shoots' of a new sustainable balanced recovery.

But notwithstanding what may or may not be the growth and productivity trend in the UK in the future the verdict on the Eurozone appears dire. On many counts – including the plight of the periphery countries, many of whom, like Greece, would have been better off not joining the euro in the first place – the whole experiment appears a failure. As was clear from the beginning, the twelve countries that joined the euro at the early years of its creation did not form a feasible common currency area, and that created problems.[3] There were too many differences in their relative development and in the structure of their economies: the system was doomed to failure without a system of transfers from the richer to the poorer members of the currency union, particularly at times of crisis. That was precluded due to resistance from Germany, which also insisted that the Maastricht Treaty that established the single currency signed in 1992 would contain a 'no bail-out' clause – of course, in the end there were many! There were bail-outs in Portugal, Ireland, Greece and Cyprus, and extra support given to Spain to rescue the banking system, which was really a bail-out by any other name. If anything, since the onset of the financial crisis in 2007/08, the differences have become even greater given the particular problems experienced by the troubled periphery countries, and new countries joining the euro from the former Eastern bloc, taking the total Eurozone membership to eighteen, have not helped in this respect. As Martin Wolf himself argues in his book *The Shifts and the Shocks*, 'a small Eurozone that contained Germany and its long-standing partners, together possibly with France, would surely have worked'.[4]

So, what should the UK do?

All this is hardly likely to be endearing the Brits to 'more Europe'. And yet 'more Europe' is exactly what is being attempted in the Eurozone, encouraged by the European Commission at present. To deal with the crisis, European institutions have been strengthened; the European Central Bank (ECB) is assuming the role of single banking regulator across the Eurozone; there is now a single-resolution regime for closing big banks across countries at the suggestion of the ECB and the Commission; EU countries that support weaker ones seem to have a direct say in their budgets; and there is serious concern about the emergence of a democratic deficiency that is worrying not only the UK but also many countries in Europe.

The result in the UK is a return to serious Euroscepticism, which has culminated in the Prime Minister, David Cameron, pledging a referendum in 2017 on whether the UK should stay in or leave Europe should the Conservatives win the next election. The Lib Dems, their current coalition partners, have said they will not support this unless there is sufficient reform that will need treaties to be renegotiated. And Labour has said that it will not support a referendum. The issue was very pertinent in the May 2014 European Parliament elections, with UKIP coming first with 26.6 per cent of the vote and a rise in seats from thirteen to twenty-four; Labour second with 24.43 per cent of the votes and a win of seven seats, taking them up to twenty; the Tories third with 23.05 per cent of the vote and the loss of six seats, dropping to nineteen; and the Liberal Democrats a very poor fifth below the Greens, with just 6.6 per cent of the vote and only one MEP elected, making it a loss of ten MEPs compared to where they were at the previous elections in 2009. This sent shockwaves throughout the UK political system. It has encouraged the fierce debate about Europe to become even more vociferous, with seminars taking place each week on the pros and cons of continuing EU membership and countless books appearing arguing the case from the two widely different perspectives. I am sure that even before this book comes out, the very informative books by Roger Bootle (against),[5] Hugo Dixon (for),[6] John Peet and Anton La Guardia (middle of the road, pragmatic),[7] David Marsh (pulling hair out),[8] the Centre for European Reform findings of their Commission on the UK and the EU single market (despairing but pro)[9] and Philippe Legrain's *European Spring* (critical)[10] will have been joined by many others.

The fundamental issues

What this demonstrates is that the case is often emotive and the politicians play on it by not outlining the economic case properly. And yet it will be through the impact on the economy that we will see the fallout from any wrong decisions our politicians make. So it is even more important that the facts are there for all to see but also that the evidence is looked at again, and clearly by anyone thinking how to vote on what is actually happening on the ground – not only in economics but also on the political front to attempt to kill off the myths that circulate and which tend to engender fear about what the EU can do to us.

First, the worry about the emerging European 'state'. Yes, Brussels is promoting the EU as a region with the institutions of statehood, having a Parliament (that we all, after all, vote for), an executive with a powerful head of the European Commission, a President of the Council of Ministers, now a single currency, a new constitution, the creation of the post of a European Foreign Minister (held until the elections by our very own Baroness Kathy Ashton), a flag and an anthem! But it is not a state. It has a tiny budget, just 1 per cent of the European GDP, and the UK has been instrumental in limiting its growth. Moreover, some 85 per cent of this budget returns to the member states. It is true, however, that there are concerns about the inefficiency of the European Commission and it is years since its accounts have been properly verified.

Second, the facts about *ever closer union*. It is true that the preamble to the Treaty of Rome, signed by the EU's six founding countries, famously says that they 'were determined to lay the foundations of an ever closer union among the peoples of Europe'. These words have hung around the necks of Europeans ever since. That grandiose language harked back to the words that backed the League of Nations when it was set up in 1920 'to secure international peace and security'. For all its faults, the Treaty of Rome has weathered better than the League of Nations; its magnetism is such that countries still queue to join. Croatia has just done so, and others, like Serbia, Moldova or Kosovo, hope very much to get in.

Nevertheless the fact remains that the common market that was created by the Treaty of Rome in 1957 was not much more than a customs union, and tariffs within it were not finally abolished until 1968. In France, General de Gaulle ignored many aspects of the treaty, and also treated Brussels with contempt. And the real questions surrounding an ever closer union were only to become sensitive in the 1980s. The Single European Act, which was strongly promoted by Margaret Thatcher, marked the single biggest transfer, or at least sharing, of sovereignty ever seen in Europe. It was followed by the Maastricht Treaty in 1992 and then a decade ago by the constitutional treaty, which paradoxically removed the reference to ever closer union because by the early years of this century politicians were getting more and more nervous about the growth of Euroscepticism in their countries' politics.

Do we need to worry about the loss of sovereignty?

The term 'ever closer union' was reintroduced in the Lisbon Treaty, which generally recycled the language of older treaties. At the same time, however, it allowed lots of opt-outs, which were hardly tantamount to harmonisation. They were there to accommodate the different needs of different countries and, in the UK, to allow the country to steer clear of social policy. There has of course been an increasing closeness brought about by free movement of people, the closer integration of standards easing the costs to businesses selling to and operating across Europe, and there has also been an increasing pressure from Brussels to open up competition and allow a level playing field across the single market area. And although there are a number of examples of successful harmonisation initiatives pushed through by the European Commission and brought into national legislation, in reality many national governments have been successfully resisting or delaying the opening of their markets. The result, therefore, is that many markets across Europe are still far from being integrated. Look at the very slow liberalisation of the service sector or the fact that countries still pursue different taxation regimes and that tax competition between countries remains intense.

In reality moves towards political union have so far been limited. In Britain, the House of Commons library examines each year the total number of laws adopted in the UK, and can never find more than 8 per cent of primary legislation that originates from the EU. As an article in *Europe's World* in February 2014 argued:

> Despite the moves to greater integration since the euro crisis first struck, the fact is that if one looks at the legislation making headlines across Europe – gay marriage, education policy, health care provision, whether to have contributory or free systems of pension and student fees, welfare reform, voting systems, pay control, or even speed limits on motorways – it is Europe's national governments that are still firmly in the driving seat.

In the meantime as the article highlights, English is becoming the international business language. That should be good news for those who worry about Europe taking over. But on the ground, national cultures continue to thrive, as do different national and very often strong regional languages. So what we are seeing is the creation of more nation states rather than fewer. And it could be argued that the rise of nationalism in many countries – France and Greece being good examples – is, if anything, pulling countries further apart. The Greeks, for example, make it abundantly clear that they don't want to be run by Germany.

So, far from getting closer together, nations seem to be moving further apart. What we have effectively witnessed is the rebirth of the nation state. As a *Europe's World* article[11] notes:

> It is doubtful that the founding fathers of the European project ever dreamed that Lithuania would one day preside over their Europe, or that Slovakia and Croatia would have the same veto rights in European affairs as Germany and France. Catalonia has its own 'embassy' in Brussels, as do Scotland and most of the major regions and provinces.

When Angela Merkel talks about 'more Europe', as she often does, she certainly does not envisage spending any money to achieve this – at least that is not what she wants to tell her electorate, which is very sceptical about any help going to the periphery economies, whom they blame entirely for the problems of the Eurozone!

There is also no sign of ever closer union in foreign policy. Look at Europe's division over whether or not to intervene in Syria. There is no unanimity on the stance towards Israel and the Palestinians, as became amply evident in the escalation of hostilities between Israel and Hamas in the summer of 2014. The length of time it has taken to start reacting to the advance of the Islamic State in Iraq is further testimony to this. And although defence sales form a large part of the exports of a number of countries, there is no joint military force as such and there is still huge divergence in the willingness to intervene in combat situations around the world and in the share of GDP spent on defence and on the size of national armed forces. There is equally no sign so far of an ever closer union in areas such as energy policy. After the Fukushima nuclear disaster in 2011, Germany announced that it will be closing its nuclear power stations by 2030. Countries like Poland stick to brown coal for their electricity generation despite the obvious negative impact on CO_2 emissions, while Britain is keen on fracking for gas despite environmental concerns. The levels of subsidy in each country vary widely, as do the prices paid by industry and the consumers.

All this does not mean that ever closer union, however defined, is not a good thing. The Eurozone attempted to achieve a bit more of it but assumed that simply tying the economies closer together would do the trick. The rushed way in which it happened without considering the possible consequences has given 'union' a bad name and fuelled, as we said before, increased Euroscepticism. Many people argue that political union should have happened first, followed by economic and monetary union, which would have been easier to achieve successfully. But nobody in 2002 was ready to take that step and many assumed that it could all happen by the back door. Well, it didn't – and arguably it should have. As it is, the euro experiment may well end up being seen as an expensive mistake, with lots of extra money being thrown at it, mainly by the ECB under Mario Draghi, to rectify its flaws.

The problem with the euro

There was too much complacency by the architects of the euro and the European Commission and the national politicians allowed no dissent. The euro was 'a good thing' as far as the leadership was concerned and a question of national pride to be part of it. Anyone saying otherwise in the Continent could not be heard. National debates within the countries were muted and countries joined the euro even though in a number of cases polls suggested that the majority of the population was against entry. But the most extraordinary thing is that markets also swallowed the story wholeheartedly and failed to see the fault lines.

Now those fault lines have become evident, the question is whether this further integration of policies that must happen, at least in the economic sphere, will be acceptable to the citizens of Europe. The May 2014 European elections were a protest vote throughout Europe that showed people's dissatisfaction with austerity and low growth. But the belief and trust in the European institutions remains, even in places like Greece. That can be developed further, but it will only be retained if there is a will to use that trust to actively address people's worries and focus on returning the European economy to a path of recovery and hope. All attention is now on whether the new European Central Bank head Mario Draghi, who promised on 26 July 2012 in a conference in London to 'do whatever it takes to preserve the euro', will be allowed by Germany to be true to his word and pump enough money through quantitative easing (buying government and corporate bonds from across Europe) to stimulate the economy, which is in dire need of extra ammunition. Europe's economy is hardly moving and one can sense that the desperation in a number of countries is rising. If not enough is done – and done soon – there will be a question mark as to whether the Eurozone will be able to remain intact in its present form for long. Italy has slipped back into recession, prices are rising by far less than the target of 2 per cent (the latest reading was an inflation rate of just 0.4 per cent across Europe) and there is deflation in countries like Greece. The ECB has reduced interest rates to negative in some cases and has provided more support to the banks for lending to SMEs in particular, but this is not felt to be sufficient to reverse the trend.

In an article in *Europe's World* in February 2014,[12] Ferenc Miszlivetz, Director of the Institute for Social and European Studies in Hungary, argues that:

> The return of the nation state … is the natural result of the failures of the post-1989 integration process, in which the EU has remained a non-democracy, super-imposing rules, legal regulations and economic and financial policies upon fully fledged national democracies. At the same time a new–old hierarchy of EU member states became obvious, with Germany beginning to act as *primus inter pares* [first among equals] and unilaterally deciding the fate of other countries. Instead of a European demos, a 'German Europe' recently has started to assert itself.

It is interesting to get that perspective from one of the newer members of the EU. A lot of what Mr Miszlivetz is worried about has come as a result of the creation of the Eurozone and the forces that it has unleashed. British Eurosceptics point to the Eurozone crisis as proving the failure of the attempt to move to a closer 'union' through the adoption of a common currency across much of the Continent. Even the most devoted supporter of the euro must surely admit that too many countries with too many different levels of development rushed into the euro at the same time. And in the excitement they failed to set up mechanisms to spot the housing bubbles, to assess the implications of a flood of cheap money from the rich northern to the poorer southern ones which used it to expand their public sectors, or to import goods from Germany and others instead of investing it in productive capacity. And they failed to spot the failure of some national economies to align their spending and revenues, which has now landed them with debts so huge they can never afford to repay them, dragging the whole euro economy down. The banking sector remains under stress despite the better than expected results of the ECB Asset Quality Review,[13] announced in late October 2014, just before the ECB was due to take over as the single supervisor of the largest 130 banks in Europe as part of the progress towards a banking union in the Eurozone. UK banks also submitted to the tests. When the findings were finally published there was relief that so few had failed. The reason, of course, was that most of them had furiously, and under a lot of guidance, been putting their house in order over the previous year and so were deemed to be properly capitalised. Only twenty-five banks failed the 'static' tests in relation to their balance sheets as of end December 2013 (nine in Italy, three each in Greece and Cyprus, two each in Belgium and in Slovenia and one each in Ireland, Portugal and France). But half of them had spent at least the previous year engaging in restructuring and capital-raising activities, or had approved plans in place and were deemed to have passed the slightly softer 'dynamic' stress tests, i.e. were able to have satisfied the ECB conditions of where they should be moving to.

The ECB has asked for only some €10 billion of extra capital in the banks but a very substantial increase in provisions to make up for bad loans – mainly in Italy and Germany and also in Greece, where the ratio of non-performing loans may be as high as 40–50 per cent. With a fragile economic recovery, things may in fact get worse in 2015. But the ECB probably hopes that, at the least, it has laid the foundations for improving confidence in the banking system. The greater transparency and the determination to avoid unforeseen crises in individual banks by the deployment of 1,000 personnel, formed in 'joint supervisory groups', one for each individual large bank the ECB will look after, should help. The important thing will be to reintroduce trust into the system, now very much part of the process towards a banking union, and encourage once again the funding of cross-border transactions that will be all to the good. The jury is out. But I think the greatest impact will be if it allows the ECB to claim that now that it has complete understanding and control of the system it can limit any risks of its proposed bond purchases and be allowed to finally engage in proper QE, without which the Eurozone may sink back into recession.

Is there an economic case for leaving the EU?

In the same *Europe's World* article,[14] Ferenc Miszlivetz argues:

> The EU is in disarray. It reached a crossroads some time ago, but clearly hasn't found the right form to take. The most urgent question now is not whether we need an ever closer union, but whether Europe's citizens are willing and able to keep the union at all. If so, new rules and better methods of cross-border integration and co-operation need to be identified.

Many in the UK share that view. Moreover, they argue that the UK should cut its losses and leave the sinking ship, since Europe's influence is rapidly reducing as its weight in the global economy is being cut by the growth of the likes of India and China. They cite also the problems of an ageing population across most of Europe and also an expensive social support structure that is no longer affordable. They cite the fact that Europe accounts for 7.5 per cent of the world's population, 25 per cent of its GDP and 50 per cent of all welfare spend as an unsustainable combination.

But these are not sufficient reasons in themselves for leaving. The percentage share of GDP hardly matters if one is still growing and in no way would one be able to compete with growth rates of 7 to 10 per cent enjoyed by emerging markets still in the early or middle stages of development. Those fast growths will soon come to a stop or at least will moderate significantly, as we have seen with Japan, Taiwan and South Korea in the past. And the high percentage of welfare spending by Europe is because those countries in their urgent search for growth have done little so far to offer sufficient welfare provision for their populations. As those populations get richer they will demand it increasingly and it will come.

No, the real problem is that there is very little authoritative work that is easily conveyed to the public outlining the benefits of EU membership to the UK citizen. And yet that evidence exists in lots of places, but it is bitty. It must be stressed that most of the benefits of the single market were always expected to come through lower prices of goods and services, with those lower prices induced by the removal of tariff and other barriers and regulation, opening up competition while offering consumers across Europe greater transparency of prices. There would then be additional dynamic effects from greater competition, exports, innovation and investment.

Anecdotally, many of the anticipated benefits of the single market have indeed been felt. But the evaluation of the impact of the single market analysis has partly been obscured by the very rapid globalisation that has been taking place with the emergence of China and other less developed countries as global production centres with very cheap labour. Inflation has stayed lower than it otherwise would have been and so have interest rates, boosting not only real incomes but also willingness to borrow by both companies and individuals, and increasing demand. World Trade Organization (WTO) rules also helped bring down tariff barriers globally and those benefited the Europeans too in terms of lower prices for imported goods, which also spurred further competition. There has also been a certain amount of consolidation taking place, which has allowed firms to enjoy economies of scale, keeping prices for European consumers lower than they would otherwise have been.

It is therefore difficult to disentangle the wider influences towards lower prices from the direct (and indirect) impacts of the single market alone. A number of studies have tried to calculate those costs and benefits through the years. Inevitably, views are polarised. Those who focus on the costs of regulation imposed by Europe tend to put them as high as possibly 10 per cent of GDP, while those who look at dynamic effects are attributing net benefits to be as high as between 2 and 5 per cent of extra GDP we would not have enjoyed otherwise. But there are also concerns that some of the benefits of specialisation that a single market allows (thanks to the economies of scale that the single market enables) have not necessarily come through fully, thus casting doubt on the argument that the single market has the potential beneficial effect of allowing European 'champions' to develop that can compete globally like the Microsofts of this world.

Strict competition regulations both within countries and also across Europe have arguably prevented this from happening, and the legal and regulatory environment continues to differ. But this calls for greater rather than less harmonisation in Europe so that the proper benefits can begin to come through. Already, studies have demonstrated the huge benefits of standardisation of technical products, which makes it easier and cheaper for products to be sold across the EU rather than having to face a myriad of different standards per country. This also allows the EU more of a chance to set international standards in a number of areas where it has a comparative advantage, something a single country operating alone couldn't do easily.

Size matters. It is interesting when you look at Europe how it has consistently lagged behind the US in productivity growth during most of the post-war period. It is true that the US spends more on average in innovation and also has more funds devoted to start-ups and to funding fast-growing high-tech firms. When you itemise the sectoral trends, however, the areas of greater disparity in productivity are retail and financial, where the advantages of size are instantly obvious. The problem in Europe is that those are the types of sectors where there has been less integration.

More integration and harmonisation is a good thing (in parts)

Indeed, the actual problem is that the process of integration and harmonisation has not necessarily been as fast and trouble-free in all sectors. There is also still considerable variation on qualifications across countries, making it difficult for people to work across in a number of skilled professions – such as lawyers, for example – in addition to language barriers. Different national insurance and welfare systems and different laws in relation to bankruptcy, pensions, retirement ages, eligibility for housing and benefits also tend to restrict the movement of people across borders. Talking about the impact of the single market is therefore difficult if the single market in fact hardly exists in so many areas of the economy. In particular, services have been very slow to integrate and there is still a considerable amount of work to be done to achieve a single market in a number of sectors like, for example, insurance. And even in sectors which have seen rapid falls in prices it is often due more to technology or an individual country's own internal competition regimes, such as the early utilities, airline and telecom privatisations in the UK, than actual harmonisation – see the continued struggle over roaming charges.

And yet there can be no doubt that the elimination of national barriers and the push for greater competition in the EU as a whole have had some considerable and very visible benefits – one sector that stands out, of course, is air travel, where the markets have been transformed by the EU policy of open skies.

National flag carriers had a monopoly in ferrying people between countries – so Lufthansa and BA, for example, were the only airlines doing the trips between Britain and Germany. In most case the airlines were state-owned and heavily subsidised by their governments. Fares were high and travel infrequent. The sector has now been revolutionised.

It happened gradually. The UK led the way with the privatisation of British Airways in the 1980s, which was then followed by the appearance of the first low-cost carriers, such as EasyJet and Virgin, and later Ryanair and many others. The consumer has enjoyed a very substantial reduction in the real price of travel and a huge increase in choice of carrier, and although service standards may have dropped as those new airlines have to operate with relatively low costs, the availability of destinations has gone up exponentially. The old 'flag carriers' had to compete: for many routes they dropped prices, and if enough slots were available they expanded their services. Airports were also privatised and began to compete to attract airlines, with special offers on slots and other service facilities. As Hugo Dixon analyses in his book *The In/Out Question*, between 1992 and 2010 passenger traffic within the EU doubled and the number of intra-EU routes increased by 140 per cent.[15] At the same time, prices have hardly moved so, in real terms and on a good day it costs less to fly between London and Paris than it does to take the train and pay full fare between London and Manchester.

Another example is telecoms. Here too there used to be national monopoly operators. The system was expensive and the range of services restricted. When she was Prime Minister, Margaret Thatcher privatised BT and allowed new entrants in the 1980s to bring in competition. Later, Gordon Brown, the then Chancellor, authorised the auctioning of spectrum to mobile operators offering 3G licences, which not only swelled the coffers of the Exchequer but also gave space to new mobile operators, competing with BT to invest and grow – and effectively create a new market, which is what academics like Marianna Mazucatto argue is the best role the state can play to encourage growth and innovation in an economy.[16]

The development of the single European Global System for Mobile Communications standard helped by allowing easier access across Europe, and the standards themselves (as we have seen earlier) did lead to a number of firms becoming global players like Nokia, Ericsson and, in terms of service providers, also Vodafone, something that would not have happened otherwise. Hugo Dixon in his book *The In/Out Question* quotes from the evidence to the UK government's review of the EU competences that 'Europe has given British companies like Vodafone the opportunity to acquire scale on the European continent and to use this as a stepping stone into the US, Japan, China and India'.

There is still a lot to do in the mobile sector and the latest focus has been on the still-too-high roaming charges imposed by mobile operators. The Commission is now trying to put an upper limit on the cost of making calls on mobiles when travelling abroad and to scrap the charges we incur when we receive calls abroad. What is clear from all this is that important markets have been revolutionised by the liberalisation forced on the UK by Europe through the European Commission, and the increase in competition that has resulted has ultimately benefited the consumer and continues to provide a dynamism that keeps the sectors reinventing themselves and continuing to innovate and grow.

And there is still more to come. The services sector accounts for 75 per cent of the European economies – admittedly many of those are public services but there is no reason why they too should not be open to change and cross-border trading. The UK of course has a comparative advantage over services, which account for 78 per cent of the UK economy and would have benefited most if the service sector had been liberalised as intended. A services directive signed in 2006 has been repeatedly diluted, mainly under the influence of France, and the Commission is periodically trying to press for completion of the single market in individual services. The latest are energy and retail banking, both of which, as mentioned earlier, would benefit hugely from economies of scale if they operated in a proper single market of 600 million consumers. The single passport which allows everyone registered in one country to provide services elsewhere is in fact rarely implemented due to different qualifications, concerns about professional quality and also different regimes in each country. Implementation of course varies widely. It is commonplace here in the UK, for example, to be working alongside lawyers, architects, engineers, academics, civil servants etc. born elsewhere in the EU. However, this is a rarity across most of the rest of Europe.

What about jobs?

A report in 2000 entitled 'UK Jobs Dependent on the EU' by Brian Ardy, Iain Begg and Dermot Hodson of South Bank University's European Institute estimated that in 1997, 3,445,000 jobs in the United Kingdom were associated with demand from exports to the European Union. Of those, 2,500,000 jobs were the direct result of that demand, while 900,000 were indirectly created from demand from those jobs. In 2014, analysis carried out by the Centre for Economics and Business Research on behalf of British Influence updated that work. The new analysis showed that in 2011 there were 4.2 million jobs, or 13.3 per cent of the UK workforce, associated with demand from exports to the EU. Some 3.1 million UK jobs were directly supported by exports to the European Union in 2011 and 1.1 million jobs were indirectly supported. The result was that total income associated with demand from EU exports was £211 billion or £3,500 per head of the population in 2011.[17]

The main areas of job growth between 1997 and 2011 were in professional, technical and scientific services and also business and administration support services. Manufacturing lost jobs over that period, but this has to be seen against a background of structural decline in the sector and also the impact of the recession on the sector since 2008. According to the research, the region that gained the most jobs was London, which now has 27 per cent more EU-supported jobs than it did in 1997. On average, the CEBR suggests, the UK gained 12 per cent more jobs than it had in 1997 as a result of the EU. The only region to have fewer EU-associated jobs now than it did then was the West Midlands. Nevertheless, CEBR figures indicate that the West Midlands still had 385,000 jobs linked to EU demand in 2011.

These jobs figures were the ones quoted by the Lib Dem leader Nick Clegg in his famous radio and TV debate with Nigel Farage before the May 2014 European parliamentary elections. They did little for the Liberal Democrat Party, which lost ten of its eleven MEPs, and had no impact on the rise of UKIP's popularity: they gained an extra eleven to send twenty-four MEPs to the European Parliament – which they want to actively campaign to leave! But the economic figures are nevertheless stark, even if one accepts that more jobs and therefore higher spending by the UK economy also means higher imports and possible job creation in other countries to meet that demand. However, the counterfactual would have been lower growth for both the UK and the countries we trade with. And of course the CEBR work does not imply that the estimated jobs linked to the EU would necessarily all be lost if the UK were to leave the EU. Much would depend on what sort of status the UK negotiated with the rest of the EU – a Swiss or Norwegian relationship, for example – or the extent to which some of those exports, if lost to the EU, were replaced by exports to other parts of the world.

But of course trade is not a zero-sum game. It is true that the EU is our natural trade partner because of its proximity and because we enjoy tariff free movement of goods and no meaningful restrictions of people or capital. There are serious advantages in dealing with a large bloc that provides us with an instant market of some 600 million people. It should nevertheless be perfectly possible to sell more to other parts of the world too while remaining within the EU. The argument often made that not being part of the EU would allow us to trade more actively with other parts of the world makes no sense.

Interestingly, the recent analysis for the Mayor of London by Volterra Economics[18] which looked at how London would fare if it left the EU seems to suggest that being in what they term a 'reformed' EU and being out of it makes little difference if the country is also actively seeking to expand its trade relations with the rapidly growing emerging markets. The assumption there is, quite correctly, that Britain can do this active trading with the rest of the world irrespective of whether it is in or out of Europe. But what must not be underestimated is how much easier it is for the UK to achieve preferential trade status if it is part of a bigger bloc such as the EU that has the clout to negotiate on its behalf. That means more influence with the WTO than we would have as a single country fighting our own corner and also better chance of success in WTO disputes. At the same time it makes it easier to strike bilateral trade deals with large countries outside the EU which lead to beneficial tariff reductions than would be the case if we were striving to reach agreement on our own as a relatively small country. Even the Eurosceptic Roger Bootle in his book *The Trouble with Europe*[19] acknowledges that should Britain choose to leave the EU it should nevertheless aim to align itself with another big trading bloc.

Some facts and figures

The European Movement, a not-for-profit, non-governmental organisation funded exclusively by their members, publishes regular facts and figures on Europe. It is a pro-European organisation but there are no doubts about the accuracy of the data they present. What comes across vividly is the sheer size of the economy of Europe.

Its GDP at just over £11 trillion is just a bit higher than the US at £10.3 trillion, more than twice the size of China's and four times the size of Japan's. Some 34 per cent of world trade originates in Europe, valued at some $5.5 trillion annually. There are also some areas where Europe dominates. It accounts for some 50 per cent of all cars, 70 per cent of all pharmaceutical exports and all exports of aircraft and satellites in the world by value. That is huge. Companies come willingly to set up their headquarters here – some twenty-eight of the Forbes 100 companies are headquartered in Europe. The EU is involved in negotiating bilateral trade agreements with other nations on behalf of the EU as a whole. The free trade agreement with South Korea is expected to provide benefits of some £1.35 billion a year to EU exporters because of reduced tariffs and the EU is currently negotiating deals with India, Canada and Singapore that are estimated to lead to a further gain of some £75 billion to the GDP of the EU. The EU–US trade deal currently being negotiated is expected to create 2 million jobs in the EU and add some $80 billion worth of benefits to the economies of the member countries.

For the UK, there are clear additional advantages to being part of the

EU. Some 50 per cent of foreign direct investment coming into this country originates in another EU member state – and is worth £351 billion a year. In addition, some 40 per cent of UK exports go to the EU – in the automotive sector, the EU received some 51 per cent of all UK cars and commercial vehicle exports in 2012. In food, the figure is a staggering 78 per cent. And proximity to Europe is a very crucial factor in investment decisions. The European Movement quotes a City UK survey where 40 per cent of respondents volunteered that proximity to Europe was a main reason for setting up operations in London.

And being part of Europe is an important part of what attracts companies to the UK. By courtesy of the European Movement website, 2014, we reproduce below what business leaders are saying about Europe.

The UK in the EU: what they say

There are distinct benefits from being part of the EU. I would be concerned there would be an impact on British jobs directly as a result of pulling out of the EU.

Jill McDonald, McDonald's North West Division President

The EU remains the UK's largest overseas market, accounting for around 60 per cent of national exports. The negative impact of the UK leaving the EU would be significant on UK companies and the balance of trade.

Lesley Bachelor, Director General at the Institute of Export

That's the chief reason we're in favour of the UK maintaining its long-established place at the heart of the European Union: it provides greater investment stability and certainty. But, as a global business with feet planted firmly on both sides of the Channel, we also believe that the UK's national interests are best served by a close relationship with Europe.

Ben van Beurden, Shell chief executive

We benefit from and support the UK being in the EU.

Ivan Menezes, chief executive of Diageo, the world's biggest spirits maker

[The UK] acts as a gateway to Europe for many financial institutions and corporates from around the world. Their establishment and subsequent growth in the UK is no coincidence but is linked to the country's membership of the world's largest single market, the European Union.

Daniel Pinto, co-chief executive of J. P. Morgan's corporate and investment bank in Europe, the Middle East and Africa

We are a positive contributor in that sense to the UK economy and we [would] have to look at that then for the UK *v.* Europe, just like we do in any other country that is not in the EU.

Paul Polman, the Dutch chief executive of the consumer multinational Unilever

Jobs and the growth of Britain's economy depend on maintaining and increasing exports to the EU, particularly as the European economy begins to recover. This will be a much more difficult task if businesses have to contend with a Britain that has decided to exit the EU. Existing trade arrangements will be at risk and Britain will have no influence in making the rules in the future.

James C. Cowles, Citi chief executive for Europe, the Middle East and Africa

We all need to know where Britain's future lies in a changing global economy. We have looked beyond the political rhetoric to examine the pros and cons of EU membership and British business is unequivocal; the single market is fundamental to our future.

We are better off in a reformed EU than outside with no influence. Each year, membership is worth £3,000 to every household in this country.

John Cridland, CBI Director General

But what do we mean by a 'reformed' Europe?

Well, no one can agree on this. John Cridland's quote above is, interestingly, the only one to refer to a 'reformed' Europe. We all want reform – and most European countries would say the same. The issue is that 'reform' means something different for different nations – and possibly also for individuals. UKIP and a number of other organisations like Open Europe estimate that the UK bears a great cost from regulations emanating in Europe and voted in by the European Parliament. And yet we all know that most regulation that costs companies is national and much of the EC legislation – not all, of course, by any means – would probably have needed to be developed by the national governments anyway and be enacted by their parliaments. Arguably some institutions may need rethinking and in some areas their role may need to be curtailed. In others, perhaps their role needs to be seriously expanded, such as in the EC competition and internal markets division, which has an important role in ensuring the further opening of the market and the preservation of competition in the conducting of companies' business affairs. And we know that liberalising and opening up markets and creating standardisation requires legislation and monitoring – and the occasional fines – for it to work.

There is, though, a gulf between what we here in the UK, at least as exemplified by David Cameron's pronouncements, mean by a reformed Europe – less control, more national sovereignty, less bureaucracy, less City supervision by the European Commission – and what is wanted by other countries which are also agitating at present. In the majority of cases what they want is a focus on growth policies that tackle chronic unemployment, underemployment and the considerable drop in living standards that is alienating a generation of young voters; less direct influence from Brussels and from Germany in particular; and, for those countries which have received bail-outs during the crisis, less control from the 'Troika' of the ECB, IMF and EU, with freedom to restructure debt and start focusing on growth rather than austerity. We in the UK should also strive to change that focus so that the right policies are adopted. We want growth for Europe too, because the prosperity of our people and our cities, including London and the City, is directly linked to developments in Europe – not exclusively, of course, as the Volterra research has indicated, but to a very considerable extent.

The voter therefore needs to decide whether the gains from staying in the EU can ever possibly be outweighed by any benefits from leaving. We have explained again and again the help that a proper cost–benefit analysis can give in identifying and enumerating the pros and cons of policies and policy proposals so that proper decisions can be made. There are occasional areas where the evidence is not very clear. Europe is a case in point as there are all sorts of conflicting forces. But overall the analysis would very much indicate a case for staying in and influencing, and of course focusing on the reforms that matter for jobs and growth. The truth is, of course, that we will never know all the facts and can't say for certain what would have happened if we had not been part of Europe all these years – or what will happen in the future if we stay or leave. But it is worth reflecting on one final thought. We have been talking about '*staying together*' a lot recently around the Scottish referendum. We were all keen to keep Scotland as part of the United Kingdom as we could see the benefits to both countries of retaining the union. If we felt that the United Kingdom was greater than the sum of its parts, why is it different for us and our union with Europe?

CHAPTER 10

Never Got a Lift Out of Lear Jets

T OWARDS THE END of the 1980s, a friend returned from a night out in the East Midlands. Like many teenagers in the late 1980s he (let's call him 'K') smoked, and, lighting up a cigarette, he sat down in his dad's favourite front-room chair to contemplate the evening. The next thing K remembers is waking up with a large burn hole in the chair and his dad standing over him, ready to go to work.

For those who weren't around in the late 1980s in the East Midlands, things did get a bit grim – miners' strikes, industrial decline and stubbornly high unemployment. At the time things weren't going well for K and his family; but he always remembers his dad's words as an important 'design for life'. As K looked up and abjectly apologised for the large burn and the near death experience he had treated his unwitting family to, his dad said, 'Don't worry, it's only things – things don't matter, only people matter.'

K's dad is not a behavioural economist but in fewer than ten words he did a good job of summarising the key findings from about twenty years of research into the economics of happiness – or, to use the more technical term, *subjective well-being* (SWB). This is something of an over-simplification, but the suggestion that 'things' (material possessions) do not make you happy, whereas people ('your relationships') do, is as good a summary as you are going to get with fewer than ten words. Particularly for those readers in mid-life, this chapter will hopefully help in your own design for life.

Let's start with a bit of background on how the dismal science came to be interested in happiness. Traditionally, economists have inferred well-being, happiness or (more accurately) 'utility' from the choices individuals make. The rationale goes something like this:

- An individual chooses how long to work, how long to play and how to spend their income based on underlying preferences, and we assume that these individuals are rational, in that they aim to maximise their overall 'utility' (which can be interpreted as satisfaction, happiness or well-being).

- If this is true, then the consumption, investment and work/life choices we observe people making are true reflections of these underlying preferences.

- The outcomes we observe *must* maximise their well-being/happiness. If happiness is what an individual wants to maximise, economists have always assumed that what we observe them doing by definition maximises their happiness.

This approach does not necessarily limit us to a world where only things, not people, matter. Many people work long hours and rarely see their families, but secure a good income. We may infer that they are making rational choices about the long-term needs of their children (financial stability) over the quality of their relationships, based on their own preferences. Somebody may take a lesser-paying job to spend more time with their children. In both cases we assume individuals are acting rationally and therefore observed outcomes represent fulfilment of their underlying individual preferences. They are doing things that, by definition, maximise their satisfaction, given constraints of time and finance – most importantly, nobody else is better placed to make those decisions because only the individual is fully aware of their unique underlying preferences.

The assumption of individual rationality does not drive us to the conclusion that people value 'things', rather than other 'people', but it does assume that what we observe them doing leaves them as happy as they can be. The assumption is that they are best placed to make these decisions. Economics is, at its heart, a libertarian discipline, believing that people are best placed to make their own decisions on how long to work, what to spend their money on and how much time to devote to leisure/family.[1]

Perhaps unsurprisingly, these assumptions have faced challenge in recent decades. The suggestion that we need to collect information on 'happiness' is part of a wider challenge to rationality from *Behavioural Economics*. As Daniel Kahneman, a well-known behavioural economist, has suggested, only an economist would be surprised to find that we don't always act rationally. Essentially, the behavioural economics movement draws on the findings from disciplines such as psychology, where there is a strong experimental tradition and clear evidence of behaviours that contradict rationality.[2]

The challenge – the fact that we are not always rational – is one that most people would recognise. In other parts of this text we consider the reasons why, as economists, we tend to stick to underlying assumptions of rationality, even in the face of evidence to the contrary. Usually these arguments are based on a desire to answer questions in a practical, useful way, which in the social sciences tends to require simplification. However, for those who diverge from this assumption of rationality, the first question for happiness researchers is: how do you measure happiness?

You are attempting to capture a very subjective concept that will vary across individuals. Asking someone whether they are 'happier' depends on how happy they normally are. There have been various attempts to come up with theoretically consistent approaches to this issue. The approach that has come to dominate is the 'evaluative interpretation', which comes from positive psychology. This 'emphasises SWB as an evaluative judgement across all areas of life as to how people think and feel about their lives'.[3] Its popularity is perhaps based on the fact that it is easy to measure and aligned with a policy approach. You can imagine how interested politicians are about the happiness or otherwise of the electorate and how it changes with each government. One can also see this as an alternative way of getting round the limitations of purely financial measures such as GDP, but in some ways we simply supplant these with a range of different, but no less severe, limitations.[4]

Having said this, the UK has made great strides in this area. We have the Whitehall Well-being Working Group (W3G), and in April 2011 the ONS embarked on its first attempt to systematically measure national well-being.[5] Furthermore, the findings from research carried out by academics and various bodies are now quite extensive, and while we need to retain an amount of critical detachment, issues of measurement are no longer seen as major concerns.

What does this evidence tell us about the behaviour of individuals, and what should we do to make ourselves happier?[6]

Dipping into your forties

The first finding that is of particular interest to the (ageing) authors is summarised in Figure 17. This is a simple chart showing how the average SWB score varies according to the age of respondents.[7] Often in the social sciences we read findings that simply confirm urban myths, common conceptions or other anecdotal evidence. Figure 17 confirms what the 45-year-old lead author of this chapter could have told you before he saw this chart – on average, individuals tend to report being less happy (in terms of SWB) in their middle ages.

FIGURE 17: AVERAGE LIFE SATISFACTION SCORE

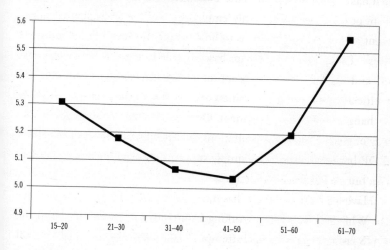

Source: British Household Panel Survey

However, the drop in average happiness from your twenties to the 'mid-life crisis' in your forties is much less than the rebound in average happiness from your forties to sixties – the good news is that 'things can only get better' and they don't actually deteriorate that much.[8] Assuming that we can compare the happiness scores of those in their sixties with those in their twenties, the former group seem to be much happier. Obviously this is not accounting for many other differences between older and younger people – but who cares, you'll take what you can get at this age!

I wish this were the end of the story, but as economists we are doomed to always see the dismal side. If you are sitting there feeling particularly middle-aged and grumpy, but can feel the gloom lifting as you look forward to a future of steadily rising happiness from an SWB of 5 to just over 5.5, be aware that the chart suggests one of two things. It is either the case that, on average, people can expect their happiness to improve quite dramatically past their forties, OR that the grumpy die young, and the higher average satisfaction for sixty-year-olds is a result of being left with only those who were always happier, whatever their age (more technically, we may be suffering from 'attrition').

I must admit that, while there is some possible truth in the last point about attrition, I'm painfully aware that the inclusion of a chart with scales and a line graph is the equivalent of bromide in a boudoir – the suggestion that rising happiness could be due to miserable people dying earlier is, believe it or not, an economist's attempt at humour. In reality, there are studies that suggest happier people die younger, but this is a finding likely driven by the extremes of those who have more volatile characters and the (often accompanying) mental health issues (such as bipolar disorder).[9]

It is therefore probable that the pattern in Figure 17 is simply driven by rising happiness past your forties, but if this is the case, why is it the case? Here the research is of little help, but you probably get grumpy because (along with the main protagonist in the film of a similar name) you ask yourself, 'What if this is as good as it gets?' While ageing is non-linear, in that the staging posts of thirty-five and forty seem to be particularly physiologically important, between the ages of forty and fifty most of us seem to realise that we have the life that we are going to have: we're unlikely to change careers at this stage; we either do or do not have kids; future sporting glory is no longer an option; nor is that No. 1 single – the list is, pretty well, endless.

It would seem reasonable to suggest that, beyond the age of fifty, the rising levels of happiness imply acceptance of this fact. It seems a more realistic assertion than the alternative, that many of the unhappiest do achieve sporting glory, or that elusive No. 1, in their fifties and sixties; and a more attractive proposition than the suggestion that grumpy middle-agers die young. Do not despair ... acceptance is coming.

'We hate it when our friends become successful'

Those of you who are concentrating will notice that the drift into age differences is something of a digression – I promised to show you why K's dad is a great behavioural economist. However, we have not digressed as far as you might think. Work on age and happiness implies that everything is relative, and this starts us off on the road towards some important insights. To be clear, there will be those among the population who feel less grumpy in old age, but no matter who you are and how successful you have been, at some point this will be behind you – we all experience *relative* decline to a greater or lesser extent, and it seems to particularly hit home in your forties. Perhaps at this very moment, Thom Yorke and Damon Albarn are sitting in a café coming to terms with the almost certain knowledge that for them, there are no more *OK Computer*s or *Parklife*s.

This issue of 'relativity' pervades the findings from research into happiness, and perhaps most important are the implications that arise from the study of whether money makes you happy. This branch of happiness research has the longest heritage and can be traced back to the work in the early 1970s of Richard Easterlin, who noted an apparent paradox in the data.

The Easterlin paradox suggests that in developed countries the growth of well-being has become detached from growth in national income. This proposition is still hotly debated[10] and some would argue that it comes down to technical questions of exactly which measures one uses.[11] However, as with most academic arguments that generate more heat than light, the truth probably lies somewhere in between. Generally, we seem to have a situation where individuals in rich countries are happier than those in poor countries; but consideration of happiness as rich countries become richer suggests diminishing returns – continued rises in income do not seem to make us happier, or at least not to the same extent. The literature provides two sets of seemingly contradictory evidence:

a) Studies considering cross-country variation suggest that individuals in higher-income countries are happier than those in lower-income countries;

b) Within each country, average measures of SWB through time remain relatively unchanged as populations become wealthier.

Easterlin suggests that this observed relationship between income and happiness can be explained by the suggestion that we have a relative income effect that 'dominates' an 'absolute' income effect. Populations that, for instance, cannot feed themselves, are unlikely to be as happy as those that can (there is an absolute income effect), but when we start to move to higher levels of income from this point within a particular country, individuals do not feel much happier if everybody else is also getting wealthier (a relative income effect). As Andrew Oswald puts it, 'Prosperity next door makes you dissatisfied.' Depressing, but (it would seem) true.

Here we have an important piece in our jigsaw puzzle. At its most basic level, 'things' clearly do matter – if you are hungry, thirsty or without shelter then this is your overriding concern. However, for societies that have moved further up the income ladder to cover these basic needs, happiness is determined by your perceived position relative to your peers. The situation may have been bad in the '80s in the East Midlands, but we can safely assume that K's dad was commenting on a situation in which we had moved beyond basic need.

This has interesting implications for our consideration of income equality and inequality, and we tackled this in Chapter 5, which considered the arguments for and against strongly redistributive welfare systems. However, returning to the matter at hand, we are getting closer to our initial goal, but still not quite there: while it is our relative position in society that seems to determine happiness, beyond the meeting of basic needs, it is still the possession of 'things' that seems to determine this relative position. Happiness research that looks at the relationship between income and happiness within a country suggests that increased prosperity does not necessarily bring increased happiness,[12] but the suggestion is that this is possibly a result of us needing to have more things than others to feel better.

This would be unfortunate, as it would leave us with the prospect of not being able to increase overall happiness, because a country's income growth cannot be distributed in a way that makes everybody *relatively* better off, on *average*. This finding would suggest that happiness peaks at a certain level of income and then all we can do is mitigate against its decline. But this ignores the findings from research on happiness at the level of the individual.

First, consider the work that finds some positive relationship between the level of income for individuals and their level of happiness: researchers[13] find that Forbes's 100 wealthiest Americans are slightly happier than the average American. While this is a 'slight' difference, we have the situation where wealthier individuals are happier than their compatriots. Does this suggest that, while things don't make us happy per se, having more things than most other people does make us happier? No, because we have no way of knowing what is driving this apparent relationship – it is quite possible that happier people are more likely to become rich (and join the Forbes 100 list), and this could be driving our findings.[14]

What we need is a study that follows the same individuals through time and measures how their happiness changes as they experience different events. Jörn-Steffen Pischke uses variation in the use of bonuses by firms across different sectors to look at the relationship between income and happiness. He suggests some tentative evidence of a link, with bonus-winners being slightly happier. However, this type of study suffers from the same sort of problem – imagine that individuals who are naturally more highly motivated also report higher happiness (we would then observe a strong relationship between happiness and bonuses, without bonuses making you happy).

Studies of lottery winners get round these problems, because the money is distributed purely at random. The findings, due mainly to Jonathan Gardner and Andrew Oswald of Warwick University, seem to suggest that lottery winners experience immediate euphoria after the win, then for a period afterwards they report being less happy. The researchers suggest that after these periods there is some evidence of increased happiness, but the findings are dogged by small sample sizes (there are not many lottery winners in datasets with happiness indicators) and the raised happiness is only observable for the year after the win.

If you're happy and you know it...

It is worth spending some time explaining why these studies are problematic, because they reflect a common problem in economics – that we work so hard to design a study that is statistically robust that we obtain results that (while robust) have lost much of their relevance to the issue at hand ('bear with', as my son the *Miranda* fan would say).[15]

Take the work with lotteries: the first thing to remember is that the results only apply to those who take part in lotteries – half the British population would be missing from a UK-based study. When we carry out a study based on individuals who take part in the lottery, our findings will relate only to this section of the population and these are people who are likely 'flagging' that they feel a need for a bit more money. At the very least, I would suggest there is an under-representation of statisticians in the sample, as they are aware of the vanishingly small odds of a win. You have to ask yourself if evidence of lottery winners (who select into lotteries because of a perceived need for more money) being a little happier in the first year after a win actually constitutes evidence that money brings long-term happiness to the average person (I would suggest not).

In fact, many lottery winners report that the win has ruined their relationships with friends and family. This is exactly what we might expect, as these friends and family, who have not experienced any change in their income or wealth, are now relatively much worse off. They now have incomes that look puny next to the winner's and will therefore feel less happy than they did. The bonuses analysed by Pischke are designed to do just this – to make the receivers feel better rewarded than those who do not receive an award.

The problem is that the relationship between individual income and happiness seems to be asymmetric – having much less than everybody else makes you feel much worse off, but having much more only seems to make you feel a little bit better. If we consider the amount of happiness in existence between an individual and their group of friends before the lottery win, it would seem reasonable to suggest that this overall 'cup' of happiness has become less full. While the lottery winners may feel slightly happier one year after the win, we have no evidence that this persists and the fall in their friends' levels of happiness implied by the decline in their relative position likely more than offsets this.

I have to flag up that there is no specific evidence to prove this last suggestion: it is more the case that it is consistent with a number of pieces of evidence. If we pull these together, we come to our final proof of the prescience of K's dad.

- We have already suggested that more income does not seem to make people significantly happier – if there is a return to having more things, it is minimal.

- In contrast, having less than everyone else (even when you have 'enough')[16] makes you pretty unhappy. It is what we call an asymmetric relationship, with relative losses looming larger than relative gains.

- Studies[17] of exceptionally happy people find that these individuals are only different to others in that they have rich and fulfilling social lives, strong friendships and a current love interest. Along the same lines, studies routinely find that people who are married or cohabiting are happier.

As we would perhaps expect from these findings, those who report that they desire wealth are less happy, possibly because, by definition, they are comparing themselves to others in a way that leaves them perceiving their situation as relatively disadvantaged.

Finally, it is interesting to note that studies of how people spend their money suggest that purchases of inconspicuous goods (for instance, reducing your commute)[18] make you happier than the sort of conspicuous consumption, or 'bling', that permeates modern society. Recent work[19] suggests that spending your money on others is a universal happiness improver.

Because we are happy … or are we?

Before bringing all this evidence together to create our design for life, it is important to first recognise that we do not need the happiness research to tell us that absolute income matters. Individuals who are unable to feed themselves or their children on a weekly basis, who find themselves homeless or otherwise unable to meet basic needs, are a priority for all societies. However, for those who have achieved a level of security that can be considered comfortable but continue to ask the questions 'Am I really happy?' and 'How can I make myself happier?', here is the recipe from behavioural economics.

First, stop comparing your financial situation to everybody else, especially those who are much wealthier than you. No matter how wealthy you get, there will always be someone who is wealthier (and even the wealthiest person will one day be less wealthy than the newly wealthiest person).

Second, give priority to your relationships with friends and family. Focus at least some of your spending on helping others, rather than pursuit of relative positional goods designed mainly to engender envy in others. It is not the number of Facebook friends but the quality of your relationships with a few true friends that drives happiness.

Finally, do not desire wealth for its own sake, but provide yourself with targets that are achievable. Most importantly, make sure you relate your targets to things that you think you should do, rather than things you think other people think you should do.

These three behaviours could have been taken from a '60s hippy manifesto and, in the view of Oswald, 'The hippies were right all along about happiness.' However, there is a little more to it than this. Perhaps the hardest lesson to learn from the research is that, while people feel unhappy when they look around and feel materially worse off than other people, the pursuit of material possessions does not make them much happier. Do not be drawn into the belief that you can overcome a sense of relative material deprivation by getting a big brash car with personalised number plates. The key is to do things that make you feel happy (see above) and this will help you feel a lot less worried about how well (or badly) everybody else is doing.

Oswald says that the hippies had it right and K's dad says that things don't matter, only people matter. It may seem rather base to suggest that we only feel happier if we are doing better than others, but it simply reflects the fact that we are social beings, for whom relationships with other people matter more than things. If we take heed, we may just be able to overcome our natural, but rather unedifying, desire to be one up on the Joneses.

So, what does an analysis of 'happiness' tell us about how we will vote? It tells us a lot about the likely attitude towards policies of higher personal taxes for the very rich, a mansion tax for houses over £2 million, taxes for foreign owners of prime property in the UK, caps on bonuses and executive pay, extra taxes for those near good schools, caps on welfare benefits etc. Why? Because all of these would improve our relative position – and who cares about the unintended consequences, which could be that we are all poorer as a result?

Perhaps, when thinking about how to vote on these issues, we need to remember that in a world where we are all made better off, you would possibly feel worse if your relative position worsened (even if you were wealthier in absolute terms). This is human nature, but being aware of this is hopefully half of the battle. One of the insights from this area of economics and psychology is that we are all walking around in the modern world with instincts and desires developed for primitive societies – the body you have is a result of hundreds of thousands of years of development to survive in jungles and on the plains. We have had less than 1 per cent of that time to adapt to the modern world – don't always follow your instincts.

CHAPTER 11

Saving the Earth or Simply on Another Planet?

From blue to green and back again

WAY BACK IN the '70s and '80s, environmentalists were seen as hippyish cranks and eccentrics, epitomised by 'Swampy', the grubby but endearing eco-warrior who earned his fifteen minutes of fame by climbing trees and hiding down dug-outs in the hope of obstructing the path of new roads. More respectable, but equally naïve, was the 'self-sufficiency' of Barbara and Tom Good in the classic sitcom *The Good Life*. Since those fun days it has all got more serious. Respected commentators have brought green issues into the mainstream of political debate. For example, the hugely influential Stern Review on the Economics of Climate Change by the eminent economist Sir Nicholas Stern, now Lord Stern of Brentford, led to the 2008 Climate Change Act, which commits the UK to reduce its greenhouse gas (GHG) emissions by at least 80 per cent, compared to a 1990 baseline, by 2050.

It also didn't go unnoticed by politicians that votes for the Green Party had been growing, to the extent that in 2010 they had their first MP elected, the bright and articulate Caroline Lucas. Heavyweight commentators, the increasing certainty of the science and the winning of votes had by then attracted strong commitments from all the three main parties. So much so that, in May 2010, Cameron pledged that his new coalition administration would be 'the greenest government ever', adding, 'I mean that from the bottom of my heart'. Although it soon became very apparent that many of his Tory colleagues were of a very different heart, including Owen Paterson, the minister whom he actually put in charge of the environment. Paterson's view was less enthusiastic about the biggest green issue there is than his leader: 'People get very emotional about this subject and I think we should just accept that the climate has been changing for centuries.'

It might be thought his comments are why Cameron subsequently gave Paterson more leave to air his personal views – from the Conservative back benches. But George Osborne has survived despite having reduced his own earlier enthusiasm for green policies down to the wholly dismissive sound bite: 'We won't fix the climate by putting the country out of business.' Osborne was, of course, much more important to Cameron than Paterson in his July 2014 shop-window reshuffle to detox his Cabinet of the 'pale, male and stale', so as to persuade the electorate that his government is not dominated by a clique of privately educated middle-aged men out of touch with ordinary people. That might explain why he has replaced Paterson with former Shell employee Liz Truss, who had also previously dismissed renewable energy as extremely expensive and damaging for the economy, and who in 2009, when deputy director of the free market think tank Reform, said energy infrastructure in the UK was being damaged by politicians' obsession with green technology: 'Vast amounts of taxpayers' money are being spent subsidising uneconomic activity.' So we can expect renewed struggle between Truss and Cameron on the one hand and the Lib Dem Ed Davey, Secretary of State for Energy and Climate, who has a real commitment to tackling climate change. We cannot be sure where Cameron's green commitment went; perhaps his original promise had relied more on the electorate being green.

'Armageddon, my arse': the science of global warming

The greenhouse effect was first hypothesised by Joseph Fourier in 1824, though he used the analogy of a bell jar rather than a greenhouse, and then the physics was demonstrated experimentally by John Tyndall in 1859. Carbon dioxide (CO_2) in the atmosphere, and other greenhouse gases,[1] trap the sun's energy like a greenhouse does and so warms the Earth. This could be a very big problem as there is now far more carbon dioxide in the atmosphere than at any other time over the last 800,000 years. It is estimated that since 1850 we have burned more than 360 billion tonnes of fossil fuels, although our output of 29 gigatons of CO_2 is tiny compared to the 750 gigatons passing through the Earth's natural carbon cycle each year: it builds up because the natural absorbers of CO_2 cannot absorb all of the extra CO_2, and this may well have tipped the previous natural balance.

The balance of world scientific opinion is overwhelmingly that human-induced, or *anthropogenic* if you want to sound expert, GHG emissions are dangerously changing our planet's climate. Since the 1950s, after over 150 years of CO_2 build-up in the atmosphere, changes in our climate have occurred that are unprecedented over decades to millennia. The Earth has warmed, snow cover and ice have diminished, exacerbating warming by reducing reflection of the sun, and this has in turn contributed to the sea level rising. Only a small minority of scientists believe that this has merely been coincidence: the vast majority think increased concentrations of greenhouse gases will inevitably lead to more droughts, floods and other weather extremes such as tornadoes, shifts in animal and human populations, changes in crop yields and species extinction; some even think that could include us.

The largest and most influential group of climate scientists, the UN's Intergovernmental Panel on Climate Change (IPCC), warns that we are only seeing the beginnings of catastrophic climate change: in two or three decades' time the world will face nearly inevitable warming of more than 2 degrees. That does not sound like much, but it is a huge increase in the amount of energy trapped in our atmosphere – like water near the boil, a few degrees massively changes volatility. We can expect floods, heatwaves, droughts and generally extreme weather to become more and more frequent. Lord Stern warns that this will lead to huge economic costs, widespread human misery and increased world conflict as people migrate and squabble over the remaining most habitable and fertile places. So overwhelming is the weight of scientific opinion on this – perhaps over 90 per cent of all those with scientific credibility and with all of the world's national science academies – that those who challenge this near consensus of scientists often have to resort to the claim that global warming must be a 'hoax foisted upon an unsuspecting public by conspiratorial environmentalists'. And so this is indeed what they do.

Hereditary peer Lord Monckton obviously feels that his ancestral pedigree as 3rd Viscount Monckton of Brenchley is qualification enough for him to promote his 'expertise' on the science of climate change, despite having no formal scientific background himself. He energetically, and with blissful confidence, dismisses it all as a hoax. Lord Lawson of Blaby, an ex-Chancellor of the Exchequer under Thatcher but who also has no scientific credentials, may feel his life peerage earns him the right to denounce climate science too. He does this from his organisation the Global Warming Policy Foundation (GWPF). The GWPF has been very influential in the Conservative Party and is frequently invited in by the media to provide a contrary view, as a consensus is too dull, despite the fact that it has repeatedly refused to reveal its sponsors, a stance that usually debars someone from being taken seriously, especially in science. The red-top tabloids and the 'Torygraph' eagerly and regularly run articles by climate change doubters,[2] and Rupert Murdoch didn't really amaze anyone by recently declaring his own belief that climate change is not much to worry about at all. Even Boris Johnson, the Tory London Mayor, feels he is a scientist, writing in the *Telegraph*, 'We have become so blind with conceit and self-love that we genuinely believe that the fate of the planet is in our hands.'

The Global Warming Policy Foundation made an immediate impact. In just the first four months of its existence, from September 2009, its leaders Lord Lawson and Dr Peiser were quoted more than eighty times in newspapers, and, in stark contrast to its persistent complaint that it is censored, much more since. It makes for lively debate, but it hardly reflects the balance of views in the scientific community. The message of the GWPF is a simple one: that because of the uncertainties of climate science we have no compelling reasons to reduce our dependence on fossil fuels. An obvious response is that waiting until we are certain may well mean we are too late to do anything about it. But there are some serious and respected scientists who hold this view too, or variations of it. And some of the activities of the GWPF have even been praised by scientists who are strong advocates of action on global warming themselves. For example, Professor Piers Forster from Leeds University has noted that 'climate sceptics such as the Global Warming Policy Foundation have really focused our attention to understand part of the climate problem we had poor understanding of. This is a good thing and it will make our science more robust.' But then he added, 'What I don't like about the Global Warming Policy Foundation is that they try to use uncertainty in science to destabilise the policy debate.'

Eventually, following complaints about misinformation and lack of balance, the Charity Commissioners stepped in on the grounds that 'some of the Global Warming Policy Foundation's activities breached what is expected of an educational charity, namely that the material lacked balance and promoted a particular line of opinion'. So the GWPF will now be split into an educational charity and a political campaigning wing but has vowed to fight on, as it will no doubt continue to do forcefully, being supported by anonymous sponsors with deep pockets and undeclared interests. All this lobbying and the miles of column inches devoted to 'disproving' global warming does seem to be having an impact on public opinion. UK Energy Research Centre reports that in its polls the percentage of UK respondents who think the world's climate is changing fell from 91 per cent in 2005 to 72 per cent in 2013.[3]

'Climategate'

Climate doubters made much of, and probably made in the first place, 'Climategate'. Climategate, as it was dubbed by the media, was a highly publicised episode in 2009 in which more than 1,000 emails and 3,000 other documents belonging to climate change scientists at the University of East Anglia (UEA) were hacked into – by whom, we can only speculate. This booty was then used to claim that UEA scientists had been cooking the books to produce false evidence for global warming. Lord Lawson was quick to wade in indignantly: 'The integrity of the scientific evidence … has been called into question. And the reputation of British science has been seriously tarnished. A high-level independent inquiry must be set up without delay.' Again, far from the suppression of their voices, as is so often claimed by the doubters, the media had a field day with this story.

By contrast, what was later hardly reported on was that no fewer than nine audits had subsequently crawled all over the UEA evidence. Their conclusions were clear: UEA's science was fundamentally sound, the hacked emails had been very cherry-picked and their interpretation twisted and taken completely out of context so as to give a false impression that the science had been concocted. For example, the report of an Independent Science Assessment Panel, published in April 2010, concluded that it had seen 'no evidence of any deliberate scientific malpractice in any of the work of the UEA Climatic Research Unit'. Its work had been 'carried out with integrity' and had used 'fair and satisfactory' methods with 'no hint of tailoring results to a particular agenda'. Former Republican House Science Committee chairman Sherwood Boehlert condemned Climategate as a 'manufactured distraction', and as 'highly orchestrated'. From all this scrutiny there were, however, criticisms of the scientists' loose banter and one scientist was criticised for being too reluctant to release his data. He explained it as due to weariness at being constantly harassed by requests for his data by those whose only motive was to attack the science in spurious or biased ways, or simply to bog him down with requests to prevent him from getting on with it. In this respect he did fall short of scientific standards, for which he apologised, and released all his data, none of which disproved his previous scientific conclusions.

A fundamental problem with the conspiratorial scientific hoax claim is that it would require that thousands of mostly mild-mannered scientists from across the world, respectable in all other walks of life and with brains enough to work in any other field of science they choose, and whose modest professional incomes could be completely transformed through whistle-blowing, have somehow operated a vast clandestine global network with vice-like control over science that has yet to be discovered by the world's frenetically probing journalists and the vastly resourced industrial interests who actively and purposely sponsor anti-environmentalist organisations.

Bad science

Given the incredulity of their conspiracy theory, which does not prevent them from repeatedly asserting it, many global warming 'non-scientists' do have a go at taking the science apart themselves. So, ignoring the plain silly objectors who think that global warming implies that each year will be hotter than the previous (remember, just a slight increase in the average is likely to increase volatility), doubters make much of anything they hope could be construed as contrary evidence. They call on things like the probably true fact that many, many, millions of years ago the Earth's atmosphere had more CO_2 in it but the Earth was cooler than it is now. Or they assert that because CO_2 emissions have risen but for the last fifteen years average atmospheric temperature has not (but see below), anthropogenic warming can't be true. The problem with this approach is that it implies that the genuine scientists are blissfully unaware of all this supposedly contrary evidence themselves – but it is their job to know all about it and to take it all into account! Even when they do take it into account, and some are too slow to do this, they still come out from their consideration of it with the conclusion that climate change is real, costly and dangerous, and mostly anthropogenic.

So why isn't 'higher CO_2 yet a cooler earth in the past' conclusive evidence? Well, as climate change doubters are so fond of pointing out, CO_2 is not the only factor that affects the temperature of our planet. For example, the sun does not emit a completely constant temperature and there are other GHGs to consider as well as a host of other climate factors. In statistician's language, climate change is a multi-variate and multi-causal phenomenon. CO_2 concentrations change over long periods because of natural processes, for example volcanic activity, but just because 500 million years ago there was more CO_2 in the atmosphere and the Earth was cooler it does not follow that the scientists must be wrong about GHGs and global warming. Looking at all the evidence together, the scientists conclude that the other factors were acting to cool the Earth in that age so long ago, compared to what would be the case today. In short, CO_2 now and ancient CO_2 is not a like-to-like comparison. If we had the same level of CO_2 today we would be in very serious trouble. The problem is that anthropogenic CO_2 – and they can identity which is and isn't anthropogenic by their isotopic signatures – has been tipping the natural balance in the direction of net accumulation in CO_2 concentrations. Today, the other factors are likely to combine to exacerbate and not mitigate the effects of this.

The doubter's 'global warming has stopped' claim is also suspect. Skeptical Science[4] publishes two graphs of Earth's surface temperature. Their first graph shows how easy it is to draw lines showing long periods of no global warming, but their second graph leaves little doubt about the longer-term trend.

Surface temperature is greatly affected by movements in the atmosphere, and is probably increasingly so as trapped energy makes the atmosphere more volatile. This makes it a 'stochastic' variable. This means that temperatures will fluctuate greatly even when the overall direction is up. In short, looking only at short periods is unlikely to give a clear picture; the natural internal variability of the Earth's climate system is short-term noise that averages out to zero over long time frames. That said, some researchers who accept the consensus do acknowledge that such a long pause as fifteen years is more difficult to explain. Though it's worth noting that fourteen of the fifteen warmest years on record have all occurred in the twenty-first century and that 2014 looks as if it will be the warmest year ever recorded.[5] For a more consistent guide to the warming trend, look at something that is less stochastic because it is denser, like the sea. Then the long-term trend is even plainer to see:

FIGURE 18

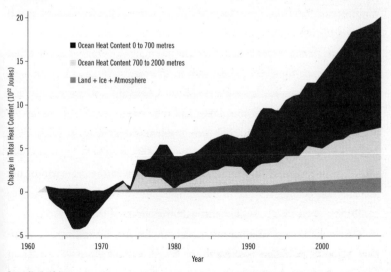

Source: Skeptical Science

There are lots of other arguments that doubters use, but all of these have been answered, or considered non-conclusive, by the scientists who make up the overwhelming scientific majority view that global warming is anthropogenic and very unwelcome.

Science is not 'unequivocal' – but then for economists that isn't a requirement

We should note here that there has been complaint, even from their own 'side', about climate scientists themselves being too ready to seize on supporting evidence for anthropogenic warming. For example, the UN's Intergovernmental Panel on Climate Change has over the years upped the level of rhetoric it uses. This has led it to use the word 'unequivocal'. This is unwise as it is a very common misunderstanding about science, even among many scientists, to think that something can be proved beyond any doubt, especially on something with so many variances and unknowns as climate change. That is why even the IPCC itself dares only to say that it is 95 per cent confident that humans are the main cause of current global warming. It is also right to point out that there are hundreds of reputable and well-qualified scientists, albeit a very small percentage of the total, who do contest the evidence on climate change. And although the percentage is small the list is long, 400 on a list published by the Republican Party.[6] Even Professor Robert Watson, who himself chaired the IPCC between 1997 and 2002 and is a prominent scientist warning of the dangers of global warming, has criticised the IPCC for not being open enough about its own, remarkably few, errors, and its complacency in addressing the contrary evidence.

Each camp has accused elements of the other of vilification and censorship. Both sides may have some justification for their claim, but we won't be looking any further into the science, as this is a book about economics. It's time to get back on to territory that the authors are more at home with, economics. Economists are very used to addressing risk; it's a large part of our trade. The insurance principle comes into play in economics: this means that for economists the relevant question is not 'Is anthropogenic global warming true?' but rather 'Is there a significant risk that it is true?' If there is, and if the consequences would be awful, then economists have no real option but to take climate change seriously and therefore to factor it into our advice to policy-makers. Put in stark everyday terms, few of us would step on to an aeroplane that even one scientist has warned is dangerous; no sane person would put all of our children on an aeroplane that over 90 per cent of the world's scientists say is dangerous!

That is not all that should be said about the insurance principle: it does not all go just the one way. As Lord Lawson has pointed out, it is possible to be *too* careful. It is also important to weigh the cost of insurance against the likely risks of climate change. If the costs of insurance outweigh the possible adverse consequences, then it may not be worth paying for the insurance. Clearly, we are now well and truly back into the domain of economics again. Unfortunately, the economics is less certain than the science.

Good economics is as important as the science

So having briefly looked, as amateurs, at the scientific and the non-scientific debate, let's now take the science as read. Hopefully the science is wrong, which seems highly unlikely, but accepting it allows us to move on and look more closely at the economics. A good starting point for this is again the eminent economist Lord Stern: 'The science tells us that GHG emissions are an externality: in other words, our emissions affect the lives of others. When people do not pay for the consequences of their actions we have market failure. This is the greatest market failure the world has seen.'[7] To understand the economic concept of externality it is useful to know that economists usually assume, with good reason, that when you personally incur the costs of your actions then you will take this into account in your decisions. So in a well-functioning market there is reason to suppose that you will consume more of something whenever the extra benefit to you is greater than the extra cost; if the cost goes up you will tend to consume less. If the benefit you enjoy from consuming extra falls as you consume more within a given time period, as is also usually assumed by economists, then there will come a point at which the extra benefit from extra consumption is no more than what it costs. This will then determine the amount that you will buy, and it produces a result that is very significant to economists in welfare terms: at the 'margin' – that is, for the last unit consumed – the marginal benefit from consumption will be just about equal to the extra cost, the marginal cost, incurred. So you will have consumed all those units with a marginal benefit higher than their marginal cost, as they provide you with a net addition to your welfare. You would stop short of consuming any units that would cost you more than the benefit they would provide to you, i.e. they have a net loss of welfare for you. In short, your free decisions will have led you to maximise your own welfare. Of course, this only works if you are fully aware of all the costs and benefits, and of the fact that you can choose so precisely across all the consumption opportunities open to you!

The vast majority of economists are very fond of markets because of these welfare-maximising attributes. But there are many things that can cause markets to fail to maximise welfare: lack of information is one, and externalities are another important one for environmental economists. An externality is the 'spill-over' effects you have on others. They can be positive, such as when you buy flowers for your front garden that bring unintended pleasure to passers-by, but the ones that matter for climate change are mostly negative ones. When firms produce, because we as consumers buy what they produce, they invariably create GHGs. Manufacturing is particularly energy intensive and therefore, unless it's done using renewable energy, it is also very CO_2 intensive. Incidentally, farming is not very green either. It uses many chemicals that have to be

produced in industrial processes and the tummies of cattle can also produce a prodigious amount of methane, which is also a significant GHG!
So vegetarianism is often advocated by those worried by the effects of tree
clearance and cow burps and farts on climate change.

The point is that when you buy your Big Mac you are probably not taking into account the cost in terms of global warming; only the price you
personally pay. If you had more information you might take into account
these bad effects, but even then you may well not factor in the bad effects
on other people – that's the externality bit. This will mean that you will
be maximising your welfare but decreasing the welfare of others. The
welfare of others is not factored into your decisions. If other people had
property rights over the bits of their life that you affect, then they could
charge you for the destruction you cause to 'their' bit of the atmosphere.
Then you would take the cost that they would charge you into account
in your decision making. It's obvious, though, that they don't even know
you or know when you are spoiling it, let alone the extent of the effect or
which bit of the climate is theirs. Theoretically, if we all did know such
effects and could enforce our climate property rights and charge others,
the externality would no longer be an externality; compensation could be
arranged. But that's obviously silly and not going to happen. Take even the
much simpler example of when there's a loud party next door: we know
whose noise is invading our property but we might well have a problem
asking our inconsiderate neighbour for monetary compensation. Hang-
ing around fast food stores to ask for compensation for global warming
is even less likely to work!

To maximise welfare for everybody together, the government has to step
in and take the place of the missing property rights. In effect, to ensure that
producers cannot use the environment as a free resource. Governments
might, for example, tax the polluter so that they will take their impact on
other people into account. The tax 'internalises the externality' so that the
gain in welfare from extra production is balanced by the wider environmental costs it imposes on society.

Why the economics is complicated

The science might be the relatively easy bit. Lord Keynes, arguably one of the greatest economists of all time, once told the following anecdote: 'Professor [Max] Planck, of Berlin, the famous originator of the Quantum Theory, once remarked to me that in early life he had thought of studying economics, but had found it too difficult.'[8]

Keynes was quick to point out that it was only the uncertainties of economics that had deterred the brilliant physicist Max Planck, who preferred the precision of physics. True to Planck's observation, in economics we immediately hit problems when attempting to attach actual values to green cost and benefits. You can expect that nebulous things like the environment are bound to be difficult to value, but we can't even be that precise on the cost of renewable fuels compared to fossil ones – or rather, different economists hotly dispute each other's valuations. All the questions that follow are even harder to answer. For starters:

What are the costs, if any, of green policies in terms of lost economic growth? Could green investments actually boost growth? What are the future benefits of green policies? Even if we can get a good handle on that, how do we place a value on distant benefits? If the effects are felt differently in different countries, do we, for example, use different values for impacts on rich and poor, as perhaps they use different values themselves? How do we balance the welfare interests of current and future generations? How do we weight various costs and benefits that will occur at different points in time? Why should we worry about future generations more than the poor whom we know are living on the world today? Will future generations be richer than us, maybe have longer lives, and if so shouldn't they be made to sacrifice some of their wealth for our benefit? What is the best way to charge for climate externalities so as to incentivise the reduction of GHG emissions? Are quotas and bans better than such pricing? Will we be able to rely on a future technological fix instead? How should we incentivise green innovations? Should we rely most on the private or the public sector for R&D? Is it better to try to stop anthropogenic global warming in its tracks, or to 'enjoy' more and learn to adapt to its consequences instead? Which green policies are most effective and how do we stop profiteers exploiting misinformation and fears by selling us ineffective technologies or milking money from misguided green policies in other ways? Should the rich countries pay more to tackle climate change than poorer countries, as they are better off from having emitted free of charge much of the past anthropogenic CO_2 that remains in the atmosphere and adds to warming today? And, apocalyptically, if it's all going to end so badly, shouldn't we be partying while we can?

It's great for economists that all these questions create so much work to keep them busy, but it also clear that, as usual, there is an awful lot of room for disagreement. That's a problem, because policy-makers like simple answers. They want one-handed economists, but many real-world problems simply are intrinsically 'on the one hand but then on the other' in nature. At least we can steer policy-makers away from some of the dafter non-economists who like to pose as gifted radical visionaries, such as those who call for 'prosperity without growth' regardless of the fact that we have no moral right to try to stop poorer countries growing their way out of poverty and no feasible powers to do so in any case. The growth-without-prosperity lobby does not seem to understand about stocks and flows either: the output of a nation that is measured by GDP is not a stock but a yearly flow, so stopping growth doesn't stop CO_2 emissions anyway, it just holds them at current levels and so still adds much more CO_2 to the amount already accumulated. To reduce CO_2 emissions through controlling output would require reversing growth, as happens in recessions, but unless there were radical changes in how society is organised, it would be with all the dislocation and misery that accompany economic depressions, and a political party promising permanent self-imposed economic depression is not much of a vote winner.

If there is difficulty in reaching a consensus on climate change, there is only a snowball in hell's chance of agreeing on a new social and economic order over the timespan needed to tackle climate change. No, the only feasible way forward at the moment is to decouple growth from carbon. Easy to say, but views on just how and when we do that differ greatly: it is disagreements on what we do about it, not on the science, that now define the debate on climate change.

The political economy of climate change

Economic policy is seldom, if ever, separate from politics, and the politics of climate change is particularly fraught. How do we incentivise internationally binding agreements when each country believes that it could be damaging its own national interest, that it will merely be 'pain for no gain' unless everyone else does it as well, and then each party would individually benefit if they renege and can get away with individually carrying on with business as usual? But we'll talk about Australia later. Economists understand well that 'altruistic' cooperation will be unstable if each country fears that other countries will ignore agreements or will cheat on them. Economists often use the example of the 'prisoners' dilemma' to illustrate this: two suspects are being interrogated separately by the police. The optimum strategy for the suspects is for both not to confess, but they are told that their own penalty will be light if they confess and the other does not, but more severe if they do not confess and the other one does. Each is now likely to confess as they reason that if the other doesn't confess they will get a lighter sentence by confessing and if the other does confess they will get a relatively lighter sentence by confessing too. Whatever the other suspect does, individually each suspect seems to gain from confessing. Clearly, in such situations cooperation is likely to break down. So it is really quite impressive that achievements have been made in reaching international agreements at all, but there have also been serious fractures in international cooperation that have severely weakened the resolve to conform to them.

For example, the Kyoto Protocol began in 1997 in Kyoto, Japan under the United Nations Framework Convention on Climate Change (UNF-CCC); it was the world's first international agreement to tackle climate change by setting actual targets for GHG emissions. It was ratified by almost 200 countries and came into 'force' in 2005. The countries that were party to it agreed to reduce their greenhouse gas emissions by an average of 5.2 per cent. An immediate fracture in the negotiations was over whether poor countries should have to pay as much as rich countries. It was strongly argued by some developing countries that the rich countries should pay more as they had already benefited from their previous development, which had loaded the atmosphere with GHG at no cost. In recognition of this argument, some countries, including China and India, were exempted from the Kyoto targets because they were not the main contributors to accumulated CO_2 during the period of industrialisation. In protest, the United States and Australia promptly walked out.

Even the rich countries that remained in noted that the Kyoto agreement only applied to a small share of annual global emissions. This was then used as an excuse by some of them, including Japan, to refuse to accept further Kyoto commitments. In 2011 Canada pulled out, the Canadian Environment Minister explaining that 'the Kyoto protocol does not cover the world's largest two emitters, the United States and China, and therefore cannot work'. Significantly, he also added:

> To meet the targets under Kyoto for 2012 would be the equivalent of either removing every car, truck, ATV, tractor, ambulance, police car and vehicle of every kind from Canadian roads or closing down the entire farming and agriculture sector and cutting heat to every home, office, hospital, factory and building in Canada.

Revealing where his true interest lay, he added, '[Withdrawing] allows us to continue to create jobs and growth in Canada.'

The Kyoto Protocol is now limited to just 15 per cent of global GHG emissions, due to the lack of participation by the United States, Japan, Russia, Canada, Belarus, Ukraine and New Zealand, and due to the fact that developing countries like China (now the world's largest emitter of GHG), India and Brazil are not subject to any emissions reductions. So the hopes of the UN Framework have now shifted to agreements made at Durban and Doha in 2011/12. However, these effectively stall any binding targets until 2020, but for the first time in the UN Framework's history they now contain the – perhaps wildly optimistic – principle that richer nations could be financially responsible to other nations for their failure to reduce carbon emissions. In 2014, Australia, the rich world's biggest emitter of GHGs per head of population, showed what its Senate thinks of green policies by repealing the carbon tax previously levied on their biggest polluters. The justification given by the Australian Prime Minister was to build 'a strong and prosperous economy for a safe and secure Australia'.

In short, when economic interest clashes with climate concerns, economics has a habit of coming out on top, so getting all the world's ducks in a row ain't gonna be easy!

If I ruled the world … I wouldn't have a clue what to do!

Given that we have accepted the science, what should we be doing, assuming we had the power to do it? As you might suspect, different economists have different views. Lord Stern was very clear in setting the direction of his recommendations:

> The evidence shows that ignoring climate change will eventually damage economic growth. Our actions over the coming few decades could create risks of major disruption to economic and social activity, later in this century and in the next, on a scale similar to those associated with the great wars and the economic depression of the first half of the twentieth century. And it will be difficult or impossible to reverse these changes.

> Tackling climate change is the pro-growth strategy for the longer term,
> and it can be done in a way that does not cap the aspirations for growth
> of rich or poor countries. The earlier effective action is taken, the less
> costly it will be.[9]

More specifically, his review warned that ignoring climate change could reduce global GDP by 20 per cent by the end of the century, and that to avoid this risk the world should spend 1 per cent of global GDP a year on reducing GHG emissions, starting immediately. As we noted above, Stern was influential in the passage of the climate legislation in 2008. Asked what he thought of government action since his review, Lord Stern again praised Labour's 2008 Climate Change Act. But he criticised the coalition's record on emissions, in particular Chancellor George Osborne's attempts to overrule the Lib Dem Energy Minister Ed Davey on a decarbonisation clause Osborne had previously supported. In February 2013, Osborne blocked an obligation for Britain's electricity supply to become almost entirely decarbonised by 2030: this was even more significant as Britain's legally binding 2008 commitment to cut by 80 per cent by 2050 was predicated on decarbonising the power sector first. It is a vital measure given that so much fossil fuel replacement, e.g. in transport, will involve a further huge switch to electricity.

If Stern is wrong about the large costs of doing nothing and the relatively small costs of doing something, and if the currently available technology cannot prevent much higher energy costs at the moment, then it might be sensible just to wait until the technology makes renewable energy cheaper. What is more, the start of the decline in the oil price in mid-2014 which fell below $70 a barrel in late autumn changed the relative attractiveness of pursuing more expensive renewable sources of energy which are already costing both the consumer and industry a lot more through extra subsidies. With a carbon price floor, renewable obligations and now 'contracts for difference', the way in which nuclear will be paid for would be expected to be on an upward trend in line with energy wholesale prices; the costs to the consumer, whether individuals or companies, would be going up, while our competitors, including the US, which is benefiting from shale gas, would be enjoying a price bonanza. And the worry is that the technology we are investing in may indeed prove obsolete pretty quickly if new technological innovations occur – and then we will be locked in even more uncompetitive energy for considerably longer.

On the other hand, if the science is right, delaying makes the future worse and so we will need an even more effective technological fix. But the real rub might be that appearing to wobble on emissions targets is probably the worst thing that can be done to encourage green innovation. The threat of increasingly binding emissions works most powerfully not in current substitutions for fossil fuel but in incentivising private capital to invest in green technology innovation. They make firms fear that they might be left fossil dependent in a future that would make that an uncompetitive thing to be. But the threat/incentive is only credible if governments don't wobble: if the emissions targets are likely to be reneged on, then the alternative threat is to have sunk a load of money into new technology that nobody wants. Question marks about whether governments will honour their targets, and the open secret of ding-dongs between HM Treasury and the Department of Energy and Climate Change (DECC), act as a significant deterrent to investment in clean energy. That is not a good thing if what we need for a technological fix is the equivalent of a privately financed Manhattan Project.

More than one math

The conclusion that it's cheaper to act now rather than later is not a simple calculation. Even if the costs and benefits were known with certainty, which they certainly are not, linking them through time and adding them up to see if the costs avoided in the future outweigh the costs now depends on a host of contested positions. Economists almost always 'discount' the future; this means that mathematically the future is weighted less than the present. We can justify this in terms of time preference – 'I'd rather have things today than wait for tomorrow for them' – and then there's the risk: 'I may not even be alive tomorrow, I want a rate of return that compensates me for forgoing alternative forms of investment – maybe I can invest more profitably and use part of the money to compensate myself for environmental loss?' Besides that, there's the consideration that future generations may be richer than we are – so they should be sacrificing for us! The higher the discount rate, the more we discount the future: that is, the less important it becomes relative to the present. So if the benefits are tomorrow and the costs today, then the higher the discount rate used to weight these costs and benefits together through time, the smaller the benefits become compared to the costs. The discount rate used has a very big effect on this calculation as it is magnified through time in the same way that compound interest builds up so rapidly. As the effects of climate change are very long-lasting, this is important. For example, if a 10 per cent discount rate were used then benefits in thirty years' time would only be worth 0.0573 of what they are valued as today, i.e. less than 6 per cent of current value.

Her Majesty's Treasury's official guidance for government financed projects, known as the 'Green Book' (though the naming of it had nothing to do with environmental concerns), is to use a discount rate of 3.5 per cent. Even at this seemingly modest rate, benefits in thirty years' time are only worth about a third of what they are worth today, and become much less if taken beyond thirty years. At that rate, even complete disaster for the human species within a hundred years can become a trivial matter for us now! Nick Stern considered the low values placed on the future by using 3.5 to be, in effect, an unethical disregard for the welfare of future generations. He accepted that such a discount rate may be appropriate for projects over our own lifetimes, but considered it inappropriate for intergenerational timespans. Not only does such a discount rate value people today more than people tomorrow, but it ignores the risk of a real catas-trophe if things get much worse than expected. For example, if global warming sets off positive feedbacks such as Siberian permafrost melting, thereby releasing masses of methane and causing runaway global warm-ing that turns the Earth into another uninhabitable Venus. So to make the future matter more today, even over long time periods, Nick Stern used the lower discount rate of only 1.4 per cent. This did make allow-ance for risk and for incomes growing through time, so it was not zero, but it also incorporated the ethical judgement that a life is a life, whether it is in America or Africa, now or in 100 years' time, and that bit of the discount rate was zero.

Many economists thought that Stern's choice of discount rate was far too low. It means that effects over hundreds of years are considered as rel-evant today. But how can we know what technologies will be available then? What we are investing – and paying dearly for now – may be irrel-evant and useless by then. And if incomes continue to grow, won't people by then be fabulously rich compared to us and so isn't it actually egalitar-ian for us to enjoy higher living standards now at their expense? Of course, as is to be expected, Lord Lawson's GWPF makes much of the views of those who disagree with Stern's judgements. GWPF gave high profile to the criticisms made by Peter Lilley, a Conservative MP who, to be fair, has a Cambridge degree in economics and physics, but no expertise that even approaches Lord Stern's – or that of the rest of experts at the Gran-tham Institute, which researches climate change and is chaired by Lord Stern at the London School of Economics and Leeds University. This dis-parity in expertise was a point emphasised in the Institute's 2013 letter in response to Peter Lilley. Lilley had argued that people in the future would be much better off so we have no need to sacrifice anything now for them; it would be sacrificing today's poor for tomorrow's rich: 'Why should we try to make those people who will be seven times better off ten times bet-ter off – at the expense of stopping poor people today from enjoying the benefits of coal and gas?'

The letter of response from Bob Ward, policy and communications director at the Institute, made it clear he is not a man to entertain fools:

> I am somewhat puzzled about why you remain so confused about the economics of climate change, and indeed your response merely repeats the basic errors that featured in your pamphlet for the Global Warming Policy Foundation and in your recent statements in the House of Commons. I will do my best to address your main mistakes (again), but I also honestly encourage you to seek tuition on modern public economics to help you grasp these issues.[10]

Bob Ward's letter explains in particular that they were not impressed by Peter Lilley's grasp of the principles of discounting: 'Your claim seems to depend entirely on the circular logic of your assumption that future generations would automatically be "many times better off than us", no matter what damage is caused by unmitigated climate change.'

In other words, the growth paths Lilley had seized on are used for constructing comparisons only. The 'balanced growth' approach used, and jointly developed by Stern as a substantial contribution to economics, is not a literal description. Amateurs treating them as if they were infallible forecasts simply confirm that they are indeed just amateurs.

Nevertheless, as we might expect, Lilley's 'criticisms' were, and still are, presented by GWPF as if they are definitive and unanswerable, as if they had caught Lord Stern out. In January 2014 GWPF again cited Peter Lilley's mocking line of 'Why should we sacrifice 10 per cent of our income today to make Bill Gates better off?', without including the Grantham reply but including a link to an article that curiously stated that at the time of the Stern Review, in 2006, Lord Stern was then just 'plain Nick Stern'. This rather makes light of Nick Stern's knighthood, given in 2004 in recognition for his seminal contributions to economics, including on discounting, much of this work being done with James Mirrlees, who was awarded the Nobel Memorial Prize for Economics in 1996.

There still remain, though, some very serious and credible critics of Stern's choice of discount rate. For example, the economist William Nordhaus:

> The review proposes using a social discount rate that is essentially zero. Combined with other assumptions, this magnifies enormously impacts in the distant future and rationalises deep cuts in emissions, and indeed in all consumption, today. If we were to substitute more conventional discount rates used in other global warming analyses, by governments, by consumers, or by businesses, the review's dramatic results would disappear...
>
> Suppose that scientists discover that a wrinkle in the climatic system will cause damages equal to 0.01 per cent of output starting in 2200 and continuing at that rate thereafter. How large a one-time investment would be justified today to remove the wrinkle starting after two centuries? The answer is that a payment of 15 per cent of world consumption today (approximately $7 trillion) would pass the review's cost–benefit test. This seems completely absurd. The bizarre result arises because the value of the future consumption stream is so high with near-zero discounting that we would trade off a large fraction of today's income to increase a far-future income stream by a very tiny fraction.

This is not a stupid or uninformed point to make at all, but the example is rather constructed to produce an absurd-sounding result. The discount rate has to allow for changes much sooner than 200 years from now, but to do that it has to be a rate that then means it can be used to extrapolate even further through time. If we go too far down the route that people in the future will be better off, and so they owe us as their poor relations, then we should cut back on most long-term investments. The Hadron collider would certainly fail standard investment discount rate tests! Again, Stern says the Treasury's rate of 3.5 per cent is fine for marginal changes over short time periods, such as in assessing the costs and benefits of building a bridge, but not for globally scaled, long-term and potentially irreversible changes such as those associated with climate change. We should also consider that those who will be most impacted by climate change will not necessarily be the beneficiaries of ignoring it for a while yet; this is particularly so as it is the people in poorer countries who are likely to suffer first.

An alternative approach would be to vary the rate of the discount over time, and it is often ignored that the Stern Review does include much modelling based on varying the discount rate through time. The review is explicit that the appropriate discount rate is dependent on changes in the state of the world – for example, by allowing for different rates of economic growth and taking into account the uncertainties across 1,000 runs of modelling. Using varied discount rates is technically the right approach, but rather than clarify things for the debate it simply opens a whole new can of worms that economists can argue over for the next 300 years!

In short, if the discount is high it gives the impression that we don't care enough about people in the future, but if it is too low it seems we care too much about them and are depriving ourselves. So most economists now accept that there is no single universal discount rate that is appropriate for all purposes. That is not surprising really: an appraisal of the future of many generations to come, and the condition of the Earth that we leave to them, is hardly likely to be identical in its considerations to the prospect of investing in a new road to be completed in only, say, eight years' time. The truth is that there can be no definitive answer as to what rate should be used for inter-generational discounting. Whatever the rate used, *reductio ad absurdum* arguments can be constructed to make it look silly. But while there is no correct answer, it turns out, because of the intricacies of discounting and uncertainty, which can be very intricate indeed, that when risks and uncertainty are allowed for the overall difference between Stern and his critics is not so great after all. A range of 0 to 2 per cent just about covers all the different opinions, and is not so far from Stern's discount rate anyway.

Even if the details of the discount rate turn out not to be as crucial as people thought at the time of the Stern Review, there were many other controversial assumptions and judgements that Stern had to make in order to produce an estimate of the benefit to cost ratio of cutting GHG emissions in the way he recommended. It is not true that he fiddled the figures in any way, or that he is incompetent, as is mischievously implied by the GWPF, just that you can't produce specific numbers unless you make a lot of judgements that reasonable others, and some unreasonable others, can then disagree with.[11] As the IPCC recently concluded:

> Global economic impacts from climate change are difficult to estimate. Economic impact estimates completed over the past twenty years vary in their coverage of subsets of economic sectors and depend on a large number of assumptions, many of which are disputable, and many estimates do not account for catastrophic changes, tipping points, and many other factors.[12]

The point of our going through some of these technical arguments has been to show that the Stern Review has not been 'discredited' and is certainly not 'fraudulent' as was claimed by Lord Lawson. As with most criticisms of the methodology of the IPCC as well, most of the so-called errors are no more substantiated than asserting that it is correct to like wine rather than beer.

All this confusing difficult technical stuff does suggest a possibly telling criticism of the Stern Review. Perhaps it is just too clever by half. Nick Stern considered that the best way to communicate with those he has to influence, especially corporate America, was to use the language of business. So he produced, in effect, a very detailed business case. To do this he inevitably needed to use a lot of numbers, even to produce his very simple, bottom-line message that it is cheaper to act now rather than leave it to later. But using such a technical approach might, with hindsight, have been unnecessarily sticking his chin out for fellow economists, and others who just hate any constraints on markets, to take swipes at. Given Stern's vast expertise he would have known that there was bound to be carping, but perhaps he felt that having been commissioned to write the review by no less than both the Prime Minister and the Chancellor of the Exchequer, he had to do a detailed and rigorous job. At the end of the day, as Stern himself frequently emphasises, the most compelling arguments for action probably do not lie in the details and intricacies of the maths or the many assumptions needed, but simply in the knowledge that the science strongly suggests there are very grave risks from continuing to pour GHGs into our planet's atmosphere. Uncertainty, equity and our responsibility for future generations are probably the most compelling reasons to do something about it.

In the name of green, what are you doing?

Just as vested interests campaign against green policies, it would be amazing if there were not also vested interests cashing in, or people carving out little empires for themselves, from exploiting green concerns. If a stranger knocks on your door offering to sell you plug-in energy-saving devices you would be truly green to buy one simply because you wish to be green. Apart from deliberate green scams, some deep greens simply let their hearts rule their heads and so some really stupid things are done in the name of green. One such folly did for poor Archie Wellbelove, an eighteen-year-old student run over by a taxi on the A452 near Leamington in the early hours of 7 December 2013. The coroner concluded that the switching off of streetlights was a contributing factor in his death, and the ambulance service couldn't even find his body until the lights were turned back on. There have been increasing reports of extra accidents in areas where the lights now go out after midnight, including on motorways. The law of unintended consequences is one the economists recite again and again but politicians – and some bureaucrats – have difficulty understanding what we mean.

The EU is especially adept at getting its green knickers in a twist. Its supposed green jewel in the crown for reducing carbon emissions is the European (Carbon) Trading Scheme (ETS), introduced in 2005. This is by far the biggest international system for trading greenhouse gas emission credits, covering more than 11,000 power stations and industrial plants across thirty-one countries, as well as their airlines. The ETS is a 'cap and trade' system whereby a limit, the 'cap', is set on the total amount of greenhouse gas emissions, measured in terms of their carbon equivalences. Companies are then given a yearly allowance to emit carbon in the form of credits for units of these allowances, e.g. tonnes of carbon emissions. Crucially, they can also buy and sell these 'carbon credits' permits. The total amount of these permits adds up to the overall cap, so that lowering the cap should lower total emissions. The carbon credits are tradable with all the other emitters covered by the scheme, the 'trade' part. The more binding is the cap the more expensive the credits become.

The economics of the ETS is impeccable. A simple quota system would not provide the same incentives for carbon reduction. For example, a firm might produce up to its quota and that would be it, but under the ETS it would always have an incentive to cut its emissions further when it is profitable to sell the credits freed. So where it is cheap to cut emissions that will be done and innovations will also be pursued in order to free up more of its allowance for profitable sale. In short, the ETS makes cutting emissions profitable. But critics say that, like other grand schemes based on only bare economic principles, such as Gordon Brown's beloved tax credits, it is intellectually pleasing but just doesn't work in practice.

The ETS has been in trouble since its launch. Its weakness is that it tends to obscure the direct link between intervention and emission control, giving politics more leeway to tamper with it. And besides this, it could only work as planned if the cap is based on accurate predictions of potential future emissions, which, like most economic forecasts, isn't a precise science. For example, in 2008, the recession and overly generous carbon allowances undercut the market. Prices fell from €25 a ton to just

€5 a ton. At this price, the all-important incentives just fade away. This might have been fixed by removing carbon allowances from the market and reintroducing them later when it is hoped demand would be greater. Economics is clear that this 'back-loading' would raise the price of carbon permits again, but economics does not turn into policy in a political vacuum. In addition, adding an EU renewable obligation in terms of the amount of energy that had to be sourced from low-carbon sources brought down current and expected emissions via a different route and the price of carbon permits collapsed again. Overlapping policies are never a good idea as they can outdo each other in effectiveness.

Members of the European Parliament had no wish to be seen to be adding to Europe's already considerable economic worries, or to further a loss of international competitiveness when Europe's energy costs were already relatively high compared with its competitors. When a scheme throws up lots of political decision points, as the cap does when it has to be set each year, it increases the opportunities for economic concerns to trump green ones. That is what happened when the back-loading proposal was voted down. Such outcomes are sometimes called the 'iron law of climate policy':[13] when climate policy starts to hurt economically, even the greenest states start to back away. The European carbon market collapsed, with the price of a carbon permit immediately falling by more than 40 per cent, rendering the ETS an ineffective and elaborate mess. ETS has been a victim of its own complexity and of sluggish economic growth opening it up to politics. Perhaps a straightforward carbon tax, at a rate set once and for a long period, would have been better after all. Indeed, even some greens hope that ETS will be replaced by things that might be more effective, such as R&D subsidies to encourage green innovation.

Political embarrassment over the ETS had another unanticipated side effect: it has stymied EU Commissioners' talk on setting targets for energy saving, that is, for not wasting so much of the energy that we do produce. In fact, insulation is by far the most cost-effective measure for cutting carbon and can make major contributions to meeting emissions targets. But its very success in bringing down emissions could again affect the price of the ETS carbon permits, so many EU Commissioners are now worried that greater efficiency in energy use would impact adversely on the workings of the EU's ETS green flagship. 'It's a very strange debate,' said Brook Riley of Friends of the Earth. 'They are forced to limit energy savings and renewables to avoid damaging the emissions trading system … They are actually talking about burning more coal if emissions fall faster than expected due to energy savings and renewables, purely to protect the carbon price. It's bonkers!'

Back home, the UK's expensively planned and implemented Green Deal has so far been a stupendous flop. The then Energy Secretary unveiled his brainchild in January 2013: it was to be a 'Green Revolution' for our homes, and when it had demonstrated its success in our houses, it would be rolled out to business premises too. In the event, it is not yet even out of the starting gate. In the name of green, an overly complex and expensive scheme had gained sufficient political support to pass through a distracted government. The Green Deal is meant to work by lending money to householders so they can improve the energy efficiency of their homes through insulation, boiler upgrades and double glazing. Its 'golden rule' is that energy savings each year must at least cover the costs of the equipment and the loan necessary to finance it, so overall the householder should gain from the start. To work all this out, of course, requires kite-marked 'Green Deal Assessors' to make forecast estimates of savings and to update energy performance certificates, and the deal then has to be authorised by 'Green Deal Providers', who arrange funding from Green Deal Finance and liaise with householders, energy databases, assessors and installers. There are complicated arrangements, through yet more third parties, that take the savings directly from your energy bill, so you can't dodge it, or the next householder either, if you move before the loan is paid off. All this has to be set up through complex bureaucratic paraphernalia, such as vast regulations books to support the 'Green Code', with each middle man taking his cut before you even get to the certified 'Green Deal Installers' who might actually install something in your house.

By mid-2014 the government's own figures showed just 2,439 Green Deal plans in place or pending,[14] far short of the Department of Energy and Climate Change's target of 10,000 by the end of 2013. Most of these might have happened anyway under existing plans for subsidies, indeed by replacing previously successful subsidy schemes it seems to have been a green counter-revolution! Cavity wall insulation and loft insulation are falling off a cliff, down 60–90 per cent. It's not just the daunting complexity; the finances never really stacked up. Together with all the arrangement fees, the interest being paid on the loans comes in at more than most householders would pay for a loan elsewhere anyway. To try to breathe life into this critically ill infant, the government is now combining it with revived traditional subsidies, which could have been done far more directly anyway. The numbers are reportedly going up but it is too early to know if the Green Deal, in its altered form, can be a success. However, what this sad episode highlights is the danger that ill-thought-out schemes which have not gone through thorough cost–benefit analysis by the government department that introduces them can really have completely negative impacts and in this case discredit the whole green initiative.

We could go on – there are many more examples, such as large green subsidies to wood-powered power stations that turn out to be even dirtier than the fossil fuel they replaced, or simply muddled people who drive their car to recycle a few bits and bobs. Part of the role of economists is to warn government and others of the pitfalls of acting only on good intentions, or, for those who know better, electoral gimmicks. It is simply crass stupidity to support everything that calls itself green regardless of its likely impact. If a measure requires a huge subsidy and is still uncompetitive, if it is over-complicated or does not help reduce emissions elsewhere, then it just might be the wrong thing to do. But being daft didn't start with madcap green schemes. The world is already spending half a trillion dollars on fossil fuel subsidies every year, largely only because of distortions insisted on by powerful vested interests. The Overseas Development Institute estimates that rich countries are spending seven times more supporting coal, oil and gas than they are on helping poorer nations fight climate change. That said, many businesses have understandable concerns about the extra added to energy costs by renewable fuels. Even in Germany, that major economy leader of the green pack, concerns are growing rapidly about uncompetitive fuel costs imposed as 'Energiewende' gives them the highest energy cost in the rich world.

Many politicians and businesses have expressed their concerns about the Fourth Carbon Budget agreed by the UK Parliament in June 2011, following the recommendation of the independent Committee on Climate Change (CCC) that UK annual emissions should be 50 per cent lower in 2025 compared with 1990, in order to be on track for 80 per cent by 2050. Provisional estimates do suggest that UK annual emissions of greenhouse gases in 2013 were 26.7 per cent lower than in 1990, but this includes the effect of recession, and so the CCC judges that the rate of emissions reduction is not consistent with achieving the Fourth Carbon Budget's target.

The *Economist* magazine sees the high cost of renewable generators as an obstacle to tackling climate change, even when governments dig deep to fund them.[15] The worry is that sharp rises in energy prices will drive manufacturers to set up in less green countries. That could mean that the UK loses out economically but UK consumers end up consuming even more carbon through imports from less stringent countries. *The Economist* sees the main effects of high renewable and carbon pricing as simply spurring a growing interest in even more controversial alternatives. For example, the price of nuclear power has been rising for decades, but it still costs less than many types of renewables.

In economics it is often the case, however, that things that seem obvious turn out not to be so. Some research, by Bassi and Zenghelis from the pro-green Grantham Institute, looked at a number of previous studies that had suggested that climate change policies could, in theory, lead to a small number of companies relocating from the UK to countries with less stringent policies on reducing emissions. They found that recent studies documenting the actual impacts of climate change policies show that any increase in energy costs due to carbon pricing could not have been high enough to cause any detectable relocation by companies from the UK.

Their conclusion is that green policies are not harming UK economic growth overall, but that some temporary help may be needed for smaller companies to make the transition to decarbonised energy. This they see, in line with the Grantham Institute, as a small price to pay for the advantage of positioning the UK for greater long-run international competitiveness as a low-carbon producer with cheaper renewables when the price of fossil fuels will be rising. A problem with that prediction is that fossil fuels have a habit of defying price increase expectations as new reserves and technologies of extraction appear.

Fracking marvellous?

Meanwhile gas-fired power stations are roughly half as polluting as coal-fired ones, so perhaps they could help fill the gap between phasing out more carbon intensive generators and innovations that will hopefully create more cost competitive renewable energy. Not enough of them are being built as operators argue that the current profitability of gas plants is low and there is uncertainty about future profitability. There have also been concerns about the operation of the government's strategy in reforming the electricity market and the extent to which gas will play a role in the move to low-carbon energy, so progress has been slow. And yet as the Department of Energy and Climate Change itself acknowledges, Modelling by DECC suggests that 'up to 26 GW of new gas plant could be required by 2030 (in part to replace older coal, gas and nuclear plant as it retires from the system).'[16]

The danger with this is that investing in such expensive and long-lived capital might just lock in UK dependence on this type of fossil fuel instead.

George Osborne may see this as an advantage given his enthusiasm for 'fracking' in the UK.

Fracking, as you no doubt are already aware given its media coverage, is the hydraulic fracturing of rocks to release oil and gas from shale by blasting a mixture of sand, water and chemicals into underground rock. It has been linked to a series of environmental problems such as earthquakes and water pollution, though the inevitability and extent of these side effects is disputed. However, it is not clear that fracking in the UK will bring the benefits the Chancellor supposes in any case: fracking of shale gas in the US has had a large impact, reducing some energy costs by a game-changing two-thirds, but the relatively small volume of potential fracking in the UK probably won't have much effect. The reason is that the gas can be traded on the international market, so it is simply sold to the highest bidder wherever they are. This means that any shale gas boom in the UK would be unlikely to have an impact on the world price of energy, and so Lord Stern sees the Chancellor's optimism for a UK shale gas bonanza as 'baseless economics' and has criticised the government for encouraging a rush into fracking without a thorough analysis of all its potential ramifications for homes and the environment.

Are wind turbines just spin?

The UK has a target of generating 15 per cent of its energy from renewable resources by 2020. Mainly because of the increased investment in wind power, it is well on the way to achieving this. There are currently 4,240 individual wind turbines in the UK across 531 wind farms, generating 7.4 per cent of the nation's electricity and more than a quarter of the electricity produced by British renewables, enough to save 6 million tonnes of CO_2, according to government estimates. Wind power plays a key role in reducing GHGs created by the UK's power generation and meeting its legally binding carbon budgets.

As you will have seen from train windows, on a good day turbines harness the wind to generate electricity. The 'harnessing of the wind bit' is millennia old, and even the 'using it to generate electricity' part is probably older than you think, dating from an impressively massive windmill built in 1888 by Charles Brush of Cleveland, Ohio. The development of the much sleeker aerodynamic wind turbines we see today dates from the 1970s, when research on them was kick-started by the US government, working with industry. It will not surprise you to know that onshore wind turbines are on the land while offshore turbines tend to be located out at sea, or that the onshore ones are much cheaper to build and maintain. The pros and cons of onshore wind energy, not only as replacement for fossil fuel but also because of their visual impact, are much debated. More recently, the political parties have gone in different directions about onshore turbines, perhaps because Labour's townie voters aren't much troubled by wind turbines but those living in the Tory shires have to look at them. So while David Cameron has called for a cap on new turbines in favour of building them offshore, which we know is much more expensive and so less likely to actually happen, Ed Miliband has defended the need for wind turbines in rural areas.

As expected, researchers from the Grantham Institute have quite nice things to say about wind turbines. They report that they are one of the most affordable of renewable energy sources: 'Generating electricity from onshore wind turbines typically costs around 7–9p per kWh, which is around half the cost of offshore wind and a quarter of the costs of solar photovoltaic panels. It is also slightly cheaper, on average, than nuclear power.' Even they admit, however, that onshore wind generation is still more expensive than fossil fuels, the costs of which they put at between 4.1 and 7.5 p/kWh, but they are optimistic that this cost will fall. The wind turbine over fossil cost premium is, of course, disputed. The *Economist* magazine reports the estimate that British wind farm electricity costs twice as much as that from traditional sources. A lot depends on how one accounts for their large capital construction cost, and on estimates of how long they will last once constructed.

An obvious problem with wind turbines, or windmills as they are often called even though there are no longer mills beneath them, is that they are no good unless the wind blows. In Britain it very often does, but when it doesn't, back-up is needed, and at the moment that is usually fossil-based electricity generation. A duel generating infrastructure is obviously a very expensive thing to build. A wider distribution of wind turbines plugged in across the national grid would reduce the risk of there being no available wind anywhere, but on uniformly calm days the essential problem remains. It can be hoped that solar power could provide the back-up, as the sun is often shining when the wind isn't blowing, but the problem will only really be conquered when there is an effective and cheap method of power storage. We are not there yet, though other measures such as more linking up of power networks internationally may help in the interim.

As with the new windmills, there are economic and environmental trade-offs and uncertainty right across the spectrum of renewable energies. Many economists feel that as there is no single winner the best approach is a portfolio of different technologies so as to balance out the cost to consumers with environmental concerns. In which case, onshore wind would certainly be part of this energy mix in helping the UK achieve its emission reduction targets. Of course, if you think cutting GHG emissions is pointless then it follows that wind turbines are also pointless, until they can be so improved that they become cheaper than fossil fuels, and even then country folk might not like them. Recent research has suggested that they do last much longer than first thought – not ten years but twenty-five.[17] As the extra cost of wind power is in the construction, that could really help reduce the estimated cost of this type of renewable. Against that, they also catch on fire more often than was expected!

Fossils back from the dead?

Dieter Helm, Oxford University's strident commentator on energy, and DECC scientific advisory board panellist, casts doubt on the predictions of rising fossil energy prices that so many green economic arguments rely heavily on to sell them to hard-nosed decision makers. The new supplies of oil and gas from fracking have changed the picture in energy in the eyes of many policy-makers. Helm believes that the initial widespread green enthusiasm from governments, from the '90s onwards, has now given way to a 'new realism', one that recognises and takes on board that things will be changing much slower than previous emissions agreements had bargained for. Helm reckons that the huge reserves and cheapness of US shale gas have lessened the imperative for new energy-intensive investment, as it now seems that renewable sources are not going to be competitive against conventional fuels for a long time to come: 'The illusion that European leaders had a decade ago that fossil fuel prices would rise so high as to render the renewables competitive has been exposed.'

He argues that this has changed the 'terms of trade' in the renewable versus fossil contests, the result being that previous policy commitments were largely justified by wholly mistaken forecasts of future oil and gas prices rising steeply, and so are being reassessed by national policy-makers. He also notes that the Russian annexation of Crimea has reminded Europeans that energy security is not something that can be taken for granted. For Helm natural gas, as it is half as polluting as coal, and is available in such volumes, is the only realistic option to fill the gap before a commercial carbon-neutral alternative capable of meeting the world's growing energy demands is developed.

Helm's prognosis is gloomy for those who believe that continuing emissions, even with natural gas, are already sailing too close to the wind for the future of our climate. The politics hasn't been looking promising either: the first commitment period of the Kyoto Protocol has expired and it is now clear that even its modest commitments came virtually to nothing. Of the world's eight biggest national emitters of GHGs, responsible for more than 66 per cent of global emissions, only Germany (2.4 per cent of world GHGs) agreed to legally binding reductions in the second commitment period (2013–20), and now Merkel faces increasing domestic pressure to renege. To recap, Canada (1.7 per cent) withdrew from the protocol; the United States (16 per cent) wouldn't have anything to do with it; China (29 per cent), India (5.9 per cent), Russia (5.4 per cent), Japan (3.7 per cent) and South Korea (1.8 per cent) are still nominally signatories but then they don't have binding targets. The apparent successes of the first commitment period are small enough in themselves, but also most likely are entirely illusory, as Western Europe's 10 per cent reduction in emissions since 1990 is largely attributable to a decline in manufacturing. The rest can only be claimed by ignoring the growth of our imports from other countries such as China. A lot of the energy generated in China's coal-fired power stations, which burn nearly as much coal as the rest of the world, is used to manufacture things for export to the West. So we haven't cut our emissions; we've just outsourced them.

The IPCC is more certain than before but also more fatalistic

By contrast, the IPCC's latest report in 2014 was still in line with the thrust of the Stern Review. Its team leader, economist Professor Ottmar Edenhofer, asserted, sound-bite style, 'It doesn't cost the world to save the planet.' The report held that the cheapest and least risky route to dealing with global warming is simply to abandon *all* dirty fossil fuels over coming decades. Its 1,250 international experts pooh-poohed fears that slashing GHG emissions could wreck the world economy. It repeated that the evidence for anthropogenic global warming is overwhelming and poses a grave threat, one that could also lead to wars and mass migration. The Stern Review was attacked after it was published for having an unrealistically low estimated cost – just 1 per cent of GDP – to mitigate climate change. Stern later raised this to 2 per cent to allow for faster than predicted climate change, but far from raising the estimate of these costs the IPCC now concludes that diverting hundreds of billions of dollars from fossil fuels to renewable energy and conservation would only shave an amazingly small 0.06 per cent off the expected annual economic growth rates of 1.3 to 3 per cent. The EU Commissioner for Climate Change, Connie Hedegaard, summed up the IPCC report with the same comparison as used by Stern in 2006: 'The report is clear: the more you wait, the more it will cost [and] the more difficult it will become.' US Secretary of State John Kerry enthused, 'This report is a wake-up call about global economic opportunity we can seize today as we lead on climate change.' But there were also signs that the IPCC report also took on board Helm's thesis of a 'new realism'. There is, no doubt reluctantly, now much more focus on adaptation to climate change than can be found in all its previous reports.

A new green light for green policies?

In June 2004, for the first time, the US Environmental Protection Agency proposed limits on carbon emissions from US power plants that had been polluting for decades. The limits are set to reduce US power sector emissions by as much as 30 per cent by 2030. President Obama has simply given up trying to convince the Republicans to back him on climate change measures, they remain hostile to the very laws of physics, and so he has in effect appealed directly to voters. And the signs are they liked it: a Yale University Project on Climate Change Communication published the results of its survey on 'Politics and Global Warming', a survey of 860 registered voters. The strong partisan divide was still apparent, but 62 per cent of respondents were not content to have the US wait on the side lines unless and until other nations also commit to emissions reductions. The Obama administration has argued that the US has to exhibit leadership on emissions cuts and that the US's credibility at climate talks in 2015 in Paris rests on a demonstration of American commitment.

Climate change sceptics have long argued that anything the US does will not count for much if large polluters like India and China do not also take steps to curtail their carbon output. So Obama is also reaching out to them too. The United States and China have entered into a joint commitment to reduce their respective greenhouse gas emissions, even though China has again reiterated that it should not be subjected to the full implementation and extent of the rules as it is not responsible for much of the earlier GHGs. It is easy to be cynical, and there are no numbers yet. But despite being the world's biggest emitter China is clearly making efforts to tackle greenhouse gas emissions and to curb its choking air pollution. Even while it is building more coal-powered generators than the West can shake a stick at, China is also taking rapid action to reduce dependence on coal. Coal is now down to 65 per cent of China's energy mix, compared to 70 per cent in 2010, and the country has embarked on a massive investment programme for clean energy and energy efficiency. China is also planning its own version of a carbon cap-and-trade scheme; it is thought by some that its state machinery is better suited than European democracy to avoid the failures of ETS. And although China is the world's biggest emitter, it is also the world's largest investor in global clean energy.

Meanwhile George Osborne was forced by the Lib Dem coalition partners, Ed Davey in particular, to back down on his attempt to weaken measures to tackle global warming by tampering with the UK's Fourth Carbon Budget. The news delighted green campaigners but was less welcomed by business, particularly manufacturing groups such as the Engineering Employers Federation. Osborne wanted to alter the target to clear the way for up to forty new gas-fired power stations, on the basis of his by now familiar refrain that Britain should not be 'further ahead of our partners in Europe' when it came to green energy. Green hopes now rest on the next United Nations Climate Change Conference, to be held in Paris in 2015, and the agreement to be implemented, assuming there is something to implement, by 2020. The aim of the conference is, as ever, to achieve a legally binding and universal agreement on climate from all the nations of the world. Ironically, as the 2008 Great Recession demonstrated, a restoration of economic growth will make any targets harder to hit but more likely to be agreed upon as the pain of bearing down on carbon is lessened.

Conclusions

It clearly makes no sense for the world to subsidise fossil fuels at $600 billion a year, against subsidies of just $90 billion to clean energy, but buffoons, vested interests and those who simply find any constraints on free markets anathema get far more than their fair share of media attention. They are often well resourced, as those who care more about today's profits than future generations' welfare have deep pockets to sponsor spurious science and ridiculous claims of a mass conspiracy among scientists. But there is a very small of minority of genuine scientists who doubt anthropogenic climate change or at least the magnitude and speed of its effects. Given the track record so far of nations getting together to tackle climate change, we had better hope that these rebel scientists, against all the odds, are right. But if you want to see a bit more than finger-crossing as a precaution against what could be the global disaster to end all global disasters, be careful who you vote for. If in 2010 you voted 'blue to be green' then you should be purple with rage now.

All is not bleak for green policies. Even while many Republicans ignore the scientific consensus and persist in their attack on physics, US Democrats do seem determined to work with what is still probably the majority of US voters and to set an example on emissions. China, the world's worst offender on emissions, seems truly worried about climate change. Towards the end of 2014 prospects looked brighter for green commitments. In October 2014 European leaders boosted their resolve by striking a broad climate change pact obliging the EU as a whole to cut greenhouse gases by at least 40 per cent by 2030, admittedly about the minimum agreement they could have brokered but one that can be raised later. Meanwhile the IPCC has issued a new summary repeating its findings and again attracting significant support in high places and in mid-November 2014 China and the US unveiled new pledges on GHG emissions, when their leaders met for talks in Beijing. This could be a sea change in the fortunes of green issues. President Barack Obama described the move as 'historic', as he set a target of reducing US emissions by 26–28 per cent by 2025, compared with 2005 levels. China did not set a specific target, but announced that its emissions would peak by 2030. This is genuine progress: it is the first time China, the world's biggest polluter, has set an approximate date for emissions to peak.

A UK government with real commitment on GHGs going to Paris for the UN Climate Conference sessions in 2015 could help make a balance that shames those countries that pulled out of previous commitments on the excuse that not enough was happening. But there is a rather nasty potential economic sting in the tail for these green hopes. If meaningful international targets on climate change are convincingly committed to, up to 80 per cent of the world's vast quantities of fossil fuel reserves held as assets by publicly listed companies could become near worthless. As well as the existing assets of fossil fuel companies falling through the floor, all the already capitalised expected profits from the billions they have sunk into developing new sources will have been wasted. It is no wonder that these huge corporations fight so hard to avoid this. The sting for us all, though, is that such a massive collapse in asset values could conceivably even trigger a new global financial meltdown. Is it a risk worth taking? Not as far as Mr Osborne is concerned as the charge on oil profits was cut from 32 per cent to 30 per cent in the autumn statement in December 2014 and other concessions were made amounting to some £470 million over the next parliament.[18]

CHAPTER 12

Should You Trust the State?

HS2, crime and punishment, legal aid cuts, pensions,
free bus passes, winter fuel allowances, international aid

How large should the state be?

I N THE DEPTHS of the recession that followed the financial crisis in
2007/08, people lost confidence in the efficient functioning of markets
and turned to the state for support. Yet since then, with the move to
austerity – which, as we reported earlier, many economists believe may
have started too soon – the emphasis has been on reducing the size of
the state. France, which is struggling to achieve any growth at present,

is castigated for having one of the largest shares of GDP accounted for by the public sector in the developed world, at some 58 per cent. The public sector tends to have low productivity and bureaucracy is generally believed to be reducing incentives to firms to set up and grow, so it would seem that any move of unproductive resources to where they can be put to better use must be a good thing. Of course there are benefits to be had from reducing a bloated public sector, as we are seeing in some of the southern European countries, and putting those generally unproductive resources to better use must be a good thing for the economy. That at least is the theory.

The first thing to say is that cross-country comparisons fail to demonstrate a direct link between the size of the public sector and relative growth and prosperity. Sweden and Norway, for example, have large state sectors and yet have shown steady growth. What really makes a difference is whether the country has a long-term vision which is a) clearly understood and b) supported by the main constituencies in the country. Those who often do best are also the countries in which the population is united in achieving a common goal. The World Economic Forum in one of the reports produced by Simon Zadec rated countries in terms of cooperativeness and found a direct link with economic well-being and prosperity.

The role of government

What must also be understood is that in a market-based democracy governments cannot change the structure of the economy overnight – in fact, they can only influence it at the margin. So the talk about 'rebalancing the economy' is just that – mere talk. Whether we like it or not, the UK will continue to be a service-dominated economy, in those services in which we have a comparative advantage. And the regions will have to accept that even if there is redistribution going on from London to the rest, the fundamental status of London as a world city, way ahead of any of its regional competitors, will remain – unless something goes terribly wrong with our attitude to Europe that messes things up.

However, even the most ardent free market economists agree that there is a role for government in regulating market transactions, for instance ensuring clearly defined property rights; clarifying avenues to pursue conflicts when they arise; detailing the relative rights and responsibilities of any parties in the exchange of such rights; and arbitrating in cases of conflict. In addition, many would wish a government to impose limitations on its own powers, as the state clearly has an unequal power relationship with any individual member of the electorate. It is then only a short step to suggest that employment rights need to be in place to protect the interests of employees against 'overbearing' employers. In a modern society, the idea of a legal system without laws banning the discrimination of individuals on the grounds of, for instance, gender and ethnicity would also seem unacceptable.

Any debate over the role of government and associated regulatory burden are questions of degree, not absolutes. From the perspective of an economist, one may wish to limit intervention to only those cases where there is a perceived market failure. In this book we touch upon many instances where the market fails, so it is worth spending a little time understanding what we expect when the market 'succeeds'. If there is value in a market system it derives from the signals of the price mechanism, which provide information on what is wanted, its costs, and the incentives to act on this information.

Walking around town, we notice that wicker chairs are selling for £50 each and to get in on the action we set up a business making similar chairs – we are pretty sure of making them for £30. Unfortunately, our addition to the supply of wicker chairs leaves us, and the original seller, with chairs that we cannot sell – there were only 100 people willing to buy at £50 and we now have 150 chairs flooding the market. I drop my price to £45, so that more people come to me and I sell all my chairs. There are 125 people willing to buy at £45 so my competitor drops their price to the same level. We both fight it out, until we get to the minimum price that allows us to sell enough chairs, but it is sufficiently above £30 to make it worthwhile (we get enough profit). If we get to the point where one of us can drop their price no further and our competitor still manages to capture the lion's share of the market, we will go out of business; alternatively, we may both be pushed to a similar level of efficiency, which means we both survive and the chairs sell for much less than previously.

The price mechanism has alerted us to the potential for profit; it has seamlessly coordinated the actions of buyers and sellers, ensuring survival of only those adopting the most cost-effective production methods; and, most importantly, if chairs are purchased on the market then the consumer is paying a price equal to the cost[1] of production. This last issue is important for economists, as it is key to an understanding of what we mean when saying that 'the market mechanism allocates resources efficiently'. If we allocated too many (wicker) resources to chair-making, the price would drop, as the market was flooded with chairs; producers would go out of business and resources would be allocated elsewhere.

You will not be surprised to learn that in many instances this goodnews story fails. For instance, in Chapter 11 we have considered how to save ourselves from our effects on the Earth – but global warming is all market failure. When the market sets the price of our wicker chair, we want all costs to be reflected in that price. Unfortunately, while the cost of cutting down trees to produce wicker for our chairs is included in the price, there is no consideration of our contribution to global warming and the cost of us leaving the countryside with fewer trees for visitors. These external costs seem pretty trivial, but imagine how large they are when we think of the cost of cars and motoring, burning coal to produce electricity, the by-products from chemical plants and making plastics, and the costs of secondary smoking. The government has a role in making sure that these various activities are taxed in a way that better ensures that their price includes these external, unaccounted costs. In a similar vein there are some activities that we would want to promote because there are benefits that the consumer/producer does not take into account. Think of education, which benefits the individual but also wider society.

However, it is not just this market failure where government has a role. Even when the market system is working well, it has a key weakness, in that resources are allocated according to spending power. If you are born to this system, poor and without talent, you will not be able to access many of these scarce resources, and your vote (spending power) will hold less weight than that of the millionaire across the road. The millionaire's spending power affords them a vote that weighs more heavily in deciding that resources should be allocated to production of, for instance, Bugatti Veyrons. In a democracy, our vote for policies counts for the same thing whether we are millionaires or paupers – and we often vote for policies that rectify this unequal distribution of resources.

However, this approach depends on the belief that government can rectify market failure. That's often wishful thinking. There is no reason why a government should be able to detect market failures, and the remedies it imposes may not work. In many instances, therefore, we may expect market failure to be simply replaced by *government failure*. For instance, there is the potential for *limited information* within government; we may consider that government has *limited control over bureaucracy*, and this may serve to increase the weight of legislation and regulation.[2] The aim here is not to go into further detail on the specific merits of government failure arguments, not least because it is an area where there is still no consensus,[3] but we are now set up for a discussion that admits there are no easy answers.

Increasing use of evidence

What the state could do better is in making more intelligent use of evidence in developing and formulating policy to ensure it is properly targeted and has the desired effect – and then frequently evaluate the policy to check that it is still fit for purpose. This is seldom done well and of course collecting evidence is costly – or inconvenient if it doesn't tell you what you want to hear. And often what should be evidence-based policy becomes policy-based evidence – in other words you develop a policy that you favour and then dig around to get the right evidence to prove your case. That, put simply, is the wrong way to do policy and it often leads to negative outcomes for the economy and the players within it.

In fairness to the UK government, it has increasingly drawn on evidence from academics and civil servants in its attempts to figure out whether to intervene and, if it does intervene, what form any intervention should take. In modern democracies the winning of elections is now determined by impressions of competency, rather than entrenched political tribalism. Policy-makers are aware that, while they are expert in the machinations of Westminster, they are less well informed on the potential impacts of their policies. One can see where a genuine desire for better understanding comes from, if evidence-based policy ultimately protects against impressions of government incompetence. This is one reason why the Government Economic Service grew from around 500 members in the mid-1990s to some 1,500 today, even against the tide of civil service downsizing.

However, there is another way of seeing this, which is best understood by considering the public's view of the main protagonists involved in the development of evidence-based policy. When asked by Ipsos MORI researchers in 2013, the following proportions of a sample of respondents suggested that they trusted individuals from the relevant occupations:

Profession	Percentage trust
Doctors	89 per cent
Teachers	86 per cent
Scientists	83 per cent
Civil servants	53 per cent
MPs in general	23 per cent
Politicians generally	18 per cent

Politicians and MPs clearly see a value in drawing in academic economists (a cross between doctors and scientists) and, to a lesser extent, civil servants to improve trust in what they do, if only perhaps with the aim of choosing an academic who will rubber-stamp their approach. The authors' experience is that government analysts and academics tend to stick to their guns. This causes politicians more trouble than they would have faced if going it alone and facing the electorate's cynicism, but there are many instances where a case can be made supporting two apparently contradictory views. There are also points where economics cannot help us.

So here are some examples of what the evidence basis would tell you:

Choosing one thing over another when the market isn't around to do it

We saw in Chapter 7 that sewers were one of the earliest major public investments. The market had failed to protect the rich from the socially indiscriminate germs of the poor, so the state intervened and used public monies to provide sewers. It is not beyond possibility that the private sector could have raised subscriptions and purchased the necessary land to build sewers, but it hadn't happened and it was unlikely to. To do the job, the sewers had to be freely available: charging the poor for them would have defeated the whole point, as to save the costs the poor would have found other less safe means of disposing of their effluent. But if there was to be no charge, how could the market collect venture finance for their construction or regain the investment made? Equally, each landowner along the routes of the sewers could hold out for 'threshold' payments and rents. That is, even a narrow strip of land, perhaps bought for this very purpose, could halt the whole project and so be used as a hostage to extract much more than the land's market value would be for anything else. Governments, however, can insist on a more reasonable price and even make land subject to a compulsory purchase order.

Similarly, left to the market the new high-speed rail links (HS2) promised by the coalition, connecting London, Birmingham, Manchester, Sheffield and Leeds, just wouldn't happen. Again, it is difficult to raise such large sums of finance (perhaps some £40 billion) and a lot of the benefits, such as reduced road congestion and reduction of CO_2, would not be felt directly by those using the new service and so would not factor into the fares they are prepared to pay. And the force of government is definitely going to be needed to shift the many disgruntled house-owners and land-holders. It might also not be a good idea to have the track in private hands. Railway lines on the ground are an example of a 'natural monopoly' which cannot be split up in many ways and the concern would be that a private monopolist would ignore wider economic benefits in their calculations.

Of the two, however, sewers or high-speed railways, the case for sewers is definitely much stronger. Sewers are unobtrusive, they do what they are meant to do and they are vital. By contrast, HS2 will be obtrusive, may not have the intended effects and may be a white elephant. How do we decide on whether we should build HS2 or not? There is only one sensible way: conduct a thorough cost–benefit analysis (CBA), something we have been mentioning through the book, and then trouble-shoot and challenge the assumptions like mad before making a decision! If at all possible, keep legacy-seeking, egotistical, grand-standing politicians aping statesmen away from what are really economic decisions!

But what is cost–benefit analysis all about?

Cost–benefit analysis looks at a decision in terms of its consequences or costs and benefits. You won't be surprised to read that if the benefits exceed the costs then that is evidence in favour of a proposal. To add up all the costs and all the benefits and then to compare them needs a common measure of measurement: the obvious and most convenient measure is money. Some people get really badly hung up on the use of money as a measure of value, but that is mainly because they don't understand that it's used only as a weight – it's not literally money. If we didn't use money but we came to a decision somehow then we would have used at least an implicit 'numeraire', one that would simply be less transparent than money. The point of attaching an explicit value is to make it transparent so that it can be considered by others and challenged if someone thinks it incorrect; implicit judgements and principles are less easy to challenge. For HS2 in 2012, the positive benefit to cost ratio (BCR) was estimated by government economists at 1.7, or 2.1 if 'wider economic benefits' are included. These BCRs have been heavily challenged, and these estimates have fallen since (see below).

Can we measure everything in money? No, of course not! A mother's love, hopefully, is not sensibly measured in money, but that doesn't mean that lots of things can't be usefully compared in decisions by attaching a monetary weight. We've already seen in Chapter 7 that we do in effect even put a monetary measure to the quality of human life. CBA seeks to put a monetary value to all the costs and benefits of a decision in order to appraise the desirability of a project, programme or policy. Its purpose is to provide a consistent procedure for appraising and evaluating decisions in terms of their consequences. It attempts to weight using values that reflect how much the various costs and benefits are valued by those who will be directly or indirectly affected.

Values are often read straight off directly from market costs and prices, or are imputed for non-market outcomes in term of people's willingness to pay or how much it would take to compensate them for the change. Economists can be quite ingenious at this. For example, the valuation of street improvements might be proxied by measuring changes in house prices. But such ingenuity still usually leaves room for challenge. For example, you may be able to work out why measuring of the cost of the noise from an established airport by the drop in house prices around it may not be a good estimate of the value of the noise from building a brand-new airport elsewhere.

People who complain about airport noise knew that this would be an issue when they bought their houses in Richmond in the past few decades, though airport noise over that period has been reduced despite more flights because of better, more efficient and quieter engines, but they may not be representative of the people around a newly built airport.

But there are some things that have proved clear time and time again – the best infrastructure spend in terms of value for money is roads. That may be surprising but it is true. The cost–benefit analysis is clear. They facilitate extra journeys at least cost. Of course toll roads would be good for the public purse and encourage people to use the roads at the best time to ease congestion. But they would lose a government an election, such is the popular dislike of them – as demonstrated by a petition signed by millions which was sent to Downing Street last time it was suggested.

Other infrastructure spending is not so cheap. Look at railways more generally – getting the consumer to pay the right price remains very difficult. The running of the Tube network was privatised in the early 2000s under Gordon Brown through a disastrously expensive PFI contract. One of the two main operators then could not meet the conditions of the contract it had been awarded, which then had to be taken over by the state. The result is that out of Transport for London's £9 billion annual budget, some £1.8 billion of it comes from its government grant.[4] Similarly, there have been occasions when the government has had to take over failed train operators to whom it awards multi-year franchises to run particular routes and whose prices it controls. Often those prove more efficient and more popular with passengers than the privately owned ones. Of course, the privatisation in the 1990s was in part due to the need for big investments and substantial upgrading, which the government at the time believed it could not afford. But in reality the cost to the taxpayer remains high.

In 1989/90, just before all that was set in motion, state subsidies to cover the gap between passenger fare revenues and costs were some £1.8 billion. In the financial year 2006/07 this hit a high of £7.8 billion! It came down afterwards as a result of some vicious rail price rises which have proved very unpopular, but in 2011/12 the state subsidies still amounted to £3.9 billion.[5] Figures for 2012/13 suggest a subsidy of £2.4 billion in that year and £2.3 billion in 2013/14.[6] This is of course still higher than before privatisation. One may therefore legitimately wonder whether it was worth it: did the cost–benefit of the whole operation stack up? Might not the railways have been more efficiently run if they had been kept as one, possibly in public hands?

Of course we will never know. But it is relevant to the discussion on how to make up your mind about HS2 which follows below.

HS2: back to the future?

As we explained, cost–benefit analysis is formally required to be conducted as part of the appraisal for all decision making on large public sector projects such as HS2. So, what aspects did it consider? There are the broader 'macro' economic wider benefits that HS2 may bring; as with other macro forecasts, any assessments of these will almost certainly turn out to be wrong! That does not mean that they are unimportant. For example, quicker and new commuting possibilities will allow a wider area for employee job search and for employers will improve the size and diversity of potential applicants. The better linking of human minds together also leads to higher productivity and innovation over and above IT links. Such sharing of ideas and contacts gives rise to the 'agglomeration effects', also known as 'density externalities', which are a major reason why cities are so productive per head compared to lower density populations. An implicit assumption here, though, is that linking to London will increase the economic value added per head of the populations of the other better-connected cities and so decrease regional disparities. However, there is a possible, quite likely, reverse effect: it may further marginalise those towns it passes through rather than stops at and could allow London to suck the life-blood out of the other connected cities as they are exposed to greater competition and as people start to commute to London jobs in greater numbers!

Obviously, new rail capacity should reduce both congestion on roads and existing rail services, and have other environmental benefits, but at around £40 million it is a very high cost at a time when finance is scarce and other areas of infrastructure badly need investment. In other words, there may be other more beneficial ways of spending the money. A criticism of HS2 is that it is not based on what is vital in any proper CBA: that is, that it has not compared the possible benefits from HS2 with the possible benefits from the alternatives. Such alternatives include: better links *between* the cities and towns of the Midlands and the north; upgrades to west and east coast networks; the massively cheaper alternative of the GB freight network that would allow the UK to benefit from compatibility with the gauge used on the Continent and make us part of a growing European freight network in which trains can carry lorry-sized trailers, thereby taking freight off the roads, easing congestion, cutting pollution and freeing capacity on our existing railways; or rolling out faster and wider super-fast broadband.

> Something fundamental has been lost in the HS2 debate. The point of any investment is to meet needs or goals; these are what determine why and how we invest scarce funds. The concern with HS2 – the biggest transport investment in UK history – is that the means (HS2) have overshadowed the ends (economy, environment and rail capacity), with no assurance that the two are truly connected. There could be better ways to meet our national goals, and as custodian of our public funds the government must step back from unsubstantiated rhetoric on HS2 in order to explore and assess these opportunities properly.[7]

In 2011 the Transport Secretary Philip Hammond said that 'if [the BCR] was to fall much below 1.5 then I would certainly put it under some very close scrutiny'. Well, it has: one of the official estimates put it as low as 1.4, and phase one at just break-even. Even these BCRs depend heavily on a very iffy assumption that is now anachronistic: journey time is no longer just wasted time. As anyone will know, often irritatingly, people work on trains nowadays. But these values for saved journey time largely still assume that people are cut off from work on a train. So these 'savings' still constitute the largest source of benefits in the HS2 business case. In total, user benefits (which are predominantly time savings) are about 55 per cent of the overall benefits of HS2. There are other technological innovations that could dramatically reduce the BCR still further. Driverless cars may still sound futuristic but there are plans to start testing their use in three UK cities by January 2015.[8] Over the span of time that HS2 is proposed for, this, pretty much proven technology, could transform transport patterns. If so, HS2 might be as relevant as canals.

Never missing the opportunity for a political point, the shadow Chancellor is wobbly on HS2, not quite against it but happy to say the coalition is not doing it right. The Tories are still committed to it, though for a party that sold us austerity on the premise that the international markets would punish us for the reckless use of public monies (see Chapter 2), it is odd that it should be the main champion of such a potential white elephant.

Which party is tougher on crime – and should they be?

This is an area where cost–benefit has hardly been used. First, the costs – the 2010 spending review after the coalition came to power required the Ministry of Justice (MoJ) to reduce its Departmental Expenditure Limits (DEL) from the £8.3 billion it was in 2010/11 to just £7 billion in 2014/15. How was this to be achieved given that the cuts were so drastic? The main way the government could see to achieve this was to cut down legal aid, reduce staffing and close courts. Other proposals have been to make better use of technology, which might involve holding short hearings by telephone, for example, or using web- or video-based applications instead of requiring people to come to court. There have also been suggestions that the government might curb the number of pre-trial hearings that require defendants in custody and advocates to attend court. At the same time the scope for judicial reviews is being constrained.

In addition, the government has been taking a swipe at probation services, which are effectively being privatised – except for the part that looks at the more difficult longer sentences, where expert help is required. The main body that looks after offenders, which accounts for some half of this budget, was to achieve total savings of £650 from its budget of £3.4 billion by 2015, the time of the next elections. In the meantime there has also been a review of the prison estate, some prisons have closed and women's open prisons, the ones that really focus on rehabilitation, are due to close after the election. There was a further cut of between 8 and 10 per cent by 2015/16, imposed on the Ministry of Justice in the 2013 spending review.

That may make sense from an efficiency viewpoint. The question, though, is whether they tackle the main issue, which is too many prisoners in jail in England and Wales, both by comparison to other countries and also given the declining trends in crime overall. And, besides this, do they look at the unintended consequences?

A proper cost–benefit analysis for the criminal justice system as a whole has never been more urgently needed. Nick Hardwick, the Chief Inspector of Prisons, describes it as 'not being fit for purpose'. It is time for a serious scrutiny of the prison system and what it achieves. Crime is costly and needs to be reduced. Of course, it already has been reduced, but the figures are muddied by the fact that there is serious under-reporting. Much corporate crime goes unreported as companies mostly deal with it themselves, although the recent scandals in the banking sector exposing manipulation of key interest and exchange rates are changing that. On an individual level, many people don't report minor instances like muggings or even burglaries, as the police often prove unable or too busy to solve the crime. There has also been chronic under-reporting of domestic or sexual abuse due to victims' fears, often well-founded, that they wouldn't be believed or, if they were, the crime wouldn't be seriously investigated by the police. That is now changing.

There has also been a huge amount of under-recording. It has become clear, for example, that in order to meet targets various police forces have been recording a certain percentage of rape cases as 'non-crimes'. That type of behaviour has now come under the spotlight and is being reversed.

Nevertheless, that is unlikely to significantly affect the picture of crime trends in England and Wales that has emerged over the past twenty years. Give or take a few percentages in recognition of the problems with reported crime, their number has nevertheless been falling over the past few years, though there was a flattening in the numbers in the last year. In the twelve months to March 2014 there were 3.7 million offences recorded by the police (which, by the way, is not a designated national statistic; in other words there is no guarantee of its accuracy), which was some 1.5 million below the offences recorded in 2003/4. Since then, the number has continued to fall. The more reliable Crime Survey for England and Wales showed a further 14 per cent decline in the year to March to some 7.3 million incidents against households and resident adults. That was the lowest since the survey began in 1981 and was a near 70 per cent decline compared to the record 19 million reported in the survey in 1995.

Why have the figures been falling? Not because we are tougher on crime. The evidence, since this is what this book is about, suggests that prison does not act as a deterrent for crime. Rather, the reasons for the decline – which has also been evident across the Western world – are unrelated to what the various parties may boast about in terms of their law and order credentials. They are:

- Improvements in technology – it is much harder now to steal a car, a car radio or even a mobile, which gets deactivated quickly once stolen or lost; or to enter people's houses when they are not there, as insurance companies generally now insist on house alarms before they agree to insure your house; or to steal from your retail employer, as automated cash tills at pay-outs are now electronically controlled and it is completely clear at the end of the day what the take of that cash till should have been.

- An ageing population – the propensity to commit a crime declines after the age of twenty-four.

- A richer population – except for some occasional economic downturns like the one we have just experienced we are generally getting richer. There is more to lose if you have a job; less to lose if you don't have one.

And yet over the period since 1996, and mostly under a Labour government, the number of people in prison at any one time has doubled to just under 90,000, of whom some 4,000 were women – mostly in for trivial offences, with a number also serving time for not paying the BBC licence fee. In comparison, women prisoners numbered only 1,700 at the end of the Thatcher era. This has reflected changed guidelines, with more custodial sentences being passed and longer sentences being applied – 'life' now means an extra five years compared to what it meant twenty years ago, so there are more people in prison at any one time as a result. The UK also keeps too many remand prisoners in jail. It varies from place to place and from month to month but there are periods in Holloway, the women's prison in north London, where remand prisoners represent some 60 per cent of the total number of inmates. Of those remand prisoners, some 50 per cent end up not being given a custodial sentence, but in the meantime they swell the numbers behind bars. These are people who are charged but have not yet been to court and who have been refused bail. There have been calls to restrict the length of time remand prisoners should be kept behind bars to only twenty-eight days, but that proposal has not so far been taken up. Some 200,000 people go through the prison system every year and the prisons are now full to overflowing. And yet going to prison is believed to increase rather than decrease the chances of reoffending, which costs the economy between £9 billion and £13 billion a year.

When the original cuts were announced, the Prison Officers' Association warned in 2011 that prisons were being put at serious risk of riots, jeopardising the safety of both prisoners and officers. That forecast has proved correct and the increased toughness as we approach the elections was exemplified in the move to reduce privileges – which included limiting access to books and basic benefits like watching television, and cutting release on temporary licence, a system that with very few exceptions had been shown to work well. Besides this, the continuous introduction of new offences that have custodial sentences attached to them has caused more and more people to join the Chief Inspector of Prisons in deeming the system not fit for purpose.

There are all sorts of emotional issues to be taken into account here, particularly the vulnerability of people in prison who are already disadvantaged by the system. The majority of prisoners also have learning difficulties – MoJ statistics[9] looking at the background of newly sentenced prisoners suggested that more than half of male prisoners and more than two-thirds of female prisoners had no qualifications whatsoever and a good percentage of them were homeless when they entered prison. By the time they leave, some 40 per cent of prisoners have nowhere fixed to go to having lost their homes while in prison which makes reintegration with society particularly difficult. This creates costs to the system and raises the question of whether our criminal justice system would pass a proper cost–benefit analysis. And when people come out they tend to reoffend. The rates of reoffending within a year are some 70 per cent and reconviction rates some 50 per cent across the system. If this was the National Health Service and you had to go back to do the same operation again and again there would be a public outcry and the system would be declared not fit for purpose. If the role of prisons is not only to punish but to rehabilitate, as the authorities would like us to think, then you would worry about their effectiveness and take remedial measures.

Alternatives cost less – the average cost of a community order is estimated at some £2,000, rising to some £11,500 for the very intensive orders, still considerably cheaper than the £40,000 a year it costs on average to keep someone in prison. And the reoffending rate tends to be considerably lower, so society benefits both in the short and medium term. Separating mothers in particular from their children is costly in terms of children being taken into care (only 5 per cent of children whose mothers go to prison stay in their homes after that separation). Costs of keeping children in care average some £50,000 a year and in the long term that creates extra inter-generational problems. Figures for 2009 indicated that there were 200,000 children who that year had at least one parent in prison, some for short periods, others whose parents were there for much longer. That is a large number. Children whose parents go to prison are much more likely to end up as NEETs (Not in Education, Employment or Training) and hence cost society a lot as they grow up. What is also worrying is that those kids are three times as likely to commit a display of anti-social behaviour, including a crime that might end up with them too doing time in jail.

Academic evidence and survey evidence suggest that prison does not act as a deterrent to crime. If that is the case, then what does? The simplest answer is the absolute certainty of being caught. But without police officers on every street corner and in every house, that is unachievable. The shocking figures are that only some 7 per cent of crimes ever go in front of a court. Crimes are committed all the time but the majority go undetected, except for the very serious ones. Of some 10 million crimes in 2011/12, only 1.8 million of them ended up in court.

The evidence suggests that there are two key factors in determining offending and reoffending. The first is education. As UCL and LSE economist Steve Machin[10] has demonstrated, education has a direct impact in reducing crime and reoffending. And yet only £100 million is spent on educating prisoners, from a prisons budget of £3.6 billion. The Prisoners' Education Trust has also been working to promote better education for prisoners and has most recently been working with the MoJ in a study that has now clearly demonstrated the positive impact that long-distance learning has had in reducing reoffending.

Secondly, being in employment to begin with cuts the likelihood of crime or getting employment when one leaves prison. Of course, being educated increases the chances of being employed, and the two are inextricably linked. Data so far suggests that in the first year of men leaving prison some 27 per cent of those released find jobs; for women it is a lot less at 8 per cent. A report by the Ministry of Justice found that reoffending rates for those who found jobs within a year of leaving prison had a nearly 10 per cent lower reoffending rate than the average.[11] A 10 per cent reduction in reoffending results in benefits to society of at least £1 billion a year. The reoffending rates of some of the specialist women's centres are less than 10 per cent so a drive supporting newly released prisoners to gain employment would lead to even greater benefits.

The average cost to the British taxpayer of keeping someone in prison for a year is estimated at around £40,000. For women, estimates in 2009/10 put the figure at £56,000 although more recent MoJ data put it at around £44,000. Give or take a few thousand pounds, though, it still leaves the cost at a level higher than if you wanted to let your son or daughter board at a top public school – Eton costs just over £30,000 a year. Of course, numerically as budgets fall and numbers in prison increase, there is less money to go around per prisoner, which flatters the average cost figures per prisoner, but as staffing also declines conditions are severely affected. As Juliet Lyon of the Prison Reform Trust asserted in her BBC interview in mid-August 2014 following recent assaults and violent behaviour in male prisons, staff shortages mean that many prisoners now spend twenty-three hours a day locked up – hardly what you need for rehabilitation. The staff cuts are enormous. According to the Howard League for Penal Reform the number of officer grade staff has declined by 30 per cent from 27,650 in September 2010 to 19,325 in September 2013.

Alternatives make such a big difference. The cost of a community order with restrictions and obligations involved, often including unpaid work, is considerably cheaper, with some estimates suggesting a cost of just under £1,500 per year though this could be higher depending on the supervision and the type of offenders involved. In 2010, 45 per cent of women were reconvicted within a year and the reoffending rate was probably much greater. For men and women on average, reconviction is 50 per cent within a year. Reoffending is probably closer to 75 per cent. The total cost of reoffending is reckoned at somewhere between £9.5 billion and £13 billion a year. Reducing that by, say, 10 per cent offers huge savings to society. The evidence suggests that those given non-custodial sentences reoffend at a lower rate than those coming out of prison. And yet the latest figures suggest that there was a 2 per cent increase in the prison population, including those on remand – to 85,509 in the twelve months to the end of June 2014 – and a further increase to 85,834 people by August 2014! This keeps us at one of the highest rates of incarceration per 100,000 of any large Western country except the US. In June 2014, Nick Hardwick, the Chief Inspector of Prisons, claimed 'political and policy failure' for the prison overcrowding in the UK.

Is cutting legal aid a bad thing?

The amount of money spent on legal aid is some £2 billion a year. It takes a big chunk of the government's Ministry of Justice budget, which has been under severe pressure and is to be cut back by some 30 per cent by 2015/16 by comparison with where it was in 2010/11. The result is that legal aid both for criminal and family matters has suffered seriously as a result. It is true that the legal aid budget was one of the highest in the world but it also reflects a system of justice which believes in the right of people to be able to defend themselves. There has been a serious outcry, with criminal barristers taking the unprecedented step of going on strike – following on from demonstrations by probation officers, whose service is being cut and partly privatised.

One immediate response would be: they would say that, wouldn't they? Solicitors and barristers have a vested interest in the status quo remaining. And as the Justice Minister himself, Chris Grayling, said in early 2014:

> As everybody knows this government is dealing with an unprecedented financial challenge and I have no choice but to look for the savings I have to make across the full range of the MoJ's work. I cannot exempt legal aid from this, but that doesn't mean I don't understand how challenging these reductions will be.

He added: 'Legal aid is a vital part of our justice system but we must ensure it is sustainable for those who need it, for those who provide legal services as part of it and for the taxpayer, who ultimately pays for it.'

There is indeed nothing wrong with maximising efficiency and making the system better value for money. That should be the duty of every public servant mindful of taxpayers' money and wanting to reduce waste. There is no doubt that the whole court system is inefficient, as has been observed by anyone who has had to be present and has witnessed the tremendous waste of time waiting for sessions to take place which then may only last for a couple of minutes – sometimes even less than that. But how the savings are made matters hugely in terms of long-term sustainability if one is to avoid any unintended consequences.

One concern is that the cuts are quite dramatic, even though they are implemented in two stages over this year and next. They involve a 17.5 per cent cut in criminal solicitors' and barristers' fees involved with legal aid and which, critics argue, will have a serious impact on the viability of many firms. In private cases, such as family courts, legal aid is now provided only in exceptional circumstances. And there is an increase in self-representation which is not really working, is clogging up the system and in a number of cases the judges have no option but to direct that the courts must pay for expert legal defence or else the cases cannot go forward.

In the family law cases, where the awarding of legal aid has only been allowed in 'exceptional' cases, there have been some worrying trends. Published statistics show that the number of 'exceptional' funding applications granted in family cases between April and December 2013 was eight[12] and between April 2013 and March 2014 was nine.[13] The question is whether the system as it exists now is indeed fit for purpose, as one would imagine that proper demand is probably higher than just eight or nine exceptional cases a year. So evidence has to be looked at from elsewhere: what seems to have happened is that activity has been displaced and there is a lot more help being sought, for example, from the Bar Pro Bono Unit. In 2012 there were 171 applications to the unit for assistance in family law children's cases. That number had gone up to 291 applications in 2013. There were already 205 applications in the first five months of 2014, and the unit has been unable to help in a number of cases already.

The whole system will be reviewed, according to Mr Grayling, in the summer of 2016. The question is whether that will be a review that is based on proper evidence of what works and doesn't work. It should look at the wider implications of the system and evaluate whether in the long term the initial savings have been maintained. It is entirely possible that they will in fact be offset by the damage to the system caused by the exit of law firms which provided legal aid before and the loss of skilled people who worked in this area before. It could also lead to damage to the reputation of and public trust in the criminal justice system as a whole.

Age before means? Pensions and pensioner entitlements

There is cross-party agreement that the public sector deficit must be brought down. The question is where should we wield the axe? A likely target is pensioner entitlements. About half of government spending on welfare benefits goes to pensions, more than enough to pay the £50 billion or so currently spent on servicing the UK's debt. This is set to increase significantly as the proportion of elderly increases and we all, fingers crossed, live longer. The number of people aged sixty or over is expected to pass the 20 million mark by 2030, while the sixty-five-plus population is projected to rise by nearly 50 per cent over the next seventeen years and by 2034 will have risen from about 18 per cent now to about 24 per cent of the population.[14]

The demographics are not as 'bad' as it seems, as more people are working beyond retirement age. Indeed, the whole concept of retirement age is becoming blurred. Sensibly, the default retirement age (formerly sixty-five) has been phased out since 2011 and now most people can work for as long as they want to, usually on reduced part-time hours, often in a 'grey' informal economy, even if for manual workers this will usually involve a change of occupation. If more people do work past current state pension age, that will both help with the 'real' dependency ratio and mean they are more affluent. We also saw in Chapter 7 that the impact on the NHS will be less than was once feared, as it is dying that is the most expensive part of health for the NHS, no matter when you do it! Most importantly, pensioners are no longer the most poverty-ridden cohort that we have so fixed in our mental imagery.

In fact, since the turn of the century, pensioner incomes have been increasing faster than average earnings, as a new generation of pensioners retires with occupational pensions (see Figure 19). Together with a more rapid increase in the level of pension benefits compared to working-age benefits, this has resulted in pensioner poverty falling to its lowest level for thirty years.[15]

FIGURE 19: REAL GROWTH IN PENSIONERS' INCOME AND WORKING-AGE EARNINGS SINCE 1996/97

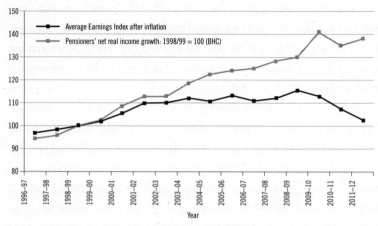

Source: http://www.gov.uk/government/uploads/system/uploads/attachment_data/file/254321/framework-analysis-future-pensio-incomes.pdf

The younger generation of pensioners and the cohort about to follow them are considerably more affluent than their predecessors. That has usually been the case, but it is significantly more so for the current generation and those about to retire. An important factor is that few final-salary or defined-benefit general pension schemes are now open to new entrants outside of the public sector. Instead, only less generous money-purchase pensions are available, effectively investing to secure a future non-specified amount of pension. The income from these schemes will depend on how well your personal pension fund performs. This switch will likely exacerbate the problem of people saving too little for their old age, and is no doubt storing up problems for the longer-term future, but this has been offset by automatic enrolment legislation enacted in 2012 that now requires all UK workplaces to enrol their staff in pensions.

For now, significant numbers of those recently reaching pension age, or who are about to do so, will have benefited from the more generous final-salary and defined-benefit pension schemes. In addition, the State Earnings Related Pension Scheme, a state-run alternative to a workplace pension that has since been replaced by the less generous state second pension, has also matured. In short, for the next decade and more, thanks to increased private sector provision, increased income from earnings, savings and investments, and pensioner benefits rising faster than earnings, those people who are only just past state pension age are likely on average to be the most affluent pensioner generation ever, and by a very considerable margin.

The Institute for Fiscal Studies[16] reports that median pensioner incomes, that is, the mid-point of pensioner incomes, are today similar to those of the whole working-age population. The picture for pensioner poverty has changed dramatically from thirty years ago. Then, more than 40 per cent of pensioners were in the bottom fifth of the income distribution and more than 66 per cent were in the bottom two-fifths. Today, barely 10 per cent of pensioners are in the bottom fifth and more than 40 per cent are in the top half of the income distribution. And this is without taking account of the fact that 75 per cent of those aged over sixty-five now own their own home (unlike most other age groups, their home ownership rates are actually rising!). Looking after pensioners is still an emotive issue in politics, but the days when we should consider almost all pensioners to be poor pensioners are gone.

Not surprisingly, then, the coalition has been asked if it intends to cut pensions or pensioner entitlements. The Tories have committed to retain the so-called triple lock on state pensions until at least 2020 if they remain in power, meaning the state pension will continue to rise with inflation, wages or 2.5 per cent – whichever is highest.[17] After just a little dithering by Cameron on the *Today* programme – apparently some senior figures in the Cabinet supported means testing – the Tories say they are 'minded' to protect free bus passes, TV licences and the winter fuel allowance from means testing until at least 2020. So Ed Miliband promised to do this too. These non-means-tested entitlements currently cost just over £4 billion per year, not a spectacular sum in public finance terms, but very well worth having as a contribution to deficit reduction. Perhaps the commitment to keep giving winter fuel allowances to millionaire pensioners, which must reduce the monies in the pot for young people who have had a rougher time overall, has more to do with politics than economics: three-quarters of voters aged over sixty-five voted in the past two elections compared with less than half of those aged eighteen to twenty-four. Another example of good politics being bad economics.

Before pensioners or anyone else is hit by austerity cuts, the next government should be tackling the tax evasion that robs the Treasury of perhaps as much as £70 billion a year.[18] But that, regrettably, is unlikely to be pursued with the vigour required, and so failing this, to spread the pain more evenly, it is only equitable that pensioners, who have so far more than ridden out the recession, take some of the burden. This must not neglect, however, the fact that almost three million people rely on taxpayer support from the means-tested pension credit, and that just above them are significant numbers with little saved. Better off as a group, but still with significant numbers of low incomes? That sounds like a good reason for means testing pensioner entitlements! The Lib Dems were not so premature in ruling out reducing these pensioner entitlements as a potential source of Exchequer savings. Originally, at the end of 2011, Nick Clegg called for universal pensioner entitlements to be means-tested, but sensibly, the Lib Dems seemed to have done a bit more thinking on that since and now seem to be leaning towards simply taxing them.

A major problem with means testing is that it is bureaucratic and potentially expensive, and means testing is well known to put off many of those who really do need the help: it can be a humiliating and demeaning experience for pensioners already sensitive about preserving their personal dignity. Means testing is also a pretty effective way to destroy the incentive needed to make people save for their old age: why do the right thing and provide for your later years if someone who doesn't will get themselves more benefits! It is also well to remember that the TV, winter and bus entitlements are all just political gimmicks brought in as populist measures to hide the fact that UK basic state pensions are appallingly low when compared to the rest of the developed world; only Mexico is worse.[19] The real issue is more about whether pensioners who have to rely on the basic pension can afford the basics of life; arbitrarily picking out a few of these necessities to get some warming headlines seems like bad economics.

Is the solution to get rid of the entitlements? Not unless any future government is serious about raising UK state pensions up to the European average, which will certainly happen if pigs fly around a moon turned blue by the next government. Meanwhile, with 20,000 pensioners dying of cold each winter it seems unwise to get rid of the winter fuel allowance, and TV licences can relieve the problems of loneliness that many pensioners face. Bus passes also can go a long way to reducing the dangers of social isolation, and anyway these should be renegotiated so that bus operators are paid less than the full fare, as the journeys wouldn't happen at all at full fare and a pensioner does not add to the cost of a bus that is running anyway – so long as the bus does run, that is!

So, there are compelling reasons both real and political to retain these entitlements for now, and yet pensioners should still share some of the burden of deficit reduction. Best turn to the UK's foremost pension expert Ros Altmann for advice: the parties should heed her four suggested solutions.[20] So we'll let her have the last word on this:

1. Make the benefits taxable. Many of the payments to pensioners are tax-free. That does not necessarily make sense, because the highest income pensioners benefit more than those with low incomes. The benefits could be made taxable, just as the state pension is subject to tax, which would raise more revenue.

2. Pay from later ages. There is also a case for considering an increase in the age of eligibility. If the benefits were paid only from a later age, and it is possible to argue that around age sixty is too young, then further cost savings would ensue.

3. Give people the option to not receive the money – or donate to others. Saga has supported the Community Foundation Network's 'Surviving Winter' initiative that 'recycles' winter fuel payments from pensioners who feel they don't need the money, to help others struggling to stay warm in winter. Such initiatives should be encouraged. Only a small proportion of pensioners are really wealthy.

4. Reform state pension so we don't need to add 'freebies' to avoid poverty. A radical reform of the state pension, leaving it as a flat-rate payment that is at a decent level, would permit a reassessment of the need for all the additional pensioner benefits. If they could be rolled into one payment, which is a higher pension than currently paid, the system could be simplified without major savings disincentives and without taking away much-needed income from many older people who will not claim their entitlements.

Hear, hear!

Charity begins at home, but it doesn't have to end there!

One target that the coalition has uniquely and unambiguously hit as a government was a long-standing international commitment, dating back even before it was enshrined by UN agreement in 1970, to contribute 0.7 per cent of UK national income to overseas aid. In 2013 the UK's total aid expenditure reached £11.4 billion or 0.72 per cent of national income for the first time. Despite austerity, this required a heroic increase from just under 0.6 per cent of national income when the coalition took office, and more than double the percentage achieved through most of the 1980s and 1990s. Overriding much opposition in his own party, David Cameron is proud of making the UK a member of a very small group of countries that have met the UN commitment of 0.7 per cent: Denmark, Luxembourg,

Norway, Sweden, the United Arab Emirates and the UK; the average for other countries party to the agreement is only about 0.3 per cent. The UK is way ahead of other major European economies, such as Germany. There is even a possibility, though now slightly diminished, that the 0.7 per cent could become enshrined in UK legislation.

The 0.7 per cent target was first adopted as a principled aspiration by the newly elected UK (Labour) government of 1974. The next Conservative government accepted the target, but without a date for its attainment. The 1997 Labour government maintained this position, but in the 2004 spending review the Labour government said that it wished to continue to raise aid at a rate that would mean it would reach 0.7 per cent by 2013. After the 2012 autumn statement, Justine Greening, the Conservative Secretary of State for International Development, reiterated the coalition's commitment to meeting the 0.7 per cent target:

> The coalition government has today reaffirmed its commitment to the world's poorest people by confirming the UK will spend 0.7 per cent of Gross National Income (GNI) on international development from 2013. We will be the first G8 country to do so. Achieving our pledge of 0.7 per cent is the right thing to do and the smart thing to do. It is in everyone's interests for countries around the world to be stable and secure, to have educated and healthy populations, and to have growing economies.[21]

Not everyone is as pleased as Cameron that the coalition is the first government to have actually achieved this historic benchmark of compassion. Predictably, our right-wing press – that is, most of our press – slammed the achievement. Sample headlines from the usual suspects ran: 'Britain leads the way in foreign aid – unfortunately' (*Daily Express*)[22] and 'Sign our petition calling on government to divert foreign aid to flood-hit British families' (*Daily Mail*).[23]

The Overseas Development Agency is in fact careful about what may be counted as aid – no general military equipment or services or anti-terrorism activities, but the cost of using a donor's armed forces to deliver humanitarian aid is eligible, as are some peacekeeping operations, such as election monitoring. This appeared to present an opening for Conservative Defence Minister Philip Hammond's 'trying it on', to quote the words of the Lib Dems' Sir Menzies Campbell. Jealous over the Department for International Development (DfID)'s expanding ring-fenced budget, the MoD sought to replenish its own non-ring-fenced budget by reclassifying some of its activities as humanitarian and peacekeeping, and even some of the cost of its new aircraft carrier, so as to get a slice of DfID's expanded budget. This bid was encouraged by Cameron, perhaps to appease his more right-wing colleagues, but the Lib Dems would have none of it. Instead, from the supporters of aid there has been severe criticism that though it has honoured its commitment to increase foreign aid the coalition has failed to take the case for aid to the British public, and that this left a political vacuum for the recent onslaught on UK foreign aid to fill.

Some opponents of aid simply think that Brits should always come first in everything, but other critics argue that the Department for International Development does not do enough to assess the effectiveness of aid, that the raison d'être is anachronistic as it is no longer a key financing mechanism for investment in developing countries (see below), that it encourages dependency in recipient countries rather than inspiring efforts to become self-sufficient, and that too much of it disappears into corrupt pockets. Despite this, the target still has the overall support of the coalition and most charities on the grounds that overseas aid plays an important role in improving the welfare of the world's poor. Many supporters also argue that it helps to reduce conflict and improve international relations with the UK.

The criticism on occasion has come from some pretty high places. In March 2012 the House of Lords Economic Affairs Committee stated that 'we do not accept that meeting by 2013 the UN target of spending 0.7 per cent (£12 billion) of gross national income on aid should now be a plank, let alone the central plank, of British aid policy'.[24]

The committee argued, firstly, that the target wrongly prioritises the amount spent rather than the outcomes by making the achievement of the spending target more important than the overall effectiveness of the programme. Secondly, they said, the speed of the (then) planned increase risks reducing the quality, value for money and accountability of the aid programme (one witness told the House of Lords committee that the target encouraged officials 'to turn a blind eye to flagrant abuse in the pressure to get the money out of the door'). Thirdly, they maintained that reaching the target 'increases the risk ... that aid will have a corrosive effect on local political systems'. This last point was given more weight by the contribution of the vastly experienced former DfID chief economist Adrian Wood, now a professor at Oxford University. He told the House of Lords Committee: 'If you give a country too much aid for too long you damage its basic governance structure because the politicians pay more attention to the donors than they do to their citizens.' The committee concluded that 'the core of aid policy should be choosing and funding the best ways of promoting international development and stability, rather than finding new ways to spend ever increasing resources'.

An alternative approach to official aid argues that any target setting is now largely irrelevant as aid is no longer the main finance for development. A 2012 European Commission report[25] pointed out that the biggest source of financing for development available to governments is their own domestic revenue, so that the primary responsibility for development lies with the developing countries themselves. In the right circumstances, aid may complement this, and could catalyse other flows, but aid is not the major element for many developing countries: rather, it is international trade, investments and money sent back home by migrants that can stimulate the real economy. In 2012, workers' remittances to low-income countries were worth $32 billion while net official aid to these countries (from all donors) was worth $30 billion. Immigration can be an effective form of overseas aid (see Chapter 8).

It is also fair to say that the empirical link between aid and economic growth is pretty patchy, but then any good economist would expect that on something so complex and overridden by issues such as effective governance and conflict. Anyway, absence of evidence isn't necessarily evidence of absence of effect and a lot of aid is also simply to cope with existing poverty and distress. It is now generally accepted that the Labour government's Prime Minister's Commission for Africa, driven from 2004 to 2005 by the giant brain of economist Lord Stern (see Chapter 11), did help many African countries achieve growth, although, as Stern freely admits, this was also helped by the massive growth of China and its demand for the primary products of Africa. Africa will grow in importance in the future: as with other countries, it may be to our advantage that we helped this process.

Compared to the extent of global poverty, and the distress in the world from wars and natural devastations, the UK's problems are mere inconveniences – and ones that we should be able to cope with while sparing a thought and some resources for others whose crime is to be born in another country. Overall, accepting that charity does not end at home, criticism of the 0.7 per cent target boils down to saying that the amount of aid for poor countries should not be based on an arbitrary spending target or some fraction of the wealth of rich countries, but rather it should be determined by how effective aid is in contributing to meeting the needs of particular poor countries. But this is to pose a false dichotomy: aid can be both generous and effective. As Lord Ashdown, UNICEF's UK President, has said: 'Scrapping the 0.7 per cent commitment would not make aid more effective, it would simply deny vital assistance to millions of poor and vulnerable people throughout the world.'

Of course, bad aid can be ineffective and even counter-productive in its effects. On average, it may only have small effects as bad aid balances out the good, but that does not mean we should lose sight of the good, of which there are copious examples, or that we cannot learn from mistakes; poor returns to aid can often be because of poor aid policies in donor countries. DfID's spending should be better scrutinised for its effectiveness, always a useful exercise after budget expansion, but the coalition has not been complacent on this: 'We will honour our aid commitments, but at the same time will ensure much greater transparency and scrutiny of aid spending to deliver value for money for British taxpayers and to maximise the impact of our aid budget.'[26]

To ensure this, the Independent Commission for Aid Impact (ICAI) was launched in 2011. The ICAI is the independent body responsible for the scrutiny of UK aid. It reports to Parliament through the House of Commons International Development Committee. The job of the ICIA is to focus on maximising the impact and effectiveness of the UK aid budget for intended beneficiaries and the delivery of value for money for the UK taxpayer. In a synthesis of its finding to date the ICIA reports:

> As Commissioners, we are often asked our views as to whether UK aid really works. This is, of course, a complex question and we are wary of easy generalisations. Nonetheless, after thirty-four reviews, including many strong results and a few poor ones, we can say that DFID at its best is capable of outstanding performance and is rightly recognised as a global leader on many aspects of development assistance. With its expanded budget and its decentralised operations, however, it has to work hard to ensure that these high standards are maintained across its global portfolio.[27]

Aid saves millions of lives, but it is also in our national interest to see other countries grow. The reason we are comparatively rich in this country is because we are surrounded by other rich people with whom we transact. If we were born in poor African countries, we would also be poor whatever our personal attributes and talents. Adam Smith, the father of economics, saw this economic mutual benefit a long time ago in *The Wealth of Nations*, published in 1776, and it works at the global level too: the richer other countries are, the more lucrative trade opportunities there are for the UK. Peace and good international relations are also in our national interest. Aid can be enlightened self-interest.

We should query giving aid to countries where it might be used to subsidise war or vanity projects, or where it significantly fuels corruption. We should find more ways of ensuring it reaches the intended target and we should recognise that immigration and trade can be even more effective than aid. Aid can be made conditional to avoid countries becoming dependent on it. Above all, it should not be cut. The 0.7 per cent should be maintained and the UK should brag loudly about it. We should use it to hold our heads high and to shame other countries into giving more. We have not held back on our criticisms in this book, but we agree that David Cameron and his coalition partners are rightly proud of their record on overseas aid; that it has been achieved in financially stretched times and against opposition close to home should only make them prouder.

CHAPTER 13

And So to the Ballot Box

A ND NOW YOU are on your own…

Endnotes

Introduction

1. Harry Truman is credited as having jokingly called for a one-handed economist so that he wouldn't have to listen to 'on the other hand' from his economic advisers.
2. http://www.instituteforgovernment.org.uk/sites/default/files/publications/The%20dismal%20science.pdf, accessed 12 December 2014.

Chapter 1

1. 'After this, therefore because of this.'
2. *Financial Times*, 14 January 2014.
3. http://blogs.channel4.com/factcheck/factcheck-50p-top-rate-tax-bring/17601, accessed 12 December 2014.

4. www.probonoeconomics.com, accessed 12 December 2014.

5. See *Freakonomics* by Steven Levitt and Stephen J. Dubner (2005).

6. http://www.npr.org/blogs/health/2013/01/02/168437030/research-a-little-extra-fat-may-help-you-live-longer, accessed 12 December 2014.

7. From an interview with the authors.

8. For example, see http://www.worldometers.info/world-population, accessed 14 August 2014.

9. See *Prisonomics* by Vicky Pryce (2013).

10. http://blogs.lse.ac.uk/politicsandpolicy/five-minutes-with-ha-joon-chang, accessed 13 September 2014.

Chapter 2

1. *Today*, BBC Radio 4, June 2014.

2. http://www.theguardian.com/politics/2011/sep/30/city-conservatives-donations, accessed 12 June 2014.

3. See http://niesr.ac.uk/media/may-2014-gdp-estimate-11856#.VHrppzGsWwU, accessed 30 November 2014.

4. Lessons from the 1930s Depression, at http://wrap.warwick.ac.uk/44713/1/WRAP_23.2010_crafts_lessons.pdf, accessed 30 November 2014.

5. http://news.sky.com/story/1062233/rap-on-knuckles-for-cameron-may-be-a-blessing, accessed 14 September 2014.

6. http://www.huffingtonpost.co.uk/2013/03/08/david-cameron-obr-economy-growth_n_2836515.html, accessed 14 September 2014.

7. George Osborne, 2006, http://www.publications.parliament.uk/pa/cm200607/cmhansrd/cmo61127/debtext/61127-0005.htm, accessed 30 November 2014.

8. http://www.telegraph.co.uk/news/uknews/1562023/Tories-vow-to-match-Labour-spending.html, accessed 14 September 2014.

9. See for example http://socialisteconomicbulletin.blogspot.co.uk/2012/07/the-incredible-shrinking-uk-economy.html, accessed 14 August 2014.

10. 'Full-time employee jobs account for only one in 40 created since recession', Angela Monaghan, *The Guardian*, 12 November 2014.

1. http://cdn.budgetresponsibility.independent.gov.uk/FER2013.pdf, accessed 14 September 2014.

2. See for example http://oxrep.oxfordjournals.org/content/27/2/241.abstract, accessed 14 September 2014.

3. http://mainlymacro.blogspot.co.uk/2013/09/sound-bite-economics.html, accessed 14 September 2014.

4. See a discussion of this at http://anotherangryvoice.blogspot.co.uk/2013/01/moneyweek-and-their-end-of-britain.html, accessed 30 November 2014.

5. http://scholar.harvard.edu/files/rogoff/files/growth_in_time_debt_aer.pdf, accessed 14 September 2014.

6. '28-Year-Old PhD Student Debunks the Most Influential Austerity Study', Paul Jay, The Real News Network, 23 April 2013; transcript of interview with Thomas Herndon and Michael Ash.

7. See http://www.nytimes.com/2013/04/26/opinion/debt-growth-and-the-austerity-debate.html?pagewanted=all&_r=0, accessed 30 November 2014.

8. See http://www.nytimes.com/2013/04/19/opinion/krugman-the-excel-depression.html, accessed 30 November 2014.

9. Stephen Machin and Paul Gregg, *The Economic Journal*, May 2014, pp. 408–32.

20. http://www.independent.co.uk/news/business/comment/david-blanchflower/david-blanchflower-economic-sentiment-has-turned--bad-news-for-george-osborne-9850240.html, accessed 9 December 2014.

21. http://www.bbc.co.uk/news/uk-politics-21190108, accessed 9 December 2014.

Chapter 3

1. *The Black Swan: The Impact of the Highly Improbable* by Nassim Nicholas Taleb (2007).

2. Bianchi, J., 'Credit Externalities: Macroeconomic Effects and Policy Implications', *American Economic Review*, vol. 100, no. 2 (2010), pp. 398–402.

3. http://www.bankingstandardsreview.org.uk, accessed 9 December 2014.

4. Pryce, V., 'Is Corporate Governance What Is Wrong with Our Economy?', contributor to 'Beyond Shareholder Value' (ed. by Janet Williamson et al.), TUC, NPI, SOAS (2014), p. 76.

5. Kay, J., 'What Became of the Stakeholder Society?', contributor to 'Beyond Shareholder Value', ibid.

6. http://www.newstatesman.com/politics/2014/03/tories-opposition-labours-youth-jobs-plan-shows-they-are-still-standing-wrong, accessed 21 September 2014.

7. http://www.dailymail.co.uk/news/article-2576662/Co-Operative-Group-pay-chief-executive-3-5m-pay-bonuses-year-job-despite-1-5bn-hole-banks-finances.html, accessed 21 September 2014.

8. http://www.thetimes.co.uk/tto/business/industries/banking/article4177952.ece, accessed 9 December 2014.

Chapter 4

1. GDP is the total value of goods and services produced within the geographic borders of the UK, even if this is within firms that are owned by foreign nationals. The figures are taken from the Office for Budget Responsibility: Economic and fiscal outlook, March 2014.

2. Generally referred to as the PSBR or Public Sector Borrowing Requirement.

3. 1,000 cars ÷ [10 workers × 100 hours].

4. As suggested by Garrett, R., Campbell, M. and Mason, G., 'The Value of Skills: An Evidence Review', UK Commission for Employment and Skills and the National Institute for Economic and Social Research (2010).

5. Spilsbury, M. and Campbell, M. 'Ambition 2020: World Class Skills and Jobs for the UK', UK Commission for Employment and Skills (2009).

6. Office for National Statistics.

7. For a more detailed discussion, see for instance Bank of England Quarterly Bulletin 2014 Q2, 'The UK Productivity Puzzle'.

8. http://www.ft.com/cms/s/0/36736292-fdd8-11e3-acf8-00144feab7de.html#axzz3B97leMC4, accessed 9 December 2014.

9. Mazzucato, M., 'Smart and Inclusive Growth: reforming the risk-reward nexus in innovation', Innovation for Growth, Policy Brief no. 9, European Commission (2013).

10. Haskel, J., Goodridge, P. and Wallis, G., 'UK Investment in Intangible Assets: Report for

NESTA', working papers 12846, Imperial College, London, Imperial College Business School (2014).

11. http://www.gov.uk/government/news/new-turing-institute-at-londons-knowledge-quarter-announced-by-chancellor, accessed 9 December 2014.

12. Garrett, R., Campbell, M. and Mason, G., 'The Value of Skills: An Evidence Review', UK Commission for Employment and Skills and the National Institute for Economic and Social Research (2010).

13. Office for National Statistics (2012).

14. Bevan, S. and Cowling, M., 'Job Matching in the UK and Europe', SSDA Research Report no. 25, Sector Skills Development Agency (2007).

15. Spilsbury, M. and Campbell, M., 'Ambition 2020: World Class Skills and Jobs for the UK', UK Commission for Employment and Skills (2009).

16. Bloom, N., Dorgan, S., Dowdy, J. and Van Reenen, J., 'Management Practice and Productivity: Why They Matter', Centre for Economic Performance, London (2007).

17. See for instance Felstead, A. and Green, F. 'Underutilization, Overqualification and Skills Mismatch', Glasgow: Skills in Focus, Skills Development Scotland (2013).

18. Chevalier, A. and Lindley, J., 'Over-education and the skills of UK graduates', *Journal of the Royal Statistical Society: Series A (Statistics in Society)*, vol. 172, no. 2 (2009), pp. 307–37.

19. As suggested by Machin, S. and McNally, S., 'Higher education and the labour market', CentrePiece (2007).

20. For instance, Dearden et al. (2004); Greenwood et al. (2007); McIntosh (2009); Dickerson and Vignoles (2007); Garrett, Campbell and Mason (2010).

21. Buscha, F. and Urwin, P., 'Estimating the labour market returns to qualifications gained in English Further Education using the Individualised Learner Record (ILR)', Department for Business, Innovation and Skills (2013); Bibby, D., Buscha, F., Cerqua, A., Thomson, D. and Urwin, P., 'Further development in the estimation of labour market returns to qualifications gained in English Further Education using ILR-WPLS Administrative Data', Department for Business, Innovation and Skills (2014).

22. Spilsbury, M. and Campbell, M., 'Ambition 2020: World Class Skills and Jobs for the UK', UK Commission for Employment and Skills (2009).

23. Blanden, J., Buscha, F., Sturgis, P. and Urwin, P., 'Measuring the Returns to Lifelong Learning', *Economics of Education Review*, vol. 31, no. 4 (2012), pp. 501–14.

24. The measure of unemployment used in Figure 11 is the International Labour Organization measure which records the number of jobless people who wish to work, are available to work and are actively seeking employment; as a percentage of all those who are in employment or unemployed (economically active).

25. For more detail see Buscha, F., Latreille, P. and Urwin, P., 'Charging Fees in Employment Tribunals', commissioned by the Trades Union Congress (2013).

26. Chittenden, F., Kauser, S. and Poutziouris, P., 'PAYE-NIC compliance costs, empirical evidence from the UK economy', *International Small Business Journal*, vol. 23, no. 6 (2005), pp. 635–56.

27. Chittenden, F., Foster, H. and Sloan, B., 'Taxation and Red Tape: The cost to British business of complying with the UK tax system', Institute of Economic Affairs (2010).

28. Or more accurately, an 'enterprise'.

29. These figures are taken from the Department for Business, Innovation and Skills' 'Business Population Estimates' (2011) and relate to the percentage of employment by size of VAT-registered business in the UK private sector.

30. See for instance Birch, D. L., *Job Creation in America: How Our Smallest Companies Put the Most People to Work* (1987).

31. See for instance Davis, S., Haltiwanger, J. and Schuh, S., *Job Creation and Destruction* (1996), and Chapter 4 of Urwin, P., 'Self-employment, Small Firms and Enterprise', Institute of Economic Affairs (2011) for a review of the relevant literature.

32. See for instance Haltiwanger, J., Jarmin, R. and Miranda, J., 'Who creates jobs? Small vs. large vs. young', discussion paper 101910, Center for Economic Studies, US Census Bureau (2010).

33. Office for National Statistics Business Demography statistics.

34. Moscarini, G. and Postel-Vinay, F., 'The Contribution of Large and Small Employers to Job Creation in Times of High and Low Unemployment', *American Economic Review*, vol. 102, no. 6 (2012), pp. 2509–39.

35. The research considers data from the US, Denmark and France, but given the consistency of findings across these countries it is unlikely that the UK experience is substantially different.

36. The most serious methodological concern is that questions are invariably asked of small firms that are, by definition, surviving under the regulatory 'burden'. Ideally, one would

gauge the extent of any costs of regulation on various firms at a particular point in time and then revisit these firms (setting up what is referred to as a panel dataset) to gauge the extent to which they had grown, retained their scale of operation or ceased trading. Asking questions only of surviving firms undoubtedly underestimates the costs of regulation and legislation.

37. Many of the ideas here are detailed in Urwin, P., 'Self-employment, Small Firms and Enterprise', Institute of Economic Affairs (2011).

38. And in the process the number of occupational categories expanded from computer analysts/consultants to occupations in 'information and communications technologies' and 'IT service delivery occupations'.

39. Quarterly Labour Force Survey 1992, 1998 and 2002.

40. See for instance Varian, H. R., Farrell, J. and Shapiro, C., *The Economics of Information Technology* (2007).

41. Drawing on ideas set out in, for instance, Kirzner, I. M., 'Entrepreneurial discovery and the competitive market process: an Austrian approach', *Journal of Economic Literature*, vol. 35, no. 1 (1997), pp. 60–85.

42. Chell, Haworth and Brearley, *The Entrepreneurial Personality: Concepts, Cases, and Categories* (1991).

43. Frank, M. W., 'Schumpeter on entrepreneurs and innovation: a reappraisal', *Journal of the History of Economic Thought*, 20 (1998), pp. 505–16.

44. 'A special report on entrepreneurship', *The Economist*, 14 March 2009.

45. Baumol, W. J., 'Entrepreneurship: productive, unproductive, and destructive', *Journal of Political Economy*, vol. 98, no. 5 (1990), pp. 893–921.

46. Though the miners' leader, Arthur Scargill, seems to have been jointly culpable in not securing such retraining for his members.

47. Crawford, C. and Freedman, J., 'Small business taxation', in Mirrlees, J., et al., 'The Mirrlees Review: Dimensions of Tax Design', Oxford University Press for Institute for Fiscal Studies (2010).

48. See for instance Blanchflower, D., 'Self-employment: more may not be better', paper presented at the Conference on Self-employment organised by the Economic Council of Sweden, March 2004.

49. The continuing IR35 threat to those seen by HMRC as being falsely self-employed acts as

a deterrent, offsetting the incentive to become self-employed purely for tax reasons, but is unlikely to have significant impacts on overall numbers of self-employed.

50. See for instance Urwin, P., 'Self-employment, Small Firms and Enterprise', Institute of Economic Affairs (2011) for a review of the relevant literature.

51. Office for National Statistics.

52. Urwin, P. and Buscha, F., 'Back to Work: the Role of Small Businesses in Employment and Enterprise', Federation of Small Businesses (2012).

53. 'Policies for a Sustainable Recovery', OECD, http://www.oecd.org/unitedkingdom/45642018.pdf, accessed 16 November 2014.

54. For a more detailed discussion see the conclusion to Urwin, P., Gould, M. and Page, L., 'Are there changes in the characteristics of UK higher education around the time of the 2006 reforms? Analysis of Higher Education Statistics Agency (HESA) data, 2002/3 to 2007/8', Department for Business, Innovation and Skills, working paper 14 (2010).

55. Chowdry, H., Goodman, A., Crawford, C., Vignoles, A. and Dearden, L., 'Widening Participation in Higher Education: Analysis Using Linked Administrative Data', *Journal of the Royal Statistical Society Series A*, vol. 176, no. 2 (2010), pp. 431–57.

56. Machin, S. and McNally, S., 'Higher education and the labour market', CentrePiece (2007).

57. Employment is not the only purpose of HE, but those who spend three or four years engaged in learning that has no financial value are unlikely to suggest that it was a good use of their time.

58. Brown, C., Hamilton, J. and Medoff, J., *Employers Large and Small* (1990).

59. While there have been some encouraging movements in this area with the set-up of the Business Finance Partnership, the Business Angel Co-Investment Fund and Enterprise Capital Funds programme, the start-up loans scheme targeted at 18–30-year-olds still only provides support of £2,500.

60. Urwin, P., 'Self-employment, Small Firms and Enterprise', Institute of Economic Affairs (2011).

61. See for example Haltiwanger, J., Jarmin, R. S. and Miranda, J., 'Who Creates Jobs? Small Versus Large Versus Young', *The Review of Economics and Statistics*, vol. 95, no. 2 (May 2013).

62. 'Companies and productivity: small is not beautiful', *The Economist*, 3 March 2012.

63. Sena, V., Hart, M., Bonner, K., 'Innovation and UK High-Growth Firms', Nesta working paper no. 13/12 (2013), http://www.nesta.org.uk/sites/default/files/innovation_ and_uk_high-growth_firms.pdf, accessed 16 November 2014.

64. Wolf, A., 'Review of Vocational Education' (2011).

Chapter 5

1. Beghin, N., 'Notes on Inequality and Poverty in Brazil: Current Situation and Challenges', background paper for *From Poverty to Power* (2008), p. 1.

2. 'An Anatomy of Economic Inequality in the UK: Report of the National Equality Panel' (2010).

3. See for instance Birchall, O., 'Family Income and Children's Outcomes: Evidence for the UK', PhD thesis, University of Westminster (2012).

4. Recognising the fact that the present downturn has distorted our view of these measures, as it has necessitated large government-financed bail-outs of banks, and other interventions.

5. Ostry, J. D., Berg, A. and Tsangarides, C. G., 'Redistribution, Inequality and Growth', IMF staff discussion note (February 2014), http://www.imf.org/external/pubs/ft/ sdn/2014/sdn1402.pdf, accessed 16 November 2014.

6. Those who have been concentrating will have noted a subtle difference in terminology – 'income' can include benefits and other transfers that are designed to rectify earnings disparities. Gross 'earnings' are what your employer pays you for your skills, abilities and effort, before any taxes are deducted.

7. The majority of figures presented on this page are taken from 'Patterns of Pay: Estimates from the Annual Survey of Hours and Earnings, UK, 1997 to 2013', Office for National Statistics (2014).

8. Much of the economic literature that looks at earnings considers only full-time employees. There are various reasons for this and we shall consider part-time working in Chapter 6.

9. Ten specific economic policy prescriptions, including trade liberalisation, fiscal discipline, privatisation, deregulation and other neo-liberal approaches that the economist John Williamson considered as a 'standard' reform package for crisis-hit developing economies.

10. Lawson, N., *The View from Number 11: Memoirs of a Tory Radical* (1992, 2010).

11. As suggested by Schmitt, J. and Mitukiewicz, A., 'Politics Matter: Changes in Unionization Rates in Rich Countries, 1960–2010', Center for Economic and Policy Research (2011).

12. For more details see Saundry, R., et al., 'Reframing Resolution – Managing Conflict and Resolving Individual Employment Disputes in the Contemporary Workplace', Acas (2014).

13. Atkinson, Anthony B., 'The Distribution of Top Incomes in the United Kingdom 1908–2000', in Atkinson, A. B. and Piketty, T. (eds), *Top Incomes over the Twentieth Century. A Contrast Between Continental European and English-Speaking Countries* (2007).

14. For more detail, see proceedings from the conference 'Increasing Inequality: Causes, Consequences and the Great Recession', Centre for Employment Research, University of Westminster, June 2012.

15. 'Living Standards, Poverty and Inequality in the UK', Institute for Fiscal Studies (2014).

16. Clearly there is not a wholly clear-cut distinction and each good or service will be more or less tradable – rather than being wholly tradable or wholly non-tradable. Most companies and individuals have to meet their accountant, financial adviser or business analyst at some point. This may reduce tradability of these goods, but the general point still holds.

17. Especially as many senior lawyers (partners) will have a stake in the company they are working for.

18. Berg, Andrew G. and Ostry, Jonathan D., 'Inequality and Unsustainable Growth: Two Sides of the Same Coin?', IMF Staff Discussion Note, 8 April 2011, SDN/11/08.

19. 'An Overview of Growing Income Inequalities in OECD Countries: Main Findings', OECD 2011, http://www.oecd.org/els/soc/49499779.pdf, accessed 9 December 2014.

20. http://www.ft.com/cms/s/0/8a45798c-7650-11e4-9761-00144feabdc0.html#axzz3LPFqQry5, accessed 9 December 2014.

21. 'Trends in income and equality and its impact on economic growth', OECD working paper 163, Social, Employment and Migration working papers.

22. See Lindley, J. and Machin, S., 'The Quest for More and More Education: Implications for Social Mobility', IZA discussion paper no. 6581 (2012).

Chapter 6

1. Which replaced the 1965 Act because the latter was seen to be too weak.

2. 'Women in the Labour Market', Office for National Statistics (September 2013).

3. For those interested in a little further reading, this is the Oaxaca-Blinder decomposition method.

4. Niederle, M. and Vesterlund, L., 'Do women shy away from competition? Do men compete too much?', *Quarterly Journal of Economics*, vol. 122, no. 3 (2007), pp. 1067–101.

5. Booth, A. L. and Nolen, P., 'Gender Differences in Risk Behaviour: Does Nurture Matter?', CEPR discussion paper no. 7198 (March 2009); Booth, A. L. and Nolen, P., 'Choosing to Compete: How Different Are Girls and Boys?', CEPR discussion paper no. 7214 (March 2009).

6. See also Gneezy, U., Niederle, M. and Rustichini, A., 'Performance in Competitive Environments: Gender Differences', *Quarterly Journal of Economics*, vol. 118, no. 3 (2003), pp. 1049–74.

7. A report by the Higher Education Funding Council for England suggests that by 2011/12, women were 22 per cent more likely to attend university by the age of nineteen when compared to men.

8. See Buscha, F., Parry, E. and Urwin, P., 'Back to basics: Is there a significant generational dimension and where does it "cut"?' in Parry, E. (ed.), *Generational Diversity at Work: New Research Perspectives* (2013). This analyses viewpoints in the British Household Panel Survey on the proportions within each generation who answer 'yes' to the question 'Does the family suffer if the mother works full-time?'

9. For instance, Blackaby, D. H., Leslie, D. G., Murphy, P. D. and O'Leary, N. C., 'White/ Ethnic Minority Earnings and Employment Differentials in Britain: Evidence from the LFS', *Oxford Economic Papers*, vol. 54, no. 2 (2002), pp. 270–97.

10. Clearly, the distinctions in many studies are not ideal, as there is much variety in the experiences of Indians, Pakistanis, black Africans, black Caribbeans, Chinese and many other groups who make up the category of 'non-white' in the UK. However, most studies are forced to amalgamate into this wider 'non-white' group because the numbers in surveys do not allow robust empirical analysis of specific groups.

11. Cabinet Office, 2003; National Audit Office, 2008; Heath and Cheung, 2006.

12. Sealy, R. and Vinnicombe, S., Female FTSE Index and Report 2012.

13. See for instance Scott, D., 'Equality and Diversity – a Good Business Proposition?', mimeo. (2011).

14. 'Women's Leadership in Public Life: Fostering Diversity for Inclusive Growth'.

15. 'Gender and Headship in the Twenty-First Century', National College for School Leadership, http://dera.ioe.ac.uk/7260/1/download%3Fid%3D17191%26filename%3Dgender-and-headship-in-the-21st-century.pdf, accessed 21 November 2014.

16. See the 2013 Diversity League Tables, produced by the Black Solicitors Network, for more details.

17. See for instance Borghans, L. and Groot, L., 'Educational pre-sorting and occupational segregation', *Labour Economics*, vol. 6, no. 3 (1999), pp. 375–95.

18. See Bibby, D., Buscha, F., Cerqua, A., Thomson, D. and Urwin, P., 'Further development in the estimation of labour market returns to qualifications gained in English Further Education using ILR-WPLS Administrative Data', Department for Business, Innovation and Skills (2014).

19. To include sexual orientation, transgender, age, disability and religion or belief.

20. See for instance Urwin, P., Parry, E., Dodds, I., Karuk, V. and David, A., 'The Business Case for Equality and Diversity: a survey of the academic literature', Government Equalities Office and Department for Business, Innovation and Skills, BIS occasional paper no. 4 (2013).

21. Ibid., p. 33.

22. Wheeler-Quinnell, C., 'How to Market to Gay Consumers', Stonewall Workplace Guides (2012).

23. While there are questions over the policy of increasing inclusion of disabled pupils in mainstream schools in Britain, it is producing a generation of schoolchildren who are much more accepting of disability.

24. An argument strongly put in Willetts, D., *The Pinch: How the Baby Boomers Took Their Children's Future – And Why They Should Give it Back* (2010).

25. For instance, Gary Becker's PhD thesis, 'The Economics of Discrimination' (1957).

26. One could call this a diversity coefficient (D). In an environment where there are seen to be gains from increased diversity, we can think of an employer perceiving a minority employee's wage as *Wage*-D (where 'D' is the additional business benefit arising from a subsequent increase in diversity).

27. Hakim, C., 'Feminist Myths and Magic Medicine', Centre for Policy Studies, http://eprints.lse.ac.uk/36488, accessed 12 December 2014.

28. Urwin, P., 'Self-employment, Small Firms and Enterprise', Institute of Economic Affairs (2011).

29. This is a form of statistical discrimination.

30. See for instance Barmes, L., 'Equality law and experimentation: the positive action challenge', *Cambridge Law Journal*, vol. 68, issue 3 (2009), pp. 623–54.

31. Urwin, P., Parry, E., Dodds, I., Karuk, V. and David, A., 'The Business Case for Equality and Diversity: a survey of the academic literature', Government Equalities Office and Department for Business, Innovation and Skills, BIS occasional paper no. 4 (2013).

Chapter 7

1. http://www.newstatesman.com/politics/2013/01/nhs-even-more-cherished-monarchy-and-army, accessed 10 December 2014.

2. http://www.commonwealthfund.org/publications/press-releases/2014/jun/us-health-system-ranks-last, accessed 10 December 2014.

3. 'Health expectancy at birth', Office for National Statistics (2009), http://www.statistics.gov.uk/StatBase/Product.asp?vlnk=12964, accessed 10 December 2014.

4. Quoted in the Institute of Government's forensic examination of the strange circumstances by which the 2012 Health and Social Care Act came to pass.

5. See http://www.nice.org.uk/Glossary?letter=Q, accessed 23 November 2014.

6. http://www.medicine.ox.ac.uk/bandolier/painres/download/whatis/QALY.pdf, accessed 10 December 2014.

7. See http://www.yesmagazine.org/happiness/want-the-good-life-your-neighbors-need-it-too, accessed 23 November 2014.

8. http://www.england.nhs.uk/2013/07/11/call-to-action/, accessed 23 November 2014.

9. https://www.gov.uk/government/uploads/system/uploads/attachment_data/file/326579/HMRC-fast-facts.pdf, accessed 10 December 2014.

10. http://www.telegraph.co.uk/health/nhs/10907823/Britains-NHS-is-the-worlds-best-health-care-system-says-report.html, accessed 9 December 2014.

11. http://www.facebook.com/ATOSM/posts/815534881808982, accessed 24 November 2014.

12. http://www.dailymail.co.uk/news/article-2832627/Farage-caught-camera-saying-abolish-ing-NHS-says-won-t-rule-forming-coalition-Labour-Miliband-s-party-fail-win-Election. html, accessed 10 December 2014.

13. http://blogs.channel4.com/factcheck/foreign-visitors-owe-nhs-2bn-factcheck/16194, accessed 10 December 2014.

14. http://www.telegraph.co.uk/news/politics/11008913/250-million-to-be-spent-clearing-NHS-operations-backlog-this-summer.html, accessed 10 December 2014.

15. http://www.pulsetoday.co.uk/your-practice/practice-topics/practice-income/10-charge-for-gp-appointments-would-raise-the-nhs-12bn-study-finds/20005100.article#. VH3WNTGsXNV, accessed 10 December 2014.

16. 'A New Settlement for Health and Social Care', interim report of the independent Commission on the Future of Health and Social Care in England (2014), http://www. kingsfund.org.uk/sites/files/kf/field/field_publication_file/commission-interim-new-set-tlement-health-social-care-apr2014.pdf, accessed 24 November 2014.

17. http://news.bbc.co.uk/1/hi/health/8569173.stm, accessed 24 November 2014.

18. http://www.ft.com/cms/s/0/02f4d940-e0d3-11e3-875f-00144feabdc0. html#axzz398DSvBLs, accessed 10 December 2014.

19. http://www.ft.com/cms/s/0/02f4d940-e0d3-11e3-875f-00144feabdc0. html#ixzz39K3zaBPC, accessed 10 December 2014.

20. http://www.bbc.co.uk/news/health-28602156, accessed 10 December 2014.

21. https://www.gov.uk/government/news/nhs-charges-from-april-2013-announced, accessed 10 December 2014.

22. http://www.pulsetoday.co.uk/commissioning/commissioning-topics/prescribing/promi-nent-gp-calls-for-end-to-prescribing-charges/20006717.article#.U-P30_ldU3k, accessed 10 December 2014.

23. Office for National Statistics (2011), http://www.ons.gov.uk/ons/publications/re-refer-ence-tables.html?edition=tcm%3A77-227587, accessed 10 December 2014.

24. http://www.independent.co.uk/news/uk/politics/tories-deleted-past-broken-promises-from-party-website-8937435.html, accessed 10 December 2014.

25. For a fascinating account see http://www.instituteforgovernment.org.uk/sites/default/ files/publications/Never%20again_0.pdf, accessed 10 December 2014.

26. See for example http://www.yourbritain.org.uk/agenda-2015/policy-commissions/health-and-care-policy-commission/21st-century-nhs-and-social-care-delivering-integration-5, accessed 10 December 2014.

27. http://www.kingsfund.org.uk/publications/new-settlement-health-and-social-care, accessed 10 December 2014.

28. Ibid.

Chapter 8

1. Bosson, J. K., Johnson, A. B., Niederhoffer, K. and Swann Jr, W. B., 'Bonding by sharing negative attitudes about others' in *Personal Relationships*, 13 (2006), pp. 135–50.

2. http://www.economist.com/blogs/blighty/2011/02/attitudes_immigration, accessed 24 November 2014.

3. See for example http://www.ipsos-mori.com/researchpublications/researcharchive/3188/Perceptions-are-not-reality-the-top-10-we-get-wrong.aspx, accessed 24 November 2014.

4. This cannot be known for certain, see http://www.migrationobservatory.ox.ac.uk/briefings/uk-public-opinion-toward-immigration-overall-attitudes-and-level-concern, accessed 24 November 2014.

5. http://www.publications.parliament.uk/pa/ld200708/ldselect/ldeconaf/82/8206.htm, accessed 10 December 2014.

6. http://www.gov.uk/government/uploads/system/uploads/attachment_data/file/257235/analysis-of-the-impacts.pdf, accessed 10 December 2014.

7. https://www.gov.uk/government/uploads/system/uploads/attachment_data/file/287287/occ109.pdf, accessed 10 December 2014.

8. http://niesr.ac.uk/blog/newsnight-immigration-report-held-back-downing-street-some-background-and-analysis#.UoFsNvldU3k, accessed 10 December 2014.

9. http://www.cream-migration.org/files/Press_release_FiscalEJ.pdf, accessed 10 December 2014.

10. http://www.publications.parliament.uk/pa/ld200708/ldselect/ldeconaf/82/82.pdf, accessed 10 December 2014.

11. http://www.timeshighereducation.co.uk/news/universities-detail-hit-to-indian-demand/2011828.article, accessed 10 December 2014.

12. http://www.dailymail.co.uk/news/article-2535110/I-Britain-fewer-immigrants-makes-poorer-says-Farage.html#ixzz2zdYNxRHu, accessed 10 December 2014.

13. http://www.ippr.org/press-releases/111/9396/britain-is-not-qa-small-crowded-islandq, accessed 10 December 2014.

14. http://www.dailymail.co.uk/news/article-1162782/British-Babel-English-foreign-language-seven-primary-school-pupils.html, accessed 10 December 2014.

15. http://www.niesr.ac.uk/blog/immigration-whats-it-doing-our-schools#.U1ltXvldU3k, accessed 10 December 2014.

16. Alan Manning, an LSE professor, has come to the conclusion that although most immigrants are likely to be eligible to apply for social housing, there is no evidence (once demographic, regional and economic circumstances are controlled for) that they have preferential access – if anything, the reverse seems to be the case.

17. See http://blogs.lse.ac.uk/politicsandpolicy/immigration/, accessed 20 August 2014.

18. http://blogs.lse.ac.uk/politicsandpolicy/immigration/#comment-328071, accessed 10 December 2014.

19. http://yougov.co.uk/news/2013/03/05/analysis-ukip-voters, accessed 10 December 2014.

Chapter 9

1. Dixon, H., *The In/Out Question: Why Britain Should Stay in the EU and Fight to Make It Better* (2014).

2. Pryce, V., *Greekonomics: The Euro Crisis and Why Politicians Don't Get It* (2013), p. 182.

3. Pryce, V., *Greekonomics* (2013), p. 26.

4. Wolf, M., *The Shifts and the Shocks: What We've Learned and Have Still to Learn from the Financial Crisis* (2014).

5. Bootle, R., *The Trouble with Europe* (2014).

6. Dixon, H., *The In/Out Question* (2014).

7. Peet, J. and La Guardia, A., *Unhappy Union: How the Euro Crisis – and Europe – can be fixed* (2014).

8. Marsh, D., *Europe's Deadlock: How the Euro Crisis Could Be Solved – and Why It Won't Happen* (2013).

9. 'The Economic Consequences of Leaving the EU', Centre for European Reform (2014).

10. Legrain, P., *European Spring: Why Our Economies and Politics Are in a Mess* (2014).

11. Pryce, V., 'Perhaps the British were right all along about the perils of ever closer union', *Europe's World*, Spring 2014.

12. Miszlivetz, F., *Europe's World*, Spring 2014.

13. European Movement, November 2014, http://ymlp.com/zv6EXV, accessed 10 December 2014.

14. Miszlivetz, F., *Europe's World*, Spring 2014.

15. Op. cit., p. 86.

16. Mazzucato, M., *The Entrepreneurial State: Debunking Public vs Private Sector Myths* (2013).

17. http://britishinfluence.org/wp-content/uploads/2014/03/UK-jobs-dependent-on-exports-to-the-EU-report-final-29-March-2014.pdf, accessed 10 December 2014.

18. http://www.london.gov.uk/sites/default/files/europe_report_2014_08.pdf, accessed 10 December 2014.

19. Bootle, R., *The Trouble with Europe* (2014).

Chapter 10

1. One of the few times economists feel that people and businesses (or 'agents') are not best placed to make their own decisions is when their actions impact on others, and agents do not take these external or spill-over costs into account. As an economist I am not concerned over the decision of some people to drink to excess (it is their body), but if they then start a fight with me as a result, they are imposing a cost that they have not accounted for in their decision to over-indulge. If alcohol was much more expensive and some of this money was doled out to the victims of violence arising from over-indulgence, as an economist I *should* be happier.

2. See the following for more information: Laibson, D. and Zeckhauser, R., 'Amos Tversky and the Ascent of Behavioral Economics', *Journal of Risk and Uncertainty*, vol. 16 (1998), pp. 7–47.

3. Rablen (2012) describes a number of interpretations that have been given to the concept of subjective well-being (SWB), as opposed to measures of objective well-being (OWB). Rablen, M., 'The promotion of local wellbeing: A primer for policymakers', *Local Economy*, 27: 297 (2012).

4. Some of the main issues that Rablen sets out are a) reliability or consistency of measures for the same individual across time, when circumstances have not changed; b) comparability across individuals, who we assume have the same understanding of what is being measured (happiness); c) are the metrics we use really capturing underlying SWB, as conceptualised by theorists?

5. Tinkler, L. and Hicks, S, 'Measuring Subjective Well-Being', Office for National Statistics (2011).

6. The following discussion draws heavily on the findings from Dolan, P., Peasgood, T. and White, M., 'Do we really know what makes us happy? A review of the economic literature on the factors associated with subjective well-being', *Journal of Economic Psychology*, vol. 29 (2008), pp. 94–122.

7. The SWB score on the vertical axis represents the response to a question which is typically asked in the following way (for instance in the World Values Survey): 'All things considered, how happy are you with your life?' The answers run from '[1] Very Unhappy' to '[10] Very Happy'.

8. It is worth noting that Frijters and Beatton (2012) find a drop in happiness after seventy-five and question the significance of the fall in happiness between twenty and fifty when we use more advanced econometric models.

9. Gruber, J., Mauss, I. B. and Tamir, M., 'A Dark Side of Happiness? How, When, and Why Happiness Is Not Always Good', *Perspectives on Psychological Science*, vol. 6 (2011), pp. 222–33.

10. Sacks, D. and Wolfers, J., 'Debunking the Easterlin Paradox, Again' (13 December 2010), http://www.brookings.edu/research/opinions/2010/12/13-debunking-easterlin-wolfers, accessed 11 December 2014.

11. Graham, C., 'More on the Easterlin Paradox: A Response to Wolfers' (15 December 2010), http://www.brookings.edu/blogs/up-front/posts/2010/12/15-happiness-easterlin-graham, accessed 11 December 2014.

12. See for instance Easterlin, R., 'A puzzle for adaptive theory', *Journal of Economic Behavior & Organization*, vol. 56 (2005), pp. 513–21.

13. Diener, E., Suh, E. M., Lucas, R. E. and Smith, H. L., 'Subjective well-being: Three decades of progress', *Psychological Review*, 125 (1999), pp. 276–302.

14. When we look at the relationship between individual incomes and happiness in data, we suffer from problems of what we term 'endogeneity'. Put simply, I may find a positive correlation (relationship) between happiness and income for a group of people, but it is quite possible that happy people make more money – not that money makes you happy.

15. More technically, we pursue internal consistency, but in the process we sacrifice a large amount of external validity.

16. 'Enough' is a fraught concept, but the idea is that you do not want for food, shelter, clothing, a fridge, cooker, television etc., but you are not able to buy expensive, branded versions of these things. This is the 'want' that a vast majority of the UK population feel.

17. For instance, Diener, E. and Seligman, M. E. P., 'Beyond money: toward an economy of well-being', *Psychological Science in the Public Interest*, vol. 5, no. 1 (2004).

18. Frank, R., 'How Not to Buy Happiness', American Academy of Arts & Sciences (2004).

19. Aknin, L. B. et al., 'Prosocial Spending and Well-Being: Cross-Cultural Evidence for a Psychological Universal', Harvard working papers (2011).

Chapter 11

1. We shall use the two terms interchangeably as GHGs are often given in equivalent tons of carbon dioxide, called just carbon equivalence.

2. The term 'climate change deniers' is often used, but that may have an unfair association with holocaust deniers. It's difficult to find the right term, especially as most of the doubters do accept that anthropogenic CO2 is responsibility for at least some, i.e. a little, of global warming.

3. Poortinga, W., Pidgeon, N. F., Capstick, S. and Aoyagim M., 'Public Attitudes to Nuclear Power and Climate Change in Britain Two Years after the Fukushima Accident', working paper, 19 September 2013, REF UKERC/WP/ES/2013/006.

4. http://www.skepticalscience.com, accessed 12 December 2014.

5. http://www.bbc.co.uk/news/science-environment-30311816, accessed 11 December 2014.

6. http://www.epw.senate.gov/public/index.cfm?FuseAction=Minority.SenateReport, accessed 11 December 2014.

7. Stern Review on the Economics of Climate Change.

8. See for example http://www.foundation.org.uk/events/pdf/20090610_Summary.pdf, accessed 11 December 2014.

9. Stern Review on the Economics of Climate Change.

10. Available at http://www.lse.ac.uk/GranthamInstitute/wp-content/uploads/2014/02/Letter-Peter-Lilley-22-Feb-2013.pdf, accessed 24 November 2014.

11. See for example http://www.res.org.uk/view/art3Apr08Features.html, accessed 24 November 2014.

12. Intergovernmental Panel on Climate Change, March 2014.

13. http://thebreakthrough.org/archive/yale360_pielkes_iron_law_of_c, accessed 11 December 2014.

14. http://www.theguardian.com/big-energy-debate/green-deal-what-next-energy, accessed 24 November 2014.

15. See 'Why are renewables so expensive?', *The Economist*, January 2014, available at http://www.economist.com/blogs/economist-explains/2014/01/economist-explains-0, accessed 24 November 2014.

16. DECC-CM 8407, Gas Generation Strategy, December 2012.

17. http://www3.imperial.ac.uk/newsandeventspggrp/imperialcollege/newssummary/news_20-2-2014-9-18-49, accessed 24 November 2014.

18. Helm, T. and Cowburn, A., 'Osborne accused of tax breaks for oil industry's Tory donors', *The Observer*, 7 December 2014.

Chapter 12

1. More accurately the marginal cost.

2. For more detail see for instance Stiglitz, J. E., *Economics of the Public Sector* (2000) or Winston, C., 'Government Failure versus Market Failure: Microeconomics Policy Research and Government Performance', AEI-Brookings Joint Center for Regulatory Studies (2006).

3. See for instance Barr, N., *The Economics of the Welfare State* (2004), which plays down its importance.

4. http://www.ft.com/cms/s/0/fd916ed8-cfa7-11e2-a050-00144feab7de. html#axzz3B97leMC4, accessed 12 December 2014.

5. http://www.publications.parliament.uk/pa/cm201213/cmselect/cmtran/329/32905.htm, accessed 12 December 2014.

6. *The Times*, 22 August 2014, p. 21.

7. http://www.neweconomics.org/publications/entry/high-speed-2-the-best-we-can-do, accessed 12 December 2014.

8. http://www.bbc.co.uk/news/technology-28551069, accessed 12 December 2014.

9. 'Compendium of Reoffending Statistics and Analysis', Ministry of Justice, 4 November 2010.

10. Machin, S., et al., 'The Crime Reducing Effect of Education', *Economic Journal*, vol. 121, issue 552, 463–84, May 2011.

11. Ministry of Justice, Analysis of the Impact of Employment on Reoffending following release, March 2013.

12. Ministry of Justice, Ad hoc Statistical Release, Legal Aid Exceptional Case Funding Application and Determination Statistics: 1 April to 31 December 2013, published 13 March 2014, p. 5, table 1.

13. Ministry of Justice, Legal Aid Statistics in England and Wales, Legal Aid Agency, 2013/14, published 24 June 2014, p. 27, figure 22.

14. http://www.ageuk.org.uk/Documents/EN-GB/Factsheets/Later_Life_UK_factsheet. pdf?dtrk=true, accessed 12 December 2014.

15. https://www.gov.uk/government/uploads/system/uploads/attachment_data/file/254321/ framework-analysis-future-pensio-incomes.pdf, accessed 12 July 2014.

16. http://www.ifs.org.uk/conferences/pensioner_incomesUK_pj2013.pdf, accessed 12 December 2014.

17. http://www.bbc.co.uk/news/uk-25609485, accessed 12 December 2014.

18. http://www.tackletaxhavens.com/Cost_of_Tax_Abuse_TJN%20Research_23rd_ Nov_2011.pdf, accessed 12 December 2014.

19. http://www.thisismoney.co.uk/money/pensions/article-2514378/Only-Mexico-worse-state-pension-UK.html, accessed 12 December 2014.

20. http://www.rosaltmann.com/press_releases/ros_altmann_121217.pdf, accessed 12 December 2014.

21. http://www.publications.parliament.uk/pa/cm201213/cmhansrd/chan43.pdf, accessed 12 December 2014.

22. http://www.express.co.uk/comment/expresscomment/408548/Britain-leads-the-way-in-foreign-aid-unfortunately, accessed 12 December 2014.

23. http://www.dailymail.co.uk/news/article-2556043/Sign-petition-calling-Government-divert-foreign-aid-flood-hit-British-families.html, accessed 12 December 2014.

24. House of Commons Library, July 2014, SN/EP/3714.

25. Ibid.

26. 'The Coalition: Our Programme for Government'.

27. http://icai.independent.gov.uk/wp-content/uploads/2011/11/ICAI-Annual-Report-13-14-FINAL.pdf, accessed 12 December 2014.

Index